ALSO BY MARY ELLEN REESE
Moving On

PUBLISHED BY SIMON AND SCHUSTER
A DIVISION OF GULF & WESTERN CORPORATION
SIMON & SCHUSTER BUILDING
ROCKEFELLER CENTER
1230 AVENUE OF THE AMERICAS
NEW YORK, NEW YORK 10020
SIMON AND SCHUSTER AND COLOPHON ARE TRADEMARKS OF
    SIMON & SCHUSTER

DESIGNED BY EVE METZ
MANUFACTURED IN THE UNITED STATES OF AMERICA

1 2 3 4 5 6 7 8 9 10

LIBRARY OF CONGRESS CATALOGING IN PUBLICATION DATA

GULLEY, BILL.
    BREAKING COVER.

    INCLUDES INDEX.
    1. PRESIDENTS—UNITED STATES—STAFF.   2. UNITED
STATES—POLITICS AND GOVERNMENT—1945–   I. REESE,
MARY ELLEN, JOINT AUTHOR.   II. TITLE.
JK518.G84   353.03′1′0922   80-11449

ISBN 0-671-24548-1

BREAKING
COVER

Bill Gulley
WITH
Mary Ellen Reese

SIMON AND SCHUSTER · NEW YORK

For Kimberly Heather Gulley

ACKNOWLEDGMENTS

I WOULD LIKE TO THANK all the movers and shakers who worked with me in the Military Office at the White House from 1966 through 1977 and four administrations. I would especially like to pay tribute to the memory of three of these former colleagues whose lives were taken by cancer: Miss Mary Margaret Crosswaite, Master Sergeant Muriel "Mac" Collins, USMC, and Mr. Fred Jefferson.

And my thanks go to Alice Mayhew, whose firm hand and light touch kept this book smoothly and happily on course.

B.G.

CONTENTS

INTRODUCTION

"THERE WAS VERY LITTLE TRAFFIC on the Capital Beltway as the White House car sped out to Andrews Air Force Base. It was just past noon on a Sunday in August, and the citizens of Washington and its suburbs were doing the things people do on summer Sundays: lying in bed, mowing the lawn, reading the paper.

"The Washington *Post* was beside me on the back seat, but I hadn't done more than glance at it. It was August 11, 1974, two days after Nixon had resigned as President; the papers were still full of it, and I didn't want to read another rehash of Friday's events. For one thing, I knew a hell of a lot more about it than they did. For another, I was tired.

"I stared out the window at the countryside and tried not to think about anything, but pictures, snapshots, kept flashing into my head. Disjointed, unrelated stills out of the past two days. Rose Mary Woods collapsing as the Nixons' helicopter left the White House lawn. My son's expression as he watched his bride walk up the aisle to meet him. The worry on Alexander Haig's and Jack Marsh's faces as we discussed my trip to San Clemente. I tried but couldn't seem to stop the slide show.

"When we got to Andrews the guard waved us through the gate and we drove out to Special Air Missions, where *Air Force One,* its backup and all the other Presidential aircraft were. I was using one of the unmarked Jet Stars that we kept for missions like this one—closely held operations known only to a few.

"We drove right onto the tarmac and directly to the plane. The pilot, copilot, engineer and steward were aboard and ready for takeoff, so I climbed up the steps. After checking to see that the twelve boxes of Nixon's papers I'd sent ahead had been loaded (they had), I told the pilot I was set to go, and we taxied to the runway.

"The interior of the Jet Star was blue and white, very restful, but it was going to take more than that to iron out my wrinkles. I'd been in a pressure cooker for the past three days, ever since Rose Mary Woods had called me at six-thirty in the morning on Thursday, the eighth, and asked me to come over to her office.

"It was obvious she had been crying, for a long time, but she had tight control of herself. 'No one is to know this, Bill,' she said, 'but the President is going to resign at noon tomorrow. Before he leaves, there are some personal things he wants done. Will you do them?'

"In addition to the private things Nixon wanted done, it was my job as administrator of the Military Office to make all the arrangements for his departure. There were no precedents for a ceremony of Resignation of a President Under Fire, or for getting him out of the White House and back home, so I was flying blind.

"But somehow by nine-thirty on the morning of the next day, when Richard Nixon and his family walked into the East Room, everything was locked into place. Which was fortunate, because the emotion that was generated in that room during Nixon's farewell to the staff was so great that people, plans, anything, could have come unglued.

"Everyone there took a pounding. It had nothing to do with politics; it was purely human. When you saw Tricia's eyes fill with tears and then watched her fight them down, it didn't matter what her father had or hadn't done. You were in the presence of pain.

"Much of the White House staff had been reluctant to leave after Nixon had spoken to the nation on television on Thursday, telling them he would resign the following morning, but they needed to let off steam. So we set up a huge bar in the Military Office and held a wake. The bar was open and people were coming in and out all night.

"There were a lot of people in the White House who were scared. Some didn't know whether they'd lost their jobs, and others knew damn well they'd lost theirs. Some didn't know if they were going to jail. Around the periphery were the Ford people, who couldn't help but give off the air of wolves waiting for the calves to finally go down on their knees.

"It was a gloomy event. You must understand what happens when you're in the White House and you go through a period like Watergate. You find yourself put on the defensive all the time, not because of what you did, or who you are, but because of where you work. In defending yourself, you were defending the White House, not because you were standing up for Richard Nixon. That had nothing to do with it. You took to the ramparts, not to defend who was in the White House, but to defend the White House itself.

"So the feeling was one of defeat. There were tears all night. Both men and women cried openly, much of it out of this sense of personal defeat, and personal anxiety about the future.

"I was in and out of my office during that time trying to work out with General Haig, Nixon's ex–chief of staff, and Jack Marsh, who was handling the transition for Ford, how contact between Ford and Nixon could be maintained without anyone knowing about it. Obviously, it would be disastrous for Ford if the press and the public got hold of it. The decision was made that I, as in-house expert on former Presidents, would go out to San Clemente and see Nixon as soon as possible, but Haig and Marsh were both uneasy about it all along.

"Now, sitting in the Jet Star, I was on my way, and by now I was uneasy, too."

The White House isn't a place for careers. Time spent there can launch them, highlight them or perhaps end them, but for the most part the White House is a way station for men and a few women who are on the move. Ironically these able professionals in their own fields become instant amateurs when they enter the White House and begin what is arguably the most important job in the world: running the American Presidency. They're amateurs because there is no training ground for the job, there is nothing like it anywhere, and there is no apprenticeship for the exercise of that kind of power.

On top of this, there is little continuity. An administration may keep some holdovers from the one before, but they are suspect and seldom last long even among administrations of the same party. The result is a lot of learning-by-doing in a place that is particularly ill suited for trial and error. Experience at the business of running the Presidency is hard to come by: four years is a long time to be a staffer in the White House, six or eight exceptional; there are few old hands to be found there.

Bill Gulley was in the White House eleven years, which made him an old hand. He went there in 1966 when Lyndon Johnson was in office, remained during the Nixon and Ford administrations, and left in 1977 while Jimmy Carter was President. Gulley spent those years at the strategic center of the White House, the Military Office, and served in three capacities: as administrator and then as director of the Military Office, as Emergency Actions Officer, and as Presidential Liaison.

That most people are unaware that there is a Military Office at the White House is not an accident. Since Lyndon Johnson's time, there has been an almost universal unwillingness on the part of those connected with the Military Office to discuss what it does. Yet its operations reach into almost every Presidential activity, public and private, and without it the Presidency literally could not function.

One of the reasons for this pervasive secrecy is the desire of every President since Kennedy to put distance between the Executive branch and the military; another is that while some of the activities of the Military Office involve matters of national security, others simply could not bear public scrutiny.

That the Military Office has been able to maintain such a low profile in the face of rampant investigation of all aspects of the Presidency is all the more remarkable in view of the size and scope of its operations. When he became director of the Office, Gulley had 2,000 people working directly for him; he called on another 1,500 as needed; and all the vast resources of the Department of Defense were at his disposal.

In addition to his responsibilities as Emergency Actions Officer and Presidential Liaison, as director of the White House Military Office, Gulley had control of ten essential and diverse entities. Among them, as the accompanying chart shows, were *Air Force One,* the Special Programs Office (Emergency Sites), Camp David and the huge White House Communications Agency.

"Basically the Military Office makes it possible for the President to do the things he needs or wants to do," Gulley says, "whether they're covert or for all the world to see. It's no exaggeration to say it's the President's Aladdin's lamp: there's nothing that can't be done, and there's a bottomless pit of money, ingenuity and resources to do it with."

Some of the things the Presidents have asked the Military Office to do have been questionable, and one reason questions weren't asked was that all the resources needed to carry out the President's wishes were shrouded in secrecy. Men, equipment and money could be and were called on without fear of exposure.

For example, only a handful of people in each administration knew of the existence of a multimillion-dollar Secret Fund held by the Military Office, which only the President and the director of the Military Office were authorized to spend. Until now the public has known nothing about this fund: why and how it was established, how it was administered, how it was kept secret and, above all, how it was used and abused.

The Military Office is the critical link between the White House and the Pentagon in case an unexpected missile attack is launched on the country. As Emergency Actions Officer, Gulley was responsible for the procedures by which the President, as Commander in Chief of the Armed Forces, could order an immediate retaliatory strike on the enemy.

In such an emergency the President would have only a matter of minutes in which to respond to an attack before the missiles landed. It was Gulley's responsibility to see that all

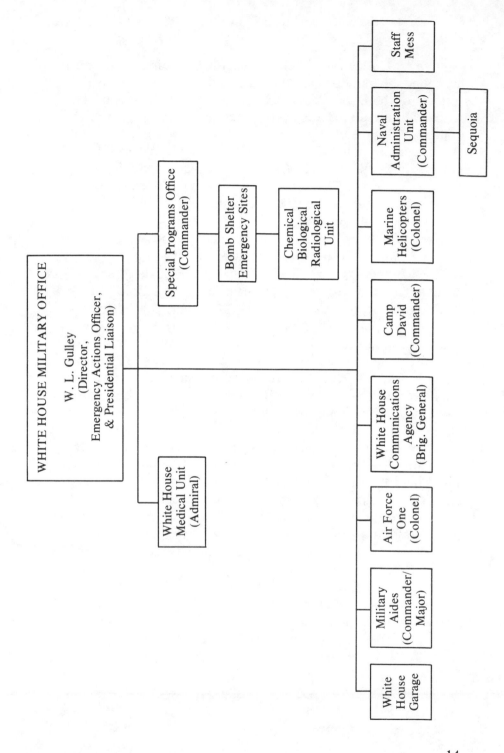

WHITE HOUSE MILITARY OFFICE

W. L. Gulley
(Director,
Emergency Actions Officer,
& Presidential Liaison)

White House
Medical Unit
(Admiral)

Special Programs Office
(Commander)

Bomb Shelter
Emergency Sites

Chemical
Biological
Radiological
Unit

White House
Garage

Military
Aides
(Commander/
Major)

Air Force
One
(Colonel)

White House
Communications
Agency
(Brig. General)

Camp
David
(Commander)

Marine
Helicopters
(Colonel)

Naval
Administration
Unit
(Commander)

Staff
Mess

Sequoia

14

the necessary information was up to date and available to the President instantly, wherever he was; that he could communicate with his military advisors; and that he was safely evacuated to a secure site.

Gulley had briefed each incoming President on the contents of the "Football," the legendary black briefcase containing, among other things, the President's retaliatory options. He had described to each the contents and the handling of the Football and the procedures for evacuation of the President and the Presidential successors, and had revealed to them just how inadequate these procedures are.

With his unique understanding of this final, vital connection between the President and the Pentagon, Gulley claims that the President is scandalously underprotected against a full military attack, or even a quasi-military terrorist attack. As an extension of this, since the President is the only one who can "push the button," Gulley asserts that our entire retaliatory strike capability is vulnerable.

"The system is brilliantly conceived and executed, from the detection networks around the world to the high-IQ computers at NORAD," Gulley says. "But then, when it gets to the White House, it's all mashed potatoes."

In his capacity as Liaison between the White House and former Presidents, Gulley occasionally carried out missions of considerable delicacy, one of which held great political risk to the incumbent. Starting August 11, 1974, two days after Nixon's resignation in disgrace, Gulley made the first of dozens of secret trips to San Clemente.

In March of 1975, Donald Rumsfeld, then Ford's chief of staff, asked Gulley to find out if Nixon would be willing to send confidential political advice to Ford on his campaign for the Presidency. Nixon agreed, and from then until Ford's defeat by Carter more than a year and a half later, Gulley secretly conveyed a constant stream of messages between Nixon and the Ford White House.

Through its vast and technically sophisticated White House Communications Agency, the Military Office handled the secret bugging of the Oval Office and Cabinet Room in Lyndon

Johnson's White House and installed taps on his telephones and those of his staff members. That such listening devices existed in Johnson's Administration has been repeatedly and hotly denied by Johnson loyalists.

Gulley not only has firsthand knowledge that these devices were in use, he has dozens of documents, from technical drawings to internal correspondence, pertaining to them, as well as to the telephone taps installed by at least one of the most prominent of the Watergate figures.

Gulley also believes he has evidence relating to the riddle of the mysterious 18½-minute gap in one of the critical Watergate tapes. As director of the agency that provided the shroud of secrecy for those in the White House, Gulley also knew what was being hidden. He asserts that an incident that took place in late September of 1973 at Camp David, which is run by the Military Office, helps explain who erased the tape.

In addition to scores of classified Presidential Emergency Sites scattered throughout the country to which the President can be evacuated in a military emergency, and the huge White House Communications Agency, other, more visible Presidential facilities are controlled by the Military Office: *Air Force One;* the Marine Corps Helicopter Squadron, with 139 men and a fleet of thirteen distinctive green and white Presidential helicopters; the Naval Support Group, Thurmont, Maryland, better known as Camp David; the Naval Administration Unit, at the Washington Navy Yard, which housed the Presidential yachts; as well as the White House garage, with its fleet of cars, and the White House stewards and the White House Mess.

"Although they were meant for the comfort and convenience of the President, these were the White House perks and status symbols," Gulley says, "and they were eagerly, sometimes even desperately, sought after by staffers.

"The Department of Defense budget is huge and largely classified; the White House budget is small and open for examination by the citizens and the politicians. Since the White House couldn't begin to support even one of the functions the military performs for it, we were the rich uncle over in the East Wing, doing anything the President wanted, discreetly."

16

This "discreet" aspect of what Gulley did in all three of his capacities explains the often shocking nature of what he reveals of life at the White House. "People," he says, "have a way of behaving differently, living by different standards, when they think nobody's looking."

Gulley started life as a bona fide Country Boy, the genuine article. Born in 1922 on a dirt farm in southern Illinois of illiterate parents, he grew up during the Depression helping his father scratch a living out of rocky soil. He shot rabbits on the way to a one-room schoolhouse three miles away, occasionally stole coal for their stove from the Central Illinois Railroad, which ran past their three-room house, and frequently raised hell. At sixteen he decided to trade it all in for something else, so he left school, added two years to his age, and in 1939 joined the Marines.

"That was the start of my informal education, and the first thing I learned was the meaning of fear. I'd only been at Marine boot camp a few days when we were taken to the range to learn how to use our weapons—this was 1939 and First World War rifles were all we had.

"I was designated stack man. That meant I was supposed to stack a number of rifles by hooking them together and then arranging them tripod-fashion. Then I was to take a step back, turn and march away, but being green and nervous, I knocked the whole goddamn stack in the sand.

"Naturally, I bent down immediately to pick the rifles up, but before I knew what was happening, the drill instructor, this Sergeant Fleming—who was the meanest son of a bitch in the Marine Corps, which is well endowed with sons of bitches—crouched down in front of me, brought his fist up, and broke my nose.

"I was throwing up and bleeding and everybody ignored it, which was bad enough. But what scared me was what happened three or four hours later. Sergeant Fleming's superior, who had seen the whole thing, came into my tent and said, 'You'd better see the corpsman about that nose. But whatever you do, don't you tell him how it happened. Not if you want to get out of here alive.' That scared me. And it was my first exposure to real abuse of power.

"My educational experiences improved after that. I refined my understanding of games of chance to the point where, as proprietor of a highly lucrative floating poker game, I was more than doubling my Marine Corps income." Gulley was also learning how to manage men and manipulate situations. "Without realizing it," he says, "I was in training all my life for my job in the White House Military Office."

Gulley wasn't the standard model of a White House staff member, but Lyndon Johnson had his own criteria for judging people. High on the list was: "Is he a 'can-do' guy?" Gulley could and Gulley did, so effectively that he was kept on by three more Presidents.

General Brent Scowcroft, who was to succeed Henry Kissinger as National Security Advisor to the President, came into the White House as director of the Military Office. Gulley served as Scowcroft's executive assistant and later was himself appointed director.

Talking about Gulley now, Scowcroft says, "Bill Gulley has a knack for imposing order on the most chaotic situation, and a rare talent for administration. It doesn't surprise me that Johnson spotted him and that Nixon, Ford and Carter kept him on.

"When Bill decided to leave the White House early in the Carter Administration, Carter asked him to stay. But the Carter people, his staff—Bill just didn't think he could work effectively with them.

"That he was in the White House at all is probably due to the Johnson style, his fitting into the Johnson style," Scowcroft says. "But that was only part of it. Bill was already one of the senior noncommissioned officers in the Marine Corps and had established a reputation as the best administrator they had. He was given a field commission after Guadalcanal, where he'd been wounded in hand-to-hand combat, so he served as an officer, too, although he later relinquished his rank.

"Bill was the first civilian ever appointed as director of the White House Military Office, and he replaced a whole string of generals in that job. Scratch the affable Country Boy that Lyndon Johnson brought into the Military Office and you'll

18

find a tough, shrewd guy who understands how things *really* relate to each other; why it is that when you push a button over here, a guy over there will jump."

General Scowcroft might also have said that Gulley is a direct man not given to mincing words. He saw beneath the polished surface of the White House and its inhabitants and doesn't hesitate to talk about what he saw.

"An incoming President makes a lot of hollow promises," Gulley says, "and the hollowest probably is 'This will be an open administration.' The guy may even believe it himself before he gets inside the gates, although he'd have to be pretty damn naive, but when he goes on promising it after the gates shut behind him, then he's lying."

Arthur Schlesinger, Jr., talks about secrecy in government in *The Imperial Presidency,* and he quotes the views of two men who went on to become President. "Government ought to be all outside and no inside. I, for my part, believe there ought to be no place where anything can be done that everybody does not know about . . . secrecy means impropriety." That was Woodrow Wilson when he was campaigning.

"The whole concept of a return to secrecy in peacetime demonstrates a profound misunderstanding of the role of a free press. . . . The plea for security could well become a cloak for errors, misjudgments and other failings of government." And, by the same author: "The new test for classifying secret documents now seems to be not whether the publication of a document would affect the security of the nation, but whether it would affect the political security of the Administration." That was Richard Nixon in May of 1961 and April of 1951.

There probably never has been, and never will be, a political figure who doesn't demand of another's administration or promise of his own that in it there will be "no place where anything can be done that everyone does not know about." When the things everyone did not know about, or some of them, started tumbling out of the Nixon White House, a lot of people concluded that it was Nixon and his men who turned it into a place where skullduggery and dark deeds of all kinds were done. It is Gulley's contention that part of the answer to the question of how it happened lies in the atmosphere that's generated in the White House itself.

The White House is a world apart. It's a palace, an ivory tower, an ego trip for its inhabitants. One of the elements that makes that world so special is the feeling of importance that pervades it. Whatever work is being done takes on a heightened significance; there's an urgency about everything. It's heady stuff. This sense of the critical quality of everything that's done in the White House interacts with the nature of those in it. Most are personally ambitious, have a tendency to be impressed with power, and are goal-oriented achievers.

So you have a small, special, isolated world revolving around truly awesome power, in which there are ambitious men and women who are convinced of the importance of what they are doing, and feel they have a better grasp of significant issues than those removed from the seat of all that power. But that's not all. If it were, the White House could be a think tank, and it's not. On the contrary, the White House is the hub of the Executive branch of the Government, where decisions of government are implemented. The Hill is the talk-about-it place; the White House is the do-it place.

All this doesn't necessarily lead to abuse; it just makes abuse easier. If you are convinced that what you are doing is right, important and urgent, you may well be impatient with anything that might slow you down or bring you to a halt.

The scene is set, the players are in place to take that next step, which will carry them over the line into abuse of power. When getting things done becomes the goal, value judgments about the means become blurred; more and more the standard becomes "Will it work?" Almost imperceptibly, expediency begins to outrank principle, and when that happens, "bending the law" becomes breaking it, and secrecy enters the picture.

The White House that Gulley saw was a palace of pragmatism where dishonesty flourished. It is a pragmatic palace because it is dedicated to the work of getting things done, not to debating the fine points. "To be efficient you have to circumvent the bureaucracy," Gulley says. "If you don't circumvent the bureaucracy you're a toothless tiger. Literally, you're a toothless tiger. Because you know if you go to Congress they're going to talk it to death, politics is going to get into it, nothing's ever going to happen. But in the White House you can get things done. You can make things happen.''

Richard Nixon posed the crucial question in his memoirs: ''What is the law and how is it to be applied with respect to the President in fulfilling the duties of his office?'' To expand: What is the law and how is it to be applied with respect to those who are trying to fulfill their duties to the President as they, and he, see those duties? It is a knotty question, which, Gulley says, hardly brushed the consciousness, let alone the conscience of those in the White House during his eleven years there.

''In the White House,'' he says, ''you never worry about the law. I never worried about the law, about breaking the law. This never entered my mind, and I doubt it ever entered the minds of people who asked me to do things—maybe for a little bit after Nixon resigned, but it evaporated almost immediately. My thinking was, If the President wants it done, it's right. I never questioned it. It never occurred to me that some sheriff might show up someday with a warrant.

''Say you are talking to the chief of staff about a project. The first thing you do is immediately try to size up the importance of what he wants. And whatever you're talking about is legal because anything's legal. You never say no. If he didn't want to do it, you wouldn't be there in the first place. He hasn't got you in there to tell him he can't do it, or why he can't do it. He wants to know how he *can* do it. Remember, the guy's not doing it for himself, for Watson or Rumsfeld or Haig. He's doing it for Johnson, Ford or Nixon.

''First you got to think, What are the percentages that we're likely to get caught?—because it's *embarrassing* if we get caught. In the back of their mind it's not that they're going to go to jail. It's the image. They're terrified of being seen to be using government money, facilities—any of its assets—for their own purposes. And the reason is that they *are* abusing those assets. All the goddamn time. And every administration's just the same.

''You need to get a thing done, and you don't care how it's

done. They would have problems on the Hill. Trying to get stuff through committees. If it was public knowledge, can't you see some guy of the opposition party standing up on the Senate floor or on 'Issues and Answers' and saying, 'Do you know how much the President's telephone bill is a year? Well, it's ten million dollars, plus he's got five hundred people full time to make sure his calls go through.' So you see, this is why. In order to make the White House work, it's not possible to stay within the law.

"Bryce Harlow, then an advisor to Nixon, said to me in the middle of Watergate, 'If we ever get out of this, one thing we're going to have is an honest budget.' I said, 'Bryce, there is no way to have an honest budget. You have no idea what the military spends on support of the White House.' And once he found out, he decided that was right. There is no honest way to do the things you need to do."

From top to bottom, Gulley says, secrecy is a way of life at the White House. According to him that is true under Carter and was during the Ford, Nixon and Johnson years and probably well before that. Only the extreme arrogance and ineptitude of what Gulley calls "Haldeman and his dog robbers," he feels, led to the exposures of Watergate. Even in the wake of that, in the sunny Post-Watergate Morality, when optimists said Ford wouldn't and cynics said Ford wouldn't dare, the secrecy went on.

With the recent quantum jump in aggressive investigative reporting, it has become more difficult to keep things from the Press, and by extension, from the public, but it can be done. Just as information is withheld from Congress.

Congress has been criticized, often bitterly, for failing to press for facts about activities at the White House. Part of its constitutional function is to serve as a check on the Executive branch of the Government. No doubt there are times when congressional investigations could be pushed more vigorously, but in the end they're no match for the White House's ultimate weapon: "Tell the bastards no."

"When I first got to the Military Office," Gulley says, "we had a call from the General Accounting Office. They had an inquiry from Melvin Laird, who was a Republican congressman then, about how much Johnson had spent on renovating an airplane. So GAO called and wanted to see the figures. When we told Johnson what they wanted, he said, 'Tell the bastards no.' So we called GAO back and said those figures weren't available, and the thing just died.

"Here it was, an inquiry from a congressman, from the General Accounting Office, and nothing ever happened. When I saw that, I decided right then I wasn't ever going to let anyone see anything. Except what I wanted them to see."

As long as the loyalty of White House staff members holds firm, "no" is an answer the poor bastards are stuck with. "If I won't tell them," Gulley says, "where are they going to go? Take how much it cost the Department of Defense—the American taxpayer—to send the Carters to Plains or the Fords to Vail on vacation. There's no way the Press, Congress, *anybody* is ever going to know unless I tell them, because nobody else knows. They can ask the chief of staff, and he's going to say, 'Hell, I don't know. Ask Gulley.' They can ask the President, and he's going to say the same thing."

But Gulley always knew, to the penny, what was spent on support of the Presidents, legitimately or otherwise. "It's just that it was in so many different baskets; even if someone else knew where to look he couldn't ever figure it out." As additional insurance against the forcing of disclosure, material Gulley didn't want released was instantly labeled "Classified," a very simple procedure at the White House. "How did I get something classified? I just said it was. And it was."

Although he has no firsthand knowledge of it—only records of questionable expenditures from a secret fund held by the Military Office—Gulley is convinced that the White House under Kennedy was secretive, manipulative and given to abuses just as it has been under the four succeeding Presidents. But it was, in Gulley's opinion, Lyndon Johnson who intensified and institutionalized these qualities, as well as adding a further dimension of paranoia to them.

Conceivably the character of the White House might have become less devious when Johnson left, but Gulley sees it as a strange act of fate that the men who followed Johnson and his men should have been so much the same. The soil was ready for them, and once the Nixon men were in place, they flourished. ''Nixon and his people came in, Haldeman came in, and it was like the engineer looking for the train—and there it is, ready to roll.''

But it is Gulley's belief that Johnson was the only one who ever really understood how to run that train. ''He was the only one of the Presidents I saw who knew what he had, really understood it, and knew what it could do. Johnson was dreaming all the big dreams, but his eye was on every detail. Nobody got full authority for anything, and he knew everything that was going on. Or you thought he did. With control like that he could do anything.''

It is this intensely personal view of the Presidency that provides a key to understanding the Johnson White House— and without understanding that, the Nixon White House will always remain an enigma, and the potential for wholesale abuses will also remain.

I
CHAPTER

The Secretive White House

"ONE THING I got a grip on as soon as I went there," Gulley says, "was the secretiveness of the LBJ White House, and how few people were told what really was going on. It was true everywhere, and it was true in our office, where sometimes we operated in gray or shady areas.

"I knew right away I was being kept on the periphery in some matters, but I didn't know what except that the President was involved. Sometimes I'd walk in where Jim Cross, the director of the Military Office, and an aide would be talking, and they'd stop, obviously because I'd come in. Or if I was there and something came up having to do with the President, Cross would say, 'We'll discuss this another time.' When this happened I'd make an excuse, leave the room, and they'd immediately close the door.

"I learned a long time ago never to press where there's something you want to know. Show little interest in the subject, never ask questions, don't make people start asking themselves why you want to know. That way, sooner or later, you'll find out. So I'd walk away from anything that looked like a sensitive area, and if the President called when I was in Cross's office, I'd leave. I acted as if things that didn't directly concern me weren't of any interest to me. By this time I'd

25

seen that Cross didn't wholly trust anyone in the office and held everything very tight. So I waited.

"At this point, of course, I didn't know there was a Secret Fund that was being abused, or anything about it."

It wasn't just the kind of secretiveness that covers up wrongdoing; there was a furtive feeling about the whole Johnson White House. "I got a full blast of it the night I went there to be interviewed by Cross for the job.

"Lyndon Johnson had appointed Jim Cross pilot of *Air Force One* and also made him director of the Military Office. The choice didn't please everybody—Joe Califano, the President's advisor, in particular—but Johnson didn't care. He thought a lot of Cross. After Cross came in, Johnson started to reorganize and streamline the office.

"Under Kennedy, and before, there had been four military assistants—generals and admirals—one from each service, each with equal status. Which made for an administrative rat's nest. Johnson restructured it so Cross was in charge and had aides from each of the other services under him, but since Cross couldn't be up in the air flying Johnson around and running the Military Office at the same time, he needed an administrator. The Marine aide, Haywood Smith, was an old friend of mine and suggested Cross interview me.

"Smith was very secretive about it, made me swear I wouldn't tell anybody he'd talked to me about going to work at the White House. He said that when I heard from him I was to take leave—I was at the Marine Corps Base at New River, North Carolina, at the time—not say where I was going, and come to Washington. Which I did.

"When I got to Washington I called a number Smith had given me to confirm my appointment and was told to come to the White House at eight o'clock that night. I remember the guard at the gate vividly. He looked about twenty-six or twenty-seven years old, but when he was opening the gate his hat fell off, and I realized he was actually forty-four or forty-five. The next summer he shot and killed his wife on the street in front of his home, and he went to jail. That's neither here nor there, but he was the first person employed by the White House, except for Smith, that I'd ever met.

"When I was escorted in I was surprised by how dark

26

everything was; it was completely dark outside and not much brighter inside. This was during the time Johnson was turning off lights to cut down on government spending, and "LBJ" stood for "Light Bulb Johnson." The sergeant on duty, George Miller, had one small lamp on his desk, and I could hardly see him.

"Smith came to get me, and as we were going up the steps, which were all shadowy, a guy who looked like Sam Spade was coming down. He was wearing a trench coat with the collar turned up, and when Smith stopped him and introduced us, telling me this was one of the President's Secret Service agents, I was really impressed. At that time, of course, I didn't know about Secret Service. I thought those guys were just terrific, that they were all Double-O-Sevens or something.

"There was nobody around but a secretary, Annie Webb, who had only been there a few weeks, a duty aide, Smith and Cross; and the lights were all low in there, too. In the Marine Corps I was used to glaring, bright lights, and I didn't realize they were hiding their lights from the President, who used to look out the windows to check on who was wasting electricity.

"Smith took me into Cross's office and left me with him, and I couldn't get over how plush it was—which later on I came to know it wasn't. They had sofas in their offices, and Cross had a high-backed chair. In the Marine Corps it would take at least a general to have a high-backed chair, and a general *might* have a sofa, but no one else would. On top of that, Cross had a stereo on, playing soft music.

"From his office I could see the outline of the Mansion, the part of the White House where the President lives. There were no lights on, but Cross was pointing out: There's the window of the President of the United States, and there's the helicopter pad, and there's the Kennedy garden. I said, 'Do you talk to the President?' He said, 'Oh, yeah. I talk to him all the time.' And I asked, 'Do you know Lynda and Luci?' and he said, 'Oh, sure. I know them well.' I was asking all the questions a boob off the street would ask, and he was the Country Boy impressing another Country Boy—and let me tell you, he was succeeding.

"I was convinced I couldn't do the job, because in the first place it sounded awfully mysterious. Cross was a guy who wouldn't lay all his cards out; he'd tell you what he wanted you to know and no more. Later I found out that this was the safest way to work for Lyndon Johnson—you always had to be able to trace what you had said, and what you were responsible for, because you might have to prove it at any time.

"As I also later learned, Cross himself didn't really know what the job was. All he knew was there was a hell of a lot of paperwork that wasn't getting done, and he was being criticized for not coming up with answers when the President wanted them, which was at the same moment he asked the questions.

"I asked Cross how he had come to know Johnson and how he'd gotten his job. He told me, 'I was given a mission one time to fly Vice President Johnson, and I flew him from then on. I'm not from Texas, or anything; I'm from Alabama.' Then Cross said, 'As a matter of fact, I wasn't even a Democrat. I voted for Nixon when he ran against Kennedy.' What I'll never forget is that as he said this Cross lowered his voice and cupped his hand over his mouth. As if he was afraid that Johnson, who was over in the West Wing of the White House, would be able to hear him. Later on I realized that this was how everybody felt about LBJ in the Johnson White House.

"About forty-five minutes after I came in Cross said, 'Well, you may be hearing from me and you may not. It might be that I'll take on a guy with a master's degree in administration,' and I believed him. This was before I knew Cross wouldn't be comfortable for five minutes with a guy who had a master's degree in anything.

"When I left, Annie Webb was still there, and she was a really nice, friendly girl. Of course she'd only been at the White House a very short time and didn't know who to smile at and who not to smile at yet.

"When Smith and I left the Military Office he said, 'How would you like to walk through the President's house and look around a little bit?' I said sure. Everything was so dark we'd walk up on a guard without even knowing he was there, and they were all over. Suddenly in the course of our tour a door opened, and some shadowy figures were moving around in the half light. We stopped. Smith grabbed me by the arm and pulled me into what I later was to know was the White House library.

"He whispered, 'Don't say anything.' We were standing there in the dark, and through the door I could see, when the figures got closer and were standing by the elevator, that one of them was Lyndon Johnson. We stood there like stone until Johnson got on the elevator, and let me tell you, Smith was so frightened you couldn't even hear him breathe. It was pretty damn frightening to me that this guy, a Marine major who had spent twelve years flying high-performance jet aircraft, was so afraid of the man he worked for. We didn't tarry long after that.

"I can't say I went back to New River and forgot all about it, but I had no expectation of getting the job. Cross hadn't been very encouraging, and I hadn't heard anything more from my friend Smith, so I had filed my visit to the White House away for future telling whenever Smith released me from my vow of secrecy. So I was genuinely surprised, shocked really, when Smith called.

"A week after that, leaving my family behind to join me later, I was working at the White House."

Money played a key role in the things that went on in what Gulley calls the gray or shady areas where the White House Military Office occasionally operated. "I discovered right away how important it is to every President to have a small White House budget—not to look extravagant," Gulley says.

"The President who cared most about this was Lyndon Johnson; he would have liked to go down in history as having the smallest White House payroll of any President since George Washington. One way he kept the budget down was by not putting new people on the payroll; he would bring them into the White House but have Defense, the Post Office, Interior, the V.A. or somebody, anybody else, pay them.

"For example, after I retired from the Marines in LBJ's last year, his chief of staff, Marvin Watson, had me put on the Post Office payroll, and I never once saw the inside of the

Post Office. I was an assistant postmaster general for administration or something, but I kept right on working at the White House and never went near the Post Office.

"Another way to keep the budget down is just to classify whatever it is that's too expensive to bear looking into; then not only is it not on the White House budget, there's no way on earth to find it. For example, in all my years there, the amount of money spent by the White House Communications Agency never came to light because all its operations were made Classified. We did this by saying White House Communications was a question of Presidential security because, in addition to providing a constant source of communications worldwide for him to use in any emergency, the agency also provided communications for his Secret Service detail. Therefore, since anything having to do with the President's security is highly sensitive, we had to classify the whole operation. That discouraged anyone from snooping—kept it away from the opposition party, the Press and the public.

"There was a guy called Snodgrass on the staff of George Mahon's Appropriations Committee who tried for years and years to examine the White House communications setup. He wanted to see what we had at Camp David, at the White House, over at Anacostia on the helicopters, on the yachts, and so on. We toe-danced this guy Snodgrass around for years and years because when they come over from the Hill they aren't after information so much as they're snooping, going fishing.

"Johnson, of course, was excellent at fixing up the figures. When he finally decided he had to let us answer a few questions about the military assets he was using, he was very skillful. We were asked about helicopters, for example—how many helicopters the President had for his own use. He said, 'Tell 'em I have one helicopter. I can only ride one helicopter at a time, so tell the bastards one's all I've got.'

"So we said he had one helicopter, one pilot and two crewmen. Of course we really had thirteen helicopters, with a crew of three for each and an additional one hundred ground crew to maintain them, but Johnson never let us report more than one helicopter and three crew."

Part of the reason for this tug-of-war with the White House

30

over expenditures is a lack of understanding of what's *legitimately* needed to support the President. "There always has to be a backup aircraft for him, for example, wasteful as it seems. If something happens to *Air Force One,* which is whatever Air Force plane the President's riding at the time, you can't have the President stranded—not because it's inconvenient, but because it's not safe. Then he has to have Secret Service, communications, staff people—the whole works.

"But Presidents don't like people to see all that. They want to look just like everybody else—like Jimmy Carter carrying his own hanging bag when there's a cast of thousands, literally, just serving him. He thinks the public will like him better if he looks like just another citizen.

"But you've got to ask yourself, What's it going to cost the country to have the President of the United States standing at the baggage claim waiting for his luggage to come off the plane? You can't put a price tag on the President's time, but you can be sure that every thirty seconds he spends on something dumb, like waiting for a plane or for a phone call to go through, is going to cost the taxpayer more than he can afford. Democracy or no democracy, the President is *not* just another citizen."

A lack of understanding of what it takes to give necessary support to the President may be part of the reason for hostile, probing questions into White House expenditures. Another is that one President and one administration after another have abused the assets at their disposal. "Presidents may not want to be seen to be extravagant," Gulley says, "but that doesn't mean they don't like the things somebody else's money can buy—especially when it comes from a source that can't be traced to them.

"Sometimes the things they liked were big things—like comfortable airplanes. In 1967, Johnson went to the memorial service for the Prime Minister of Australia, who had been lost in a swimming mishap and presumed dead. At the time the prime aircraft, *26000,* the one that brought Kennedy's body back from Dallas, was being overhauled and only the backup was available.

"The backup wasn't nearly as luxurious as *26000.* To go from the cockpit to the rear of the plane, for example, you

31

had to go through the President's cabin—which was only separated from the rest of the plane by a curtain to begin with.
When he got back to Washington, Johnson, who always had
a problem being comfortable, said to Cross, 'That's a goddamn uncomfortable airplane. I want it fitted out like *26000.*'

"When Cross looked into it, the Air Force got all shook up,
saying they'd have to go to Congress for supplemental funds.
There was no way Lyndon Johnson was going to expose himself like that, asking for funds to fancy-up an airplane for his
own use, so he said, 'We can't have that, goddamn it. Find
some other way.'

"The other way turned out to be one we were pretty familiar with in the Johnson Military Office. We took funds that
were allocated for other uses out at Andrews, and we used
Air Force manpower, so it never showed up anywhere that
money had been spent on renovating and reconfiguring a
plane for LBJ. The bill for material alone came to almost a
million dollars, and of course there's no telling what the labor
cost was since it was all done by Air Force personnel.

"Johnson took a personal interest in the work. He had a
special chair put in that would lift and lower at the press of a
button. There was a movable wall on a track so he could close
himself off at the push of another button. He designed a conference room—all in all, it came out one hell of a comfortable
airplane. Kissinger can testify to that because that's the one
he liked to use when he was doing his thing; he got very
attached to it, and in fact came to think it was his.

"His staff was aware of this, and in the last days of the
Ford Administration, when they were planning a farewell
party for Kissinger, his aide, [Larry] Eagleburger, later ambassador to Yugoslavia, called me and asked if they could
have some little memento from the plane to present to Henry.

"I called the *Air Force One* office, got [Colonel Les]
McClelland, the pilot of *Air Force One*, and asked him to have
something sent over. He said, 'Christ, Bill, Kissinger's already taken everything off the thing but the landing gear.
Does he want that, too?'

"By the time Johnson left office, and even after that, the
American taxpayer, without knowing it, had spent a fortune
making Lyndon Johnson comfortable one way or another. For

32

one thing, he had a terrible time sitting down. Whenever he was going to have to be seated for any length of time, at a dinner, or on a platform, Johnson had to have his special chair flown in for him—there was a master sergeant in our office who looked after it for him. It was a wooden armchair with a long, upholstered seat, and the reason he gave us for needing it was, 'Everywhere I go they have chairs with those goddamn short seats, and my balls hang off.' ''

Johnson's ''other way'' sometimes went over the line from shuffling allocations and ''borrowing'' labor into outright misappropriation of funds. ''The first time I got an idea of what it was all about came when the President called Cross and said the sprinkler system at the ranch was having a problem.

''The Army aide, Hugh Robinson, was an engineer, and Cross sent him right down to the ranch to look into it. After six days down there, Hugh called the office and asked for Cross, who wasn't in. So Hugh said, 'Listen. Give him a message for me. Tell him we're going to have to spend a few more thousand dollars on this.'

''I said O.K., that I'd tell him, but I thought to myself that this was strange; that it was odd that the Military Office was involved in spending the President's money. Why wasn't somebody else handling the President's personal funds?

''When Cross came back I gave him Hugh's message, and by then it was clear I was going to have to be told some things. I said, 'How come we're spending the President's personal funds?,' and this time when Cross got up and closed the door I was inside. He sat down and said, 'It's not the President's money. It's military funds, and I only hope we don't ever get caught.'

''Cross said he'd get together with me on the weekend and go over the whole thing; then he picked up the phone and called Hugh Robinson back there at the ranch, and they discussed contractors and the details of what had to be done.

''That weekend, Saturday afternoon, Cross told me about the Secret Fund and gave me the combination to the safe. I realized he had decided to trust me completely.''

''In my interview with him before I went to the White House, the commandant of the Marine Corps, General [Wallace] Green, said a couple of things that particularly struck me. One was: 'You're going to find over there that a lot of people you don't expect to, have feet of clay.' I didn't have any idea what he meant at that point; I just accepted that if the commandant of the Marine Corps said it, it must be true.

"Looking back, I see how naive I was. I'd been raised in the Marine Corps, and as far as I was concerned a general could do no wrong. Literally. It wasn't possible for a general to break the rules, in my view, because he was the one who wrote them in the first place. And you did what the general said to do for that reason, because he wrote the rules.

"When I got to the White House I transferred my adulation of generals to the President. To me he wasn't only Commander in Chief of all the generals, he was the guy who wrote *all* the rules.

"It was when I found out about what the Military Office Secret Fund was meant for, and then what it was being used for, that I suddenly realized what General Green had been talking about: this was definitely not an O.K. thing to do. I thought to myself: How far can even Presidents go in this thing? There were traces of clay on the White House carpet."

That the irregular expenditure of millions of dollars could be kept secret, that even the source of these funds could be hidden in the aftermath of Watergate when the White House was held up to such scrutiny, is indicative of a formidable ability to hide abuses of all kinds.

"In the White House you discover quickly that there's nothing you aren't able to do if it's for the President—it's just a question of money and secrecy, both of which are available," Gulley says. "First you figure out how to pay for whatever it is; then you tackle how to do it—what's to be done, what's all right for the Hill and the Press to see and what isn't. Then you make the necessary adjustments. You move a dozen planes out of sight, waive a regulation, stamp a folder of papers 'Classified,' whatever.

"The Secret Fund played an important part in this, since getting money legitimately, through channels, means going public with what's planned, taking the risk that it will be shot down, and waiting forever to get authorization. Having a se-

34

cret hoard of funds makes life a lot easier for Presidents, a lot more personally comfortable, as became very clear in the Johnson and Nixon years.

"Not that that's what was intended when the fund was set up. In 1957 when the Secret Fund was established, Eisenhower was President, more and bigger atomic bombs were being tested all the time, we were deep in the Cold War with Russia, and the threat of an attack on our country seemed more real than at any other time since the Second World War.

"With this for a background, Congress authorized a sum of money to be used for the construction and maintenance of secret sites where the President could be taken in case of military attack: Presidential Emergency Sites. The sites are literally holes in the ground, deep enough to withstand a nuclear blast and outfitted with elaborate communications equipment. At first there were only a few, in the Washington area, but now there are more than seventy-five sites around the country.

"The entire project was strictly classified; the location and every aspect of the sites were, and are, considered and treated as Top Secret. To help ensure secrecy the money, which at the end of the line was in the sole control of the Military Office at the White House, was channeled through a circuitous route the cleverest spy, or accountant, would have trouble following.

"Only a handful of people at the beginning and the end of the channel knew what the money was for. At the beginning were Representative George Mahon, of Texas, the chairman of the House Appropriations Committee and of its Defense Subcommittee; and Representative Robert Sikes, of Florida, chairman of the House Appropriations Military Construction Subcommittee. At the end of the channel were the President, the director of the Military Office and a commander at the Washington Navy Yard.

"After the money was authorized in the federal budget, the Appropriations Committee allocated it to the Department of Defense as a classified item in the Army construction program. The Army, however, was not authorized to spend it—they didn't even know what it was for.

35

"Authorization to spend the money, although it was allocated to the Army, was given to the Navy—specifically, the Chesapeake Division, Navy Engineers—who didn't know what the fund was for, either. Not even the admiral in charge of the division knew. There was only one guy in the Chesapeake Division, a commander who was assigned to them but responsible to the White House Military Office, who was aware of the actual purpose, amount and, more important, the actual destination of money from the Secret Fund."

"In the eleven years I was in the White House, money from the fund, whose *only* legitimate purpose was to construct and maintain Presidential Emergency Sites, was secretly used for a variety of purposes in no way connected with deep holes in the ground, except for the well we had dug on the LBJ Ranch.

"Other ways the fund was used to improve Lyndon Johnson's house and grounds included installing a shower and a sprinkler system, repairing roads and converting a hangar, then air-conditioning it, for use as a movie theater. Under Nixon it paid for the massive reconstruction and decoration of Camp David, including building a half-million-dollar swimming pool outside Aspen, the President's cabin.

"In Ford's time the fund was used to rent villas in Vail and hotel rooms at the Waldorf in New York and the Crown Center in Kansas City so that staff members could be near the President. In my time with Carter it was used to pay for plans for a Presidential support compound on Billy Carter's land; renting trailers for the doctor and the military aides to live in, and then for moving them from Albany to Plains for each visit; and for paying the President's friend Tom Peterson for parking our helicopters on his grass landing strip. This last cost escalated with each visit.

"Secret Fund money was also laundered through Camp David and then used to subsidize the White House Staff Mess —which is closer to a dining room in an exclusive men's club than anything called a Mess; was filtered through the Coast Guard and built helicopter pads at San Clemente and Key Biscayne; helped support the Presidential yacht, *Sequoia;* paid for landscaping at San Clemente; and installed a huge generator on Johnson's ranch."

36

There isn't any evidence to suggest that Eisenhower ever made improper use of the Secret Fund, Gulley says, but after him the picture gets cloudy. "When the Kennedy people left they took with them, or destroyed, most of the files in the Military Office having to do with that Administration, including Secret Fund records. Only a few figures have turned up.

"Kennedy seems to have held the fund very close. When Johnson went to the White House he inherited Kennedy's Military Office, where no one guy was in charge; the military assistants each held equal status. Johnson's first move in reorganizing the office, before making Cross the director, was to put the senior officer, Army Major General Chester Clifton, in charge.

"Until that moment, Clifton, who was supposed to share equal responsibility with the Air Force and Navy and Marine assistants, didn't know of the existence of the Secret Fund, although more than $5 million had been spent from it. Apparently Kennedy had dealt directly with the naval assistant.

"The bookkeeping for the fund, the fact that there was never an audit, and the secrecy around it meant that almost every trace of it could be made to disappear by the two or three people who controlled it. There is a total amount spent from the fund in the years 1961 1963 of $5,566,323.00 but virtually no indication of where the money went. There's no clear picture of what amount went into sites in Kennedy's time and what didn't, but there are individual items totaling $313,225.35 that apparently didn't go into deep holes in the ground."

Because of the way the fund was meant to be used, and how it was abused, figures for expenditures from it are fragmentary and scattered. They have turned up in out-of-the-way places, stuck in unlikely files and folders. "The Kennedy figures aren't consistent, and because of the code words, they need some explaining," Gulley says. " 'Tally Ho' and 'Bunker Hill' were in-house Secret Service code names for Glen Ora, the place rented by the Kennedys in Middleburg, Virginia, and the Kennedy Compound in Hyannisport, Massachusetts. 'Tally Ho' and 'Glen Ora' are used interchangeably, and so are 'Bunker Hill' and 'Boston.' 'Chateau' refers to the house the Kennedys built at Rattlesnake Canyon, Virginia.

"Lakeworth Shelter was a Presidential Emergency Site, which it no longer is, but I've been told that the money spent there was for alterations to the property which would make it a comfortable fishing camp. Peanut Island, Palm Beach, Florida, was a small island belonging to the Coast Guard, immediately adjacent to property owned by Joseph Kennedy, the President's father. Money for the work done there was transferred from the Secret Fund and used for landscaping and general beautification; why it should have continued until 1967 is unexplained."

The figures relating to the Kennedy Administration follow.

"Johnson got a grip on the fund immediately on assuming the Presidency and left no one in any doubt that not one penny of it was to be spent without direct authorization from him. How Kennedy made his wishes known no one knows, but Johnson had a style all his own. As soon as he decided what he wanted done at the ranch—an irrigation system installed or roads resurfaced, for instance—he'd call Cross and bitch about what the military had done to his property, how we had damaged it and had to put it right.

"One time he called his aide at dawn complaining: 'Your President is going blind!' and hung up—which put the poor guy into a panic until he got a follow-up call saying: 'You know *why* your President is going blind? It's because of all your goddamn military vehicles; they're tearing up my roads, and the dust is getting in my eyes.' It turned out he wanted some Air Force water trucks put on the ranch to sprinkle his dusty Texas roads.

"Once he'd made it clear the military was responsible for whatever it was he wanted, he'd either tell Cross to get a contractor and have it done, or tell him which contractor to use, and then he'd wind up: 'And since it's military, you bastards can pay for it.'

"Obviously, since the only money the Military Office had was the Secret Fund, the bills had to be paid from that, so when they came in, Cross would send them over to the com-

SPECIAL PROGRAMS FUND
PRESIDENT EISENHOWER
  No indication

PRESIDENT KENNEDY

March 1961	Snow removal & guard booths, Glen Ora	$ 1,549.25
April 1961	Contract "Tally Ho"	6,854.00
April 1961	Contract, electrical work, Glen Ora	1,973.00
April 1961	"Tally Ho"	2,473.82
October 1961	Presidential logistical support, Boston	55,000.00
March 1962	"Bunker Hill"	40,000.00
October 1962	Contract, floodlights, "Tally Ho"	1,131.00
November 1962	Contract, repair and replace power lines	618.00
April 1963	General construction (Nelson Construction Co.)	69,235.98
April 1963	Modify electric service, "Tally Ho"	472.43
May 1963	Fire protection and alarm system, Chateau	10,505.01
June 1963	Security screens, Chateau	12,194.02
June 1963	Presidential logistical support, Boston	13,048.54
June 1963	Presidential logistical support, San Francisco	178.00
July 1963	Presidential logistical support, Charleston, S.C. (Lakeworth Shelter)	96,995.70
April 1964	Move guard booths	996.60
	TOTAL	$313,225.35

(Because of inadequate documentation the following is presumed: built by Atlantic Fleet Seabees on land of Coast Guard next to Ambassador Kennedy residences.)

1962–67	Fallout shelter, Peanut Island	$ 96,996.00

PRESIDENT JOHNSON

Location	Description	Date	Cost	Fund
LBJ Ranch	Communications equipment,[1] construction and improvements to communications area	1964–69	$1,306,202	Classified (DCA)
LBJ Ranch	Recurring communications costs	1964–69	2,266,800 ($453,360 per yr. for 5 yrs.)	Classified (DCA)
LBJ Ranch	Road repairs	1963–69	27,458	Classified (Navy)
LBJ Ranch	Gasoline	1963–69	4,000	Classified (Navy)
LBJ Ranch	Trailer	1963–64	7,565	Classified (Navy)
LBJ Ranch	Correct electrical hazards	1967	15,434	Classified (Navy)
LBJ Ranch	Sprinklers	1966	6,000	Classified (Navy)
LBJ Ranch	Correct emergency generator	1967	11,629	Classified (Navy)
LBJ Ranch	Landscaping	1967	3,830	Classified (Navy)
LBJ Ranch	Water supply system repairs	1967	1,112	Classified (Navy)
LBJ Ranch	Power supply	1967	8,779	Classified (Navy)
LBJ Ranch	Hangar work	1968	21,500	Classified (Navy)
LBJ Ranch	Irrigation (airfield)	1968	24,000	Classified (Navy)
LBJ Ranch	Well drilling	1968	3,000	Classified (Navy)
		Total:	$3,707,309	

[1] Maintenance of grounds assumed by the U.S. Park Service.

mander at the Chesapeake Division and tell him to withdraw the necessary amount.

"Nixon was told about the fund when he took office but apparently turned the whole matter over to Haldeman since, unlike Johnson, Nixon never directly contacted us. Haldeman himself rarely called us; instead we'd hear from his errand runner, Higby, who'd say, 'Bob said to get this done and to pay for it from your fund.'

"It was all cut-and-dried. Haldeman said what was wanted; we got it done and told the commander to withdraw the money from the fund to pay the bills—which in the case of Camp David were astronomical. The figures on Camp David are incomplete, as all the figures are for each administration, but the swimming pool, for example, actually cost over $500,000 because an underground shelter had to be reinforced so the pool could be dug above it.

"Many of the numbers show up as lump sum transfers from the fund to one of the services. The helicopter pad and the office complex at San Clemente, for example, were built on property belonging to the Coast Guard adjacent to the Nixon property, and money for the work was transferred to the Coast Guard from the Secret Fund.

"I have no direct evidence that Gerald Ford knew or didn't know about the fund; I do know he never fully understood how the White House worked or who did what in support of the Presidency. His two chiefs of staff, Don Rumsfeld and Dick Cheney, did know about the fund, but their approach to it seemed to be: the guys in the Military Office are problem solvers; if you want something done, go see them.

"During the Ford years I basically made the expenditures from the fund on my own. If the President was going somewhere outside Washington, essential staff people like the doctor, who is military, or the military aide with the 'Football' had to stay near him. If no other provision was made for them, as it was not in Kansas City at the 1976 Republican National Convention, I took money from the fund and rented hotel rooms.

"When the President went to Vail, I leased villas for the military close to Ford's—and since he stayed in the high-rent district, our rent was high, too. So I took it out of the fund. On a trip to New York City the President was staying at the Waldorf, and staff members, including essential staff, were given thirty dollars per diem, which wouldn't rent them a chair in the lobby. I got them rooms near the President, which is where they were supposed to be.

"Because I became director of the Military Office while Ford was President, there are no records of how the fund was spent—I didn't keep any. For the same reason, there are no records of fund expenditures during my time with Carter. Carter was fully briefed on the fund—I briefed him, and I'll go into that in some detail later on. How the money has been spent since I left, only Carter and perhaps his cousin Hugh know."

"There were a lot of reasons Presidents abused the fund. In some cases it was a simple matter of getting the military to do and pay for something a President wanted, like the work that

PRESIDENT NIXON
SUMMARY OF UTILIZATION OF FUNDS
SINCE 1 JAN. 1969

CONSTRUCTION

PRESIDENTIAL MILITARY SUPPORT

Transfer to U.S. Coast Guard for construction of foundations, utilities, helicopter pad, earthwork, landscaping, paving and erection of structure, Western White House complex	$423,000
Support of military labor at Western White House office complex	5,600
Revert funds to U.S. Army Corps of Engineers for construction of helicopter landing structure, Biscayne Bay, Key Biscayne	418,000
Security improvements dredging, electrical improvements, building improvements, Presidential yacht support, Washington Navy Yard	151,931

CAMP DAVID

Aspen improvements, including construction of pool	238,583*
Engineering	9,400
Construction of replacement guest cottages, Phase I	159,623
Construction of replacement guest cottages, Phase II	188,588
Design, engineering	24,980
Construction of conference center	703,098
Engineering	43,500
Sentry buildings, related paving, electrical	51,321
Air conditioning, BEQ	12,170
Modernization of electrical generation and distribution system	36,039
Design	9,005
Heating–air-conditioning modernization, Aspen	1,261
Heating system expansion	9,838
Fire alarm system improvements	4,583

EQUIPMENT

Initial outfitting, Camp David Guest cottages, Phase I	18,500

* Does not include $261,417 for reinforcement of underground shelter.

42

EQUIPMENT (*cont.*)

Guest cottages, Phase II	22,064
Conference facility	75,000
Smoke detection devices	5,701
Procure office trailer, Camp David	4,000

MAINTENANCE

Roof repairs, Camp David	20,501
Air-conditioning and humidity control repairs	64,245
Steam repairs, Camp David	31,110
Replace trees for screening, Camp David	10,000
Electrical distribution system, Camp David	7,951
Total:	$2,749,592

was done on the LBJ Ranch. In others it was also a way of keeping what was being done, and the extravagance of it, secret from Congress and the people, as in the case of Camp David.

"In addition, using the fund meant that work could be done not only without anyone knowing, but it could be done immediately and without hassle. To rebuild Camp David according to the rules would have meant going to Congress and asking for funds. This would have set the Democratic cats among the Republican pigeons, and the air over Washington would have been thick with feathers. It also would have meant a three-year delay after the project was approved before the work would even begin.

"The temptation of a ready source of money with no strings attached—no questions to answer or explanations to make—is tremendous. Things you'd hesitate to do, or would never do if you had to account for them, seem O.K. when no one is looking. Then there's the confusion in the White House over whose money, or whose airplane, or whatever, it really is. Presidents and those close to them quickly come to think of such things as theirs, that they have a right to them."

Greed, expediency, concern with their image, and the simple facts that it was there, that nobody knew about it and that it was so easy to use, Gulley says, were all reasons the fund was abused. What made these abuses possible in the first place was the ease with which secrecy could be established and maintained in the White House.

II
CHAPTER

Lyndon Johnson

GULLEY MAKES CLEAR that cloaks of secrecy are readily available at the White House, and they screen all kinds of manipulations—financial, political and personal. As soon as he reached the Military Office, Gulley walked into a tangled web of money, secrecy and suspicion largely spun out of Johnson's complicated nature. His capacity for distrust, bordering on, or perhaps extending into, paranoia, was of legendary proportions. And he had been thrust into the Presidency under conditions that only stretched it further.

Johnson's affliction spread like a contagion through the White House, with aftereffects that extended through successive administrations. One way to understand how secrecy and deceit apparently took such firm root in the White House is to look at Lyndon Johnson as Gulley saw him.

THE INSATIABLE PERSONALITY

Johnson was in the Military Office one morning shortly after Gulley came to the White House, making fun of a staff member who had lavishly redecorated his office in an effort to enhance his status. Suddenly the President turned to Gulley and said, "Just you remember this: There's only two kinds at the White House. There's elephants and there's pissants. And I'm the only elephant.''

Johnson reveled in being an elephant and never let anyone forget his pissant status. No small shopkeeper ever felt more intensely than he the personal nature of the business he was running. LBJ lived over the store; the Presidency was *his*. Because it *was* his, this most manipulative of men felt that he could do more or less what he liked. And some of it he did quietly out of sight.

"Before I came into the White House," Gulley says, "what I saw when I looked at Lyndon Johnson on television was this sorrowful, huge man who convinced me that a terrible burden had been put on his back, one that he hadn't wanted; that he was trying to make the best he could of the situation he found himself in; that he really hadn't been prepared for what had befallen him; that he wasn't the eloquent speaker that Kennedy was; and that he was a father figure who was going to do the very best he could. I carried this impression of Lyndon Johnson with me from the day I saw him on television after the assassination until I went into the White House.

"Even after I knew different, when I saw him on television and he would come on with that air of the grandfather giving you advice, talking very slowly and very deliberately—when in fact he wasn't like that at all—even then I had a hard time in my mind trying to figure out how the hell this guy could give that appearance and then go around the corner and be a totally different person. But he could do it.

"The first time I met LBJ was on Saturday morning of the first week I was at the White House. Annie Webb, Cross's new secretary, was there with me when the President walked in with Marvin Watson, his chief of staff.

"Johnson had walked right past me when Watson stopped and said, 'Mr. President, I'd like you to meet Bill Gulley. He's the new Marine who's going to clean up the mess in this office and replace six people on the staff.'

"Johnson didn't smile or shake hands or anything. I'm six feet two and I don't react much to people's size, but I felt this was just a huge man who was standing there glaring at me. Finally he said, 'So you're a water walker are you? Well, those six better be gone by the end of the month or you will be,' and with that he passed right by Annie Webb and went into Cross's office.

"I'd been in the Military Office exactly five days, and this was the first I'd heard of a 'mess' or that I was supposed to do any cleaning up or replace anybody but one guy. I looked at Annie Webb, who was as bewildered as I was, and while we were staring at each other we heard Johnson talking to Cross in the next office. Even if the door had been closed we would have heard him halfway down the hall: 'That a new secretary you've got, Cross?'

"Cross said, 'Yes, sir.'

"Then Johnson said, 'Will she shuck her britches?'

"Annie Webb was a pretty little thing, no more than twenty-two or twenty-three, and newly married. She just kind of sank into her chair, very slowly. Both of us were thinking the same thing: *This* is the President of the United States?'

"After Johnson and Marvin Watson left I said to Cross, 'You know, there are a few things you've got to explain to me.' He said, 'O.K. I know it. Come into my office and I'll tell you the whole thing.' Which, of course, he didn't. He didn't tell me about the fund and a lot of other things then, but he told me some of it.

" 'First,' Cross said, 'we've still got that Kennedy crowd hanging on. The President would like to fire every goddamn one of them, but for political reasons he can't. So we're left with a lot of these Kennedy people here in the Military Office as well as everyplace else.' As he filled me in I began to get an idea of how big an influence the Kennedys, and his feelings about the Kennedys, had on Johnson, and how it affected the Military Office.

"When Johnson came into office, the Kennedy Military Office had an Army major general, Chester Clifton; a brigadier general of the Air Force, Godfrey McHugh; and a Navy captain, Tazewell Shepherd, who was a son-in-law of Senator John Sparkman, and there was a staff of fifty people. Since for the most part Clifton, McHugh and Shepherd were celebrity types, it was really a social outfit.

"Johnson didn't like pomp and ceremony, and Cross told

me that the first morning Johnson was in the Oval Office the President looked out the door and this Navy captain and two generals were standing there. He walked to the door and said, 'What are you here for?'

"They said, 'Mr. President, we're here to make our report.'

"Johnson said, 'Report of what?'

"They said, 'Report on our respective services.'

"So Johnson said, 'Look, I served for years as a member of the Naval Affairs Committee; I know more about the Defense Department than any of you, and I don't want to see you over here again unless I send for you.'

"This put a whole new perspective on the military participation at the White House. Johnson wouldn't talk to the generals and captains and made it clear he wanted to lower the military presence at the White House. He drastically cut their staffs and at the same time stopped including them in White House social functions, as they had been under the Kennedys. They naturally became unhappy.

"Looking back, you can see it was pure Lyndon Johnson. His whole point was to make them unhappy, make them want to leave, and yet not fire someone Kennedy had appointed. In the course of events Clifton, McHugh and Shepherd asked if they could leave, and Johnson brought in the guy who had flown him while he was Vice President, Major Jim Cross. Little by little, Lyndon Johnson was building his own team."

As Gulley shows later, however the Kennedys might have appeared to the world, to Johnson as to Nixon, Ford and Carter—the Kennedys were quite simply The Enemy. For Johnson, however, it went further; they became an obsession. They were everywhere, threatening his Presidency, mocking him, humiliating him—it was said the Kennedys had a pet monkey they had named "LBJ."

"This kind of thing, getting rid of the Kennedy people, was going on all over the White House," Gulley says, "but not overtly. What the Johnson people did was they just isolated the Kennedy people to the point where—and this is very easily done at the White House—they suddenly found themselves receiving no papers, not being talked to on the telephone, being excluded from meetings and all that's going on. It's really a pretty simple matter in the White House to get rid of a guy with pride.

"Or they would promote a guy up and out. Because they don't care about his status at one of the agencies, they'll make him a big duck in the pond over at Interior, for example, just so long as they get him out of the White House, because that's where the decision making goes on."

It was also a question of style, Gulley says. "The Kennedys had lived high; they acted like royalty and didn't mind showing it to the world. It was champagne and French chefs, which wasn't LBJ. He was a bourbon and chili man. He was convinced, for one thing, that the country didn't like big spenders, and for another, he was determined to change things from the way the Kennedys did them. He was going to show everyone: I'm just a Country Boy. I don't need all this pomp and ceremony. And you'll see I'm the better President.

"Before I went into the White House, General Green, the commandant of the Marine Corps, wanted to see me. My being picked for the job had been done with such secrecy and in such a high-handed way that General Green was curious. No one had known I was even being considered for the job, and then all of a sudden Green got a call from the Secretary of Defense's office telling him some sergeant major he probably had never heard of was being transferred to the White House —where a colonel is considered small fry. Naturally he was curious.

"His first question when I walked in was, 'Are you from Texas?' He was wondering how the hell they came up with me. He'd been through my record. He knew what my educational level was. He knew my background. He could only assume there had to be some reason other than the real one that I was going over there.

"The real reason, I think, was that city people, especially easterners, were alien to LBJ. Johnson was accused, and probably rightly, of considering people from Harvard, Yale and Princeton as foreigners. He wanted to get rid of them, because he considered them nonpractical intellectuals who were laughing at him behind his back. Where he was strictly an action man, they were sitting around talking about what they were going to do. He was never comfortable with them.

"It wasn't the first appointment of that kind Johnson made; Jim Cross was only a major. I'm sure it gave Johnson much, much pleasure to replace two generals and a captain, who were Kennedyites—more political than they were military—with a major.

"But probably the strongest recommendation Cross could have gotten was a memorandum from Joe Califano to LBJ about Cross's wife. During the shake-up of the Military Office, when the President first suggested he was going to replace Clifton with Cross, Califano objected.

"He told Johnson it would be a politically better move if he put a black in the job. When Johnson didn't buy that, and Califano saw the President was really leaning toward putting Cross in the job, he tried another tactic. He wrote Johnson a memorandum which said, in effect, 'I think you should know that Cross's wife isn't a college graduate. She only has a high school education, and that could create a problem from the social standpoint.'

"What LBJ did when he got that memo was call Cross in and hand it to him—which tells you something about LBJ. And Califano.

"It wasn't only the people Kennedy had put in the White House that Johnson wanted to get rid of. He not only fired anybody who might be considered a Kennedy contact himself, he fired staff people who were seen with anybody who might be a Kennedy contact.

"The White House is a very small place, really, and there's a hell of a lot that goes on within the confines of those eighteen acres that never gets out to the public. The reason it never gets out is that the people who make it to the inner circle, or to the periphery of the inner circle, are those that can be trusted to keep their mouths shut, so for the Johnson people to have a Kennedyite in their midst was seen as dangerous.

"The guy I replaced, a Kennedy appointee, had been kicked upstairs to a job in the Post Office, but occasionally he would have lunch with, and generally be seen around, people he had worked with who were still in our office. That kind of thing made the Johnson people very nervous, because they didn't want the Kennedys to be fed information about what was going on in the Military Office, or anywhere else, for that matter. From the beginning, LBJ saw Robert Kennedy as a threat to his election as President in 1968, and he didn't want to give him any edge at all.

"I had to fire two people because they were seen in the company of my predecessor. That's all they'd done, been seen with him. One had been spotted in a sandwich shop having lunch with this guy; the other was the driver of the car assigned to take this predecessor of mine to and from his office. One of them, a sergeant, had been in the White House for about ten years and was very knowledgeable about the place. He had started there with Ike and used to handle personal matters for him.

"Down in the catacombs under the White House there's a little room where he did some artwork for Ike. He would stretch a canvas across a wooden framework, something like an easel, and, using a film-projection light, he would shoot a picture onto the canvas, take an artist's crayon, and make an outline of the picture. Later on, Ike would paint in the lines.

"I hated to fire him, but word came down from Marvin Watson that since the sergeant had been seen with this Kennedy appointee, the sergeant might be a leak and would have to go."

"Johnson kept a very firm hand on even the littlest things in the White House. That's something we knew all about at the Military Office because we were the ones who held the status symbols. The planes, the cars, Camp David, the yachts, the Mess, the special telephones and radios—all those things that everybody at the White House wanted. With Nixon and Ford, I had a lot of control over who got what, but Johnson ran the White House the way a headmaster might run a school for delinquents.

"We had a violation sheet, and at the end of every month we reported to Marvin Watson how many violations each staff member had. There were rules for everything. For example, a car could be used by certain people for certain things, but not for others—and it couldn't be used to haul your wife. One time Joe Califano told a driver to drop his wife at the beauty shop. The driver immediately called me and reported the request, and I, not knowing better at the time, said O.K. But when it was reported to Watson, he called Califano in and threatened to take his car privilege away if he had another violation.

"Enforcing the rules wasn't a problem for me. I'd been raised in the Marine Corps, and I'd been a sergeant major a long time. It isn't the role of a sergeant major to be a nice guy; it's his job to get things done. I'm very direct, and that's been a plus and a minus for me all my life. I admit I came on pretty strong at the White House.

"It was the only way to get the job done, and the job was to be responsive to the President. This was particularly hard with Johnson because he was so impatient, unpredictable and demanding. When he was no longer President, Johnson told Cross, 'Gulley was the only man who worked for me that always did what I told him. I was always sure that if he knew what I wanted, I didn't have a problem.'

"From Johnson this was real praise, like Nixon's 'He's got balls' when he admired something a guy did. Maybe Johnson did feel this way about me afterwards, and maybe he said it because by then he was out of office and I was Liaison with the White House, which put me in a position to do things for him. I don't know. You never knew with Johnson. But it didn't always seem he had such a high opinion of me while he was President.

"The Russians had invaded Czechoslovakia on August 20, 1968, and tension was running high between the U.S. and the Soviet Union. The whole world was tense, in fact, when information came out that the Russians had kidnapped the Czech party leader Alexander Dubcek and taken him to an undisclosed location in Russia.

"I got a call about nine o'clock that evening asking me to go to Marvin Watson's office. Marvin, his secretary Nell Yates and the President were all there. Congress was in recess, the Administration was scattered, and the President was pacing back and forth talking to Marvin about getting hold of Rusk and other people he needed to talk to. When he went back to his own office, he left the connecting door open.

"Marvin said to me, 'The President wants you to send aircraft and get the congressional leadership back. You're going to have to find them and do whatever's necessary, because we've got to have them here tomorrow.' He added: 'I'd like you to work out of my office.'

"I thought I'd have trouble reaching these guys—Gerald Ford was off at a lodge on the Northern Peninsula of Michigan, for example—but I got him right away, and it turned out geography wasn't going to be the problem. Personalities were.

"I got hold of Wilbur Mills, in Little Rock, Arkansas, and Senator Fulbright was down there, too. But when it came to making arrangements for transporting them back, they wouldn't ride on the same plane. I had to send two planes down to Little Rock.

"The connecting door between Marvin's office, where I was, and the President's office was open, so Johnson was overhearing everything. Little by little he was getting more and more involved in this particular roundup, and his temper was getting shorter and shorter.

"When Lyndon Johnson got mad he'd let fly at the nearest target. At one point after this had been going on for a couple of hours, he came out to Nell Yates, who was Marvin's long-time secretary and highly professional, handed her a memo and asked her to type it. He wasn't back in his office more than a minute before he hollered, 'When's that memo going to be ready?'

"Nell was sitting at her desk with her back turned to the President and before she had a chance to answer, Marvin, who was standing in the doorway, said, 'It'll be ready in just a minute.' But Johnson went right on: 'The whole world is burning and you have to have the slowest goddamn typist in the world. Here the whole world is on fire, and I can't get a message out because you have to have this woman who can't type.'

"Later on I asked Nell what she thought at that moment and she said, 'I was thinking about getting up and walking out of there, but I'd kicked my shoes off and couldn't reach them with my feet. There's no way to make a dignified exit barefoot, so I stayed.'

"As the evening went on, the President was talking to the

Prime Minister of England, the President of France, many of the world leaders, and in between calls he was making input into my operation. He decided he wanted all the congressional leadership—all of them—to arrive by helicopter on the White House lawn at the same time. He saw the trouble I was having just trying to get them to ride together and knew there'd be worse trouble if one of them arrived earlier than the others and thought the President was showing preference.

"Finally, about one-thirty the next afternoon, we had all these guys assembled at Andrews, with two helicopters waiting to bring them to the South Lawn, which they did. As soon as they arrived and got off, the pilot of one of the helicopters signaled to Cliff Sharrock, the air controlman, and told him, 'We're missing one passenger. Carl Albert.'

"It turned out the pilot didn't know it, but Carl Albert had gotten off the helicopter at Andrews to go to the men's room. When the signal came for the two helicopters to take off, he took off, leaving the majority whip in the john.

"When LBJ got that piece of news, he didn't say, 'You guys did a pretty good job to get all these people here as fast as you did, and all at the same time—even if you did leave one guy in the john.' Instead, you'd have thought it took us a week and we'd left half the leadership stranded in men's rooms from here to Alaska.

"He was furious. He said, 'Goddamn it! Why do I have such incompetents working for me? You bastards can't even get the leaders of Congress here at the same time.' "

Johnson, himself a sensitive man and easily hurt, was strangely indifferent to the feelings of other people. Senator Eugene McCarthy said that Lyndon Johnson was "playful in the cruelest way." Showing Cross the memorandum from Califano about his wife was only one example; Louis Heren, the British journalist and Johnson-watcher, enlarged on it. "For all his years in politics," Heren said of Johnson, "he could never treat people as people."

"During the riots at the Glen Echo amusement park near Washington before Martin Luther King was killed," Gulley says, "Johnson was on the ranch and had told Secret Service to keep in touch with what was going on back in the capital. The Johnsons and their guests had been out on the lake, and as they were coming in, heading for the house, Bob Taylor, the Secret Service agent in charge that day, waited for the President and told him he had some news about the riots.

"Taylor walked up to the house with Johnson, and while the guests were going up the steps onto the porch, the President said to him, 'Let's go on over here; then you can tell me what it is you've got to say.' He stopped in front of the porch where there was a row of flower beds and said, 'Now, what's the problem?' As Taylor began to tell him, the President unzipped his fly and started to piss in the flowers.

"Taylor was trying to keep his voice low because there were three or four women on the porch and he didn't want to draw their attention to what was going on in the flower bed, but the President said, 'Goddamn it, Taylor, I can't hear you. Come over closer.' So Taylor went over next to the President, who suddenly put his elbow on Taylor's shoulder.

"Taylor went on telling him about the riots, but at the same time he was moving his body away from Johnson. Pretty soon he was leaning at a forty-five-degree angle. The President's elbow was on his shoulder, but Taylor was trying to move his feet out of the way because Johnson was pissing all over them.

"There was no way you could win with Johnson. Down at the ranch he had a cover for his swimming pool, not a really good cover, just thin plastic, and he also kept peacocks. The peacocks roamed all over the place, and every time we'd go to the ranch, Johnson would raise hell about them, that they were pecking holes in the pool cover. He'd order everybody to keep the peacocks away from it.

"One morning, very early, the aide looked out and saw the peacocks over by the pool, so he got dressed, ran over and tried to get them away before the President got up. Now, peacocks, when they get angry, make a screeching noise you can hear for miles, and that morning they got so angry they woke the President.

"The next thing the aide knew, Johnson had raised his window and was hollering, 'What the hell are you doing? You dumb son of a bitch, you're going to kill my peacocks, chasing them like that. Don't chase my peacocks—they'll lose their feathers. What do you think I have those peacocks for—for their beauty! And you, you dumb bastard, you're running all the feathers off them.'

"These were the things that made LBJ a legend around the White House. Even when they happened to you, you couldn't believe them, so when somebody else told you stories, you were sure they were exaggerating. But they weren't. It was Lyndon Johnson himself who was an exaggeration.

"Everybody knows he had a thing about showers, for example. He had to have tremendous water pressure, and the water had to come at him from all different angles. One day the President said to Cross, 'Goddamn it, Cross, I want a shower here at the ranch just like the one I have at the White House. Why can't I have that?' Cross told him there was a problem with water pressure at the ranch and the only way to get enough would be to lay new pipes and install a booster pump.

"The President said, 'Then do it. Do whatever it is to install that pump.' And he added: 'And remember, I don't want a lot of strangers roaming all over my ranch. I only want people who can be trusted. I want the military to handle this. And since this is a military operation, you can pay for it.' Then he walked off.

"Cross sent an Army engineer down to the ranch to supervise the job. The engineer called Cross at the end of two weeks, and told him the job was done and everything worked fine, which Cross reported to the President.

"The next time Johnson went to the ranch, Cross went as his aide, and since he was pilot of *Air Force One* as well, he was dressed in full military regalia. It was hotter than hell, but before Cross could change his clothes, the President spotted him, opened his window and hollered, 'Cross, you son of a bitch, get up here!'

"Cross went running into the house and up the stairs, and there was the President standing in the middle of his bedroom without a stitch on. The minute Cross walked in, Johnson yelled at him, 'You lying bastard. You told me that shower was fixed. That shower doesn't work.'

"Cross said, 'Well, the engineer said . . . ,' but the President roared, 'I don't care what anybody *said*—the goddamn thing won't work!'

"So Cross went into the bathroom, into the shower stall, turned the handle, and got hit with about a thousand pounds of water banging at him from all sides. When he finally found the handle again and turned it off, he was standing there in his dress uniform, as soaked as if he'd been underwater for a week. The President was outside the shower stall, still stark naked, looking at him, and he didn't even crack a smile. He just said, 'Well, the son of a bitch didn't work for me.' "

Getting what he wanted while not treating people as people applied equally to Johnson's dealings with women. "There was a secretary assigned to the Military Office when I got there. She was a divorcée, and every now and then she'd be detached from our office for a few weeks and go to work for LBJ.

"When I was new I wasn't aware of a lot of things, and what was going on with this girl was one of them, so when Johnson went down to the ranch one weekend and asked to take her with him, it didn't mean anything to me but that he was taking another secretary.

"They were gone four days, and when she came back she put in for fifty-five hours' overtime. Since I was the administrator of the Military Office, it was up to me to sign everybody's time card, but when I saw that I said no. It didn't make any sense to me. Even if she'd been working eight hours a day overtime all four days, which I knew she hadn't, it *still* wouldn't add up to fifty-five hours.

"I began getting a lot of pressure to let her have the 'overtime,' so I went to see Juanita Roberts, LBJ's number one secretary, who had been with him for years. She said, 'Sign her card. If you don't, this girl is going to go to the President and we'll all be in trouble.' So I signed.

"Coming back from Texas one time, Johnson brought three beautiful women with him, all young beauty queens. He had promised them jobs, and got the State Department to enroll them—at State Department expense—in a private secretarial school, where they learned to type and take shorthand.

"When they'd graduated and were working in the White House, he decided to take the youngest and prettiest of them on a trip with him as a 'supplemental secretary.' When he sent for her the first night she picked up her notebook and pencil and went to his bedroom, but when she realized she was expected to take more than dictation from the President, she ran out of the room in a flood of tears.

"Later that same night I sent an unmarked plane out to get her and bring her back to Washington. She was transferred to the Executive Office Building, and she never set foot in the White House again.

"Johnson's sex appetite was legendary. There was a woman around town who was a regular visitor to the President during office hours. He had a little room off the Oval Office, his 'boudoir,' where there was a small sofa, and when this gal came to visit, it was always the same routine. The secretaries in the next room would stop what they were doing and listen.

"The gal would go in. They'd hear the door being locked. Everything would be quiet. Then the john would flush, and the gal would leave.

"One of the White House doctors told me that Johnson's sex appetite was a result of B_{12} shots. He said B_{12} has that effect on certain people, and Lyndon Johnson was one of them. So if I read the picture right, he had a doctor in the wings with a shot of B_{12} always at the ready."

"Johnson was peculiar about minorities," Gulley says. "He really believed in bettering their lot, in the Great Society, but he had a problem with individual people—about thinking about them as individual human beings. In the Military Office we had an aide from each of the services, and the Army aide, Hugh Robinson, was black. He was a major who had graduated at the top of his class at West Point; he was the son of a West Point graduate and was an Army engineer. He was a fine, sharp individual who never seemed to be aware that he was just about the only black around, and neither were we.

"In April of 1968 when Johnson was going to a black affair in Chicago, Juanita Roberts called and asked, 'Who's going to

Chicago with the President?' We told her it was the Navy aide, Commander [Worth] Hobbs. About an hour later Johnson called, and all he said was, 'Shine up that nigger. I sure as hell don't need the commander out there.'

"In spite of this kind of talk, I think Johnson cared about the blacks, but most of all he had a thing about the Mexicans. Periodically he would bitch because there were no Mexicans in the Honor Guard at the White House. The reason was that most Mexicans were too short to meet the six-feet-one height requirement, but Johnson was unimpressed.

"Once, while he was reviewing some hastily assembled troops after an unexpected stop at El Toro Marine Corps Air Station in California, he singled out two Mexicans to serve in the White House Honor Guard. 'Get these men's names,' he said to Smith, who was his aide that day, 'and have them transferred immediately.'

"A week later I got a call from Marvin Watson. 'The President wants to know when his Mexicans will be here.' I said, 'What Mexicans?' and Watson, who I don't think knew what Mexicans either, said, 'You better find out what Mexicans, because he wants to know when they're going to arrive.'

"I found [Haywood] Smith, who said, 'Shit. I thought he'd forget. I didn't even take their names.' That caused a delay, and there were others along the line. The Marines didn't want to transfer them—one, they said, was too short and too fat; the other was too short and too old—and the Mexicans themselves didn't want to come. But we finally got them to the White House.

"When they arrived I took one look at them. One was five feet four and weighed 220 pounds; the other was about forty and looked it—and they were going to be in with a bunch of young privates all over six feet one. They were standing there not looking very happy, and I was thinking: If they're not happy now, wait until they get in that lineup.

"I took them right to Marvin Watson, who took them into the Oval Office, where Johnson said, 'Now you're going to be my Honor Guard. You're going to be right out there in front in fancy uniforms. And I'm going to be looking for you because I consider you to be very special men.'

58

"Everybody was stalling, including the Mexicans, and they weren't in the next two honor guards reviewed by the President. After the first one, Johnson had Watson call and ask us where they were; the second time they were missing, Johnson himself called and told Smith to come to his office.

"He said, 'All right, Smith, where are my Mexicans?' Smith could see the President was about to pop, so he said, 'Sir, one of them is on his way to California to get his family,' which was true, 'and the other one has a broken arm,' which was a lie. Smith didn't know where the hell he was.

"The President said, 'All right, Smith. I'd like to see the one with the broken arm. Bring him here. Today.'

"From then on we moved very, very fast. We found the guy at the barracks at 8th and I streets, sent a car, brought him to the White House, took him to the White House doctor, had him wrapped up, and took him over to the President's office.

"After a little wait the President told Smith to bring the Mexican in. He said to him, 'Tell me, son, do you want to be in my Honor Guard?' And this guy, who was an airplane mechanic, said, 'Frankly, Mr. President, no. I'd rather be back in El Toro.'

"The President stood quiet for a minute or two, just looking at him, and finally he said, 'All right, son.'

"We shipped him back to California and told the older one he didn't have to come to Washington after all.

"There was a little spin-off from that. A Mexican family that worked for Johnson lived near the ranch and had a son in the Marine Corps. One day not long after this affair with the Honor Guard, Jim Jones, who had replaced Marvin Watson, called me and said, 'The President has a good friend out in Texas who has a son in the Marines, and the President doesn't want the boy sent to Vietnam. Find him an embassy guard post somewhere.

"I called the Marine Corps, asked them where this guy was, and told them we didn't want him to go to Vietnam, we wanted him stationed at an embassy.

"They called me back and said, 'Look. You've got to have certain educational qualifications and test scores for embassy detail, and frankly this guy doesn't have them. He just barely made it into the Marine Corps.'

"I knew the President wasn't going to like that, but I gave the news to Jim Jones, who called me back and said, 'Are you ready? The President says, O.K., if the boy won't qualify for embassy duty, you tell the Marine Corps I want him sent to Quantico to Officer Candidate School so he can learn to be a general.'

"The last I heard, the boy was at our embassy in Caracas."

SHADOW OF THE KENNEDYS

Lyndon Johnson once said, "I always believed that as long as I could take someone into a room with me, I could make him my friend, and that included anybody. . . ." His track record for getting legislation through Congress, both while in the Senate and in the White House, bears out this ability to make men his friends, at least while he needed them.

A notable although untried exception has to be the Kennedys. Untried both because he never wanted to take any of them into a room with him for the purposes of friendship, and because they wouldn't have gone. In fact, he did try once, with Jacqueline Kennedy, and was rebuffed. As far as Gulley knows, this was the only time he made an overture to the Kennedys, although, he says, "As long as Johnson was President he always gave them everything they asked for. Everything and more."

The shadow of the Kennedys has loomed large and dark over each of the four Presidents that Gulley served, but it was Johnson who suffered most. He, an outsider, inherited the Kennedy Presidency, and he knew even as he took the oath on *Air Force One* in Dallas that he would be fighting to defend his own right to power from the claims of the dead President's brothers. It only intensified his hatred for the Kennedys, one that stayed with him past Robert's death, and past his own Presidency, so that he continued to savor any setback to them.

"On the Monday after Chappaquiddick happened, former President Johnson called me," Gulley says. "He didn't say 'hello,' he almost never did. He said, 'Bill? Are Dick and the boys whooping it up over in the West Wing?' I was caught completely unaware, so I said, 'I don't know if they are or not, Mr. President. Why?' And he said, 'Well, old Teddy got his pecker caught in the pickle cutter. That ought to make them happy.'

"We talked some, and he wound up by saying, 'Well, they're going to find it pretty hard to put a noose around a Kennedy's neck in Massachusetts.'

"There was some pretty thorough coverage of Chappaquiddick, but that's just about the only bad press the Kennedys ever got. The substance that lies behind the shadow of the Kennedys is the media. It's always favorable to them. A Kennedy child gets into trouble and the whole thing is handled in such a way that the Kennedys are never put in a bad light. The whole thing is downplayed.

"Whereas they'll go to any lengths to play up the crudeness of LBJ—how many times did we see him display that scar? Or the vulgarity of Richard Nixon—as if saying 'shit' made him unfit for office. Or the awkwardness of Ford—as if hitting his head on the low door-frame of a helicopter said something about a tall man's intelligence rather than about his size. Or about how Carter has a brother with a big mouth.

"The Kennedy kids are constantly in trouble with the law. There was one who had an automobile accident and crippled a girl for life—they're constantly getting arrested for speeding or reckless driving or something. And in the White House you can't help but say, 'Now if it had been a Johnson or a Nixon or a Ford or a Carter child, think what would happen.' But since it's a Kennedy, nothing happens.

"They have the aura of American royalty because the Press gives it to them. And a segment of the American people believe what they read. It's not only the people who are affected by this; it's the crowd around each President who see what's going on and are frightened by it.

"I'm old enough to remember that this is really not very different from the way a large part of the Press reacted to

FDR. This may tell you something about the social bias of the Press, since FDR was what you might call an American aristocrat, a genuine one. And John Kennedy was seen as being something close to it, having lots of money and a degree from Harvard. FDR had that mystique about him, too, and no matter what the situation, the Press would present him in as favorable a light as possible.

"Most Americans see the people around the President as cool, slick operators, when in fact they're all amateurs. What you really have over there is a bunch of guys who are tinkering; they're using trial and error, trying to find out ways to present the President in a good light. The result, as often as not, is that they make him look like an ass.

"If they could really manage the news and get the Press to say what they wanted it to say—and if all the writers were mindless—then they wouldn't have any problem. Instead, the writers feel that someone's trying to manage them, and they resent it. Furthermore, big news is bad news, sensational news, and that's seldom good for the President.

"I don't believe for a minute that a segment of the Press, a big segment, wasn't aware of Kennedy's shenanigans with women in the White House; yet they never reported them. But they never hesitated to spread innuendo about LBJ's bedroom activities. Where the Press is concerned, there's a double standard—one for the Kennedy's and one for everybody else.

"Look at the way the revelations about Jack Kennedy and Judith Exner were handled. She was portrayed as the villain of the piece. She was the bad guy, besmirching the image of the dead hero. Not a word about Kennedy being an adulterer, or about what he was doing to Jackie Kennedy, in the house where she also lived. Not a word about his bringing into the White House a very questionable woman with possible connections with the Mafia. Who was it that engineered those meetings? It was Kennedy, of course. But by the way the Press handled it, Judith Exner chased the choirboy into the White House and then seduced him.

"There is no question that all of this favoritism on the part of the Press had a direct and immediate effect on the President, whoever he was. With Johnson it was easy to understand. He had a long, bitter, miserable relationship with the Kennedys. They didn't bother to hide their contempt for him and shoved him into the background as Vice President, when he had been the most effective man the Congress had ever seen, probably. He had good reason to be bitter about the Kennedys, personal reasons. And he was a passionate, vindictive man.

"Beyond that, from the moment he became President on the plane in Dallas, he knew Robert Kennedy was a threat to his becoming President in his own right. The lines were drawn; it was terrible, but it wasn't hard to understand.

"With Nixon it was more complicated. But from the moment he took office in 1969 he was constantly aware of Ted Kennedy as the major threat to his Presidency. In a very early staff meeting Haldeman said, 'We've got only three and a half years to establish ourselves in a strong enough position that we can beat Ted Kennedy, or this will be a one-term Presidency.' In January 1969 Haldeman, speaking for Nixon, identified Ted Kennedy as *the* threat in November 1972. The message was that there was no time to lose even then for fighting their major enemy. He was more than a mirage, too.

"When Chappaquiddick happened, Haldeman's reaction was, Now that this guy is down, we've got to break both his legs. And that same feeling was reflected by LBJ when he called me and said that about Teddy and the pickle cutter. Having Teddy down wasn't enough for them.

"The Kennedys were always considered the Enemy Camp. They were a political party apart. Ford was less prepared for them than the others, because of the naiveté of his staff. All they did was sit around and hope Teddy wouldn't run, and of course he didn't; he took himself out early.

"At first the Carter people were just afraid, but then they were afraid of everybody. One of the main things that worried them about Teddy was that he would overshadow Jimmy Carter with his name and personality. As time went on, they realized that what they really had to worry about was that Teddy might take Jimmy Carter out of the White House.

"They each fought the Kennedys in their own way. Johnson kept extensive files on them, as he did on Hubert Humphrey, too. Bruce Thomas, who was head of the visitors' office, kept them. And of course it's well known that the Nixon people gathered everything they could on the Kennedys. But at the same time, Johnson gave them anything they wanted. Like when Bobby was killed.

"At about four-thirty on the morning of June 5, 1968, I got a call from the White House that Jim Jones, the chief of staff after Marvin Watson left, wanted me down there right away. No reason, nothing, just that I was to get there. I had a transistor radio and turned it to the D.C. news station while I was getting dressed—maybe I could find out what was going on. I tuned in on the middle of a broadcast about the Kennedy assassination. I was half listening, waiting for the hard news, when it dawned on me that they were talking about *Bobby* Kennedy—that he had been shot in a hotel in California.

"As soon as I got to the White House I called to let Jones, who was in the bedroom with the President, know I was there. Ten minutes later the President called me, and he was very subdued. He talked very low, and with a somberness I'd never heard before.

"The President said, 'I want you to get in touch with Edward Kennedy's office, and I want you to tell them that we stand ready to support them in any manner. If they need airplanes to pick up relatives, cars, whatever they need. We'll be more than happy to provide any assistance we can.' And he said again, 'Don't hold back anything.'

"I'm sure Johnson was shocked and upset, honestly, but even then I couldn't help thinking of what Marvin Watson had told me. He had said, 'Lyndon Johnson loves sad events. He loves to cry.'

"Just hours after he was shot, Bobby Kennedy was dead. I was in close contact with Ted Kennedy's office, and I found out then that they had a real bunch of tarantulas working for them; I'm sure that's why they're so successful. Robert Kennedy had just died, and those bastards were cold-bloodedly calculating how much publicity they could get out of this for the Kennedy family. They were telling me how the Press was to be handled, that all announcements and releases for the

Press were to come from them, not from the White House. I was extending the President's offer of help, but I needn't have bothered; they were telling me what they expected: heavy military participation in the funeral ceremonies and a huge chunk of Arlington Cemetery.

"They wanted an airplane to fly to California to bring Robert Kennedy's body back; they wanted to get airborne immediately, to get some of their people right out there; and they wanted a Jet Star to stand by in case they needed to get one of the girls who was away at school. I alerted one of the 707s on twenty-four-hour call at Andrews to be ready to launch as soon as the Kennedy people arrived, and told them the President's Army aide, Hugh Robinson, would be going along to California to be in charge.

"Shortly after the 707 left, Joe Chappell, the crew chief of *Air Force One*, called me from Andrews. He'd been in Dallas at the time of President Kennedy's assassination, and said that, as a technical matter, we were going to run into serious problems trying to get the casket into the body of that airplane. 'The way the door is made, it will be difficult to turn the casket and get it through,' he said.

"I said, 'O.K. What do you need to know to figure out what to do?' 'I'll need the casket dimensions,' he said, 'that's all. I'll work it out on an identical plane here.'

"As soon as he got the measurements, Joe Chappell told me there was no way it was going to get into the body of the plane, but since that's where the Kennedy people wanted it, I asked what our options were. 'You've got one,' he said. 'Take an axe.' So they took an axe and hacked away at the plane inside the door where the galley and communications were.

"On the way back we had trouble with the passengers. There were seat belts for seventy-eight people after allowing for the casket, but when Hugh Robinson tried to get even a rough idea of how many passengers we'd be carrying, he met a total stone wall. Every question he asked was either ignored or brushed aside; they acted as if he was trying to get in their way, not help them.

"Hugh told me later, 'I could see it written all over them.

As far as the Kennedy people were concerned, I represented Lyndon Johnson, and therefore I was the enemy. In effect, they seized control of the plane.'

"Eventually the family and the body arrived at the airplane, along with all the hangers-on—the Hollywoodites and the football players who behaved as if it was Noah's Ark. Everybody was crowding on, nobody would identify anybody, there were more people than seat belts—it was more like a brawl than a tragic occasion.

"Finally the pilot called me at the White House. 'What do I do?' he said. 'If I take off like this I'll be violating half a dozen FAA regulations.'

"When I asked him if he could take off safely, he said, 'I can raise the airplane safely enough; it's the passengers I'm not sure about. There aren't enough seat belts—people are scattered all over the plane—it's a zoo. What do I do?'

"I said, 'Let her rip.'

"That was just the beginning, of course. Then came the Lincolnesque train ride through the countryside, which meant thousands of guards along the route. And the huge piece of Arlington Cemetery, which is a national site, for a grave—or a shrine, really. Through it all Johnson kept saying, 'Give them anything they ask for. Anything.' And we did. They asked for plenty, and we gave it all to them.

"It was true all the time Johnson was President. He never gave less than the Kennedys asked. This extended even to Jack Kennedy's staff members. Some of them left the White House owing Mess bills and things like that, but Johnson wouldn't let us pursue it. He told us just to absorb the loss.

"But the Kennedys could always get to Johnson. He wanted to honor Jacqueline Kennedy for all she'd done for the White House—renovating it, recovering so many of the articles that are in it now, and drawing the attention of the public to its history as well as its beauty. To do that he wanted to give her the Medal of Freedom, which is the highest civilian honor that can be bestowed on an American.

"Johnson tried twice, but there was always a problem. Then in September 1966 word came to our office, which handled them, to have a Medal of Freedom With Distinction engraved for Jacqueline Kennedy. The citation was written and everything was set when Marvin Watson called and said to scrub the ceremony. Jacqueline Kennedy had turned the President down again—she refused to come.

"The President was really hurt by that. I don't know what Mrs. Kennedy's reasoning was, but I do know she didn't like Lyndon Johnson. She didn't like him at all.

"When LBJ was getting ready to leave office, I called Juanita Roberts and told her I still had the Medal of Freedom for Mrs. Kennedy and asked what the President wanted me to do with it. She called me back and she said, 'Bill, about that medal. The man's made you a present of it.' I've still got it, or rather I gave it to my son, and he still has it.

"The irony of the thing was that although the Medal of Freedom goes way back, it was revived in its present form during the Kennedy years as a way of honoring people for their contribution to the arts. Of course Jacqueline Kennedy had a lot to do with that, so, in a way, what Johnson was trying to do was bestow on her the high honor she and her husband had more or less created for other Americans. I've got to think it was a nice thought, but she turned him down, and it hurt.

"In fact, I think her reaction may have been what turned the Medal of Freedom from what it was, a distinguished honor, into what it became—a political gimmick. On the morning of the day of Nixon's coming into office and Johnson's going out, January 20, 1969, I got a call from Jim Jones telling me the outgoing President wanted *twenty* Medals of Freedom to be presented at noontime that day at Clark Clifford's home.

"Obviously there wasn't time to have them engraved or get the citations written that are supposed to accompany them. All we could do was get the medals. So, at noontime Johnson presented twenty unengraved medals to his friends, and whatever citations he gave, he gave them verbally.

"Almost the identical thing happened when Ford left office, only he gave twenty-one Medals of Freedom, all of them With Distinction. The request for the twenty-first medal came on Ford's last day as President; we had to rush it over to a jeweler and have it engraved. It was for Don Rumsfeld.

"A little spin-off from the Medal of Freedom is that it looks as though the Kennedys have got themselves a new medal of honor for the arts to give out—The Annual Kennedy Center Honors. It was done first in December of 1978, in a two-hour prime-time television special, with Senator Edward Kennedy kicking it off and President Carter looking on.''

SECRECY

"Lyndon Johnson did a pretty good job of being everywhere at once, or making you think he was, but there were still plenty of opportunities for wrongdoing, other than what he did himself.

"When I first went to the White House I was primarily interested in getting a thorough understanding of how the place worked, of the nuts and bolts. I saw right away that our office crossed paths with just about every other one in the White House, so it was important to get to know how the machinery operated.

"The guy who knew the most about the White House, and he knew everything there was to know, was Bill Hopkins, the Executive Clerk. He had come in during FDR's first administration as a clerk-typist, worked his way up to Executive Clerk, and now literally sat at the center of the web in the West Wing. Everything nonmilitary passes through the hands of the Executive Clerk; he's the coordinator of everything that crosses the President's desk.

"The Department of Defense had been complaining that their mail to and from the White House was being misdirected and delayed. I discussed it with Bill Hopkins, who suggested I have a messenger go directly to DOD twice a day to collect and deliver White House mail. Which I did.

"All the mail going to the Defense Department was coming to our office now, and I was surprised at the volume of it. I got to wondering what kind of business all these people were doing with Defense when we were the official White House contact with them. So I looked through the mail and found some interesting things. For example, there was a guy who worked in Califano's office who wrote and asked to be given information on which company was going to be awarded a huge aircraft contract.

"That looked like a pretty neat way to increase his winnings on the stock market, and it looked as if it shouldn't be happening. But my problem was, What should I do with what I knew? Should I go to Marvin Watson and tell him? How did I know Marvin Watson wasn't doing exactly the same thing? (I later learned that he was a Baptist with strong morals and didn't do things like that, ever.) I was too new to know who was who, or who did what, except I did know that Lyndon Johnson would come down on the head of anyone who was a thief on an elephant scale.

"In the end I sat on it until Nixon was elected and then used it as an example to the new director of the Military Office of what could result from direct contact between White House staffers and Defense employees. The new administration was working hard to be pure, which, in light of what finally happened, is one of the bigger White House ironies, and it was arranged that all Department of Defense communications went through our office, but that was later."

Gulley quickly learned his way around the White House, but like everyone else who worked for LBJ, he was constantly being taken off guard by the President, who rarely gave anyone advance notice of his plans. There were many reasons for the suddenness of Johnson's activities, and the secrecy that surrounded them.

Being afraid of leaks might be called a professional reason for secrecy. Johnson had more-personal reasons as well. "Two of his favorite targets for tormenting," Gulley says, "were the Press and the Secret Service.

"One thing Johnson liked to do when he made a trip was keep it a secret from the Press until an hour before he was ready to go. There was no way the Press could charter a plane in an hour, of course, so when they'd complain he'd tell us, 'O.K. Rent them one of our airplanes since they don't have time to get one of their own.' The reasoning behind this was that the Military Office would then have total control of the

Press airplane; it could only land when and where we said it could land, and the crew would respond at all times to the cockpit of *Air Force One*.

"If the pilot of the plane the Press was in was told to wait the safety period before it landed—an airport is closed to other aircraft until the President's plane has landed unless another plane is specifically cleared by *Air Force One* to land at the same time—that meant LBJ would be off and gone before the Press even hit the ground. Naturally they would bitch and yell and scream, but it didn't make any difference to LBJ.

"Johnson hated the Press. It didn't matter how effective he was, the Press still pictured him, not as a statesman and leader, but as a boor. Then there was the Walter Jenkins thing, and the Press really tore him up over that.

"Walter Jenkins was Johnson's first White House chief of staff, but, more important than that, he was a close friend and Johnson was loyal to him. Jenkins was picked up by the police on a morals charge in the men's room of a YMCA in Washington one night, and to see him mauled by the press—to see the holiday they seemed to be having over what to Johnson was a deep personal tragedy—it was too much.

"That was when he really put the clamp on the White House association with the Press. It became Them and Us. No one was to talk to the Press; any inquiry the staff got from them about anything was to be reported. From that time on, Johnson was two-faced with the Press; he'd smile at them in his office, and the minute the door was closed behind their back, they were dead.

"Another reason for Johnson's secrecy was that he was deathly afraid of leaks. He didn't trust anybody to keep his mouth shut, so sometimes he took extreme measures. When Premier Aleksei Kosygin of the Soviet Union was in New York in June of 1967, complaining to the U.N. that Israel had started the Six-Day War, Johnson decided he'd like to meet with him, but on his own terms.

"Johnson, because of protocol, said, 'I'm sure as hell not going to go to *New York*,' but Kosygin said, '*I'm* sure as hell not going to go to Washington.' Finally Johnson came up with

70

a solution: they'd find a place that was exactly halfway between. Which is what they did.

"One of Johnson's aides laid a ruler on a map to find a spot exactly halfway between New York and Washington, and came up with Glassboro, New Jersey. In the end they held their meetings at the state college there, but Johnson was so secretive about his plans that no one knew anything about them until two hours before he was ready to announce them to the Press.

"At that point he called into the bedroom the people who absolutely had to know: Watson, the chief of staff; George Christian, the press secretary; and Cross, because Johnson had to know whether a plane could land near Glassboro. Once Johnson got them in the bedroom he told them what he was going to do—and then he wouldn't let them leave. He didn't even trust *these* guys to keep quiet, so he just locked them in with him until it was time to tell the Press.

"Part of the reason why Johnson acted the way he did with the Press was that he hated them, but he also knew that if the Press found out where he was going, they would call ahead to their bureau wherever it was, which would be the same as telling the world, including all the assassins in it. The Secret Service kept Johnson scared to death. They were still in shock from the Kennedy assassination and never missed an opportunity to frighten the President. Before he went anywhere they'd tell him all about the possible assailants that were last known to be in the area, or that could be coming to the area, or that they had lost sight of but might possibly turn up in the area.

"There's a lot of romantic bullshit about the Secret Service. And they're still living off their finest hour—the Kennedy assassination when they protected Lyndon Johnson and Jacqueline Kennedy, who weren't the targets anyway, while the President got killed. The most dangerous thing about it is that if you didn't know, you might even feel safe with those guys around.

"The truth is that Secret Service is the worst, most inefficient, badly run, highly political outfit in the United States Government. In all my years at the White House I only saw two or three really outstanding agents in the Secret Service, with the intelligence and the desire to do the job they were there to do.

"One thing they did focus on, though, was taking advantage of any opportunity to better their lot. The Secret Fund wasn't the only classified fund controlled by the Military Office. There was another, much smaller one, code-named 'Greenball.' It was established in the aftermath of the Kennedy assassination to provide Defense Department 'support items' to the Secret Service detail.

"In order for the White House to keep some control over how Greenball funds were spent, Secret Service had to make their request to our office, and if we approved it, we would send it on to the Department of Defense. Some of the 'support items' they requested, in addition to cases of the sunglasses which all Secret Service agents feel they need in order to be properly dressed, were fleece-lined leather flight jackets, foul weather gear, and safety shoes—expensive, well-constructed shoes used on the decks of aircraft carriers.

"A President might go out on a carrier once in four years, or he might not, but every agent felt he needed to be prepared. Coincidentally, these articles are also great for hunting, backpacking, and all the other neat outdoor things Secret Service guys are into. As are the shotguns and other weapons and ammunition they requested but which were not used for any kind of protection.

"It was another case of 'What the hell—it's not our money,' and the fact that Greenball was classified made it easy to abuse the fund.

"This was an irritant in our relationship with Secret Service, but the trouble went a lot deeper. It was apparent to me as soon as I got to the White House in 1966 that the Secret Service had a Seven Days in May mentality. They literally seemed to think the military was going to take over the White House at any moment—which didn't encourage us to trust them. And our mistrust was well placed.

"Secret Service had teams that periodically swept all the White House offices to be sure no one had dropped any bugs, but not trusting them, we had our own guys, Charlie Sither and his crew, come in right behind them after they'd swept our office. We wanted to be sure that while they were around looking for other people's bugs they didn't drop a few of their own.

"On two occasions we did find bugs on our telephone after they'd finished their sweep, and our guys left them in place just to confuse the issue. Whichever way you look at it, whether these were Secret Service bugs or somebody else's bugs that they didn't find, it makes them look bad.

"This gives you an idea of the relationship between Secret Service and the military at the White House. The fact that our relationship was strained wasn't so important, but it led to a situation that had the potential for becoming dangerous. It got so that if Secret Service got a piece of information about the President's plans, they would withhold it from the military, and the military would do the same thing.

"Lyndon Johnson only complicated matters. He never fully trusted Secret Service, any more than he ever fully trusted anyone else. Over and over, when he was planning a trip, for example, he would say: 'Don't you tell Secret Service. Don't you tell them anything.' Part of it was his suspicious nature, and part of it was that they had come to him bearing tales about other people, and no doubt he assumed they were bearing tales about him. But most of it, I believe, was the Kennedy connection.

"The head of Johnson's Secret Service detail was Lim Johns, and the reason he got the job, in which I felt he was always over his head, was that Johnson was grateful to him. Johns had been in the car with Johnson in the motorcade in Dallas when Kennedy was shot and had immediately thrown the Vice President onto the floor of the car and himself on top of him.

"He'd then taken Johnson to a room in the hospital and kept him there with the shades drawn while they worked on Kennedy. In view of this, when Johnson became President he made Lim Johns head of his protective detail, as a reward.

"The second man on Johnson's detail, however, was Clint Hill. Hill was the one who crawled up on the back of Ken-

73

nedy's car when he was shot and pushed Jacqueline Kennedy back into it. He left the White House and stayed with Mrs. Kennedy for a time, but then came back to Johnson's detail as Lim Johns's deputy. By the time he returned, I feel sure, the Kennedys had a special interest in him and he was keeping them informed about what was going on in the White House. And I believe that's what Johnson thought, too.

"This question of where the Secret Service's loyalty really lay extended past Lyndon Johnson's time and got a pretty good airing as late as 1974, just after Nixon resigned.

"About two weeks after Nixon left office, Rose Woods, who was still at the White House, called me and said there had been a threat on Julie Nixon Eisenhower's life. Rose had called Secret Service and asked them to do something, but they refused. Just said a flat no. So Rose called me and said Julie was arriving at National Airport and was there something *I* could do.

"I called Alex Butterfield, who by then was head of the Federal Aviation Administration, which has Dulles and National airports under its direct operational control. He arranged with his own security people and the FBI to get Julie off the plane and into a car in an underground garage.

"The thing that was particularly galling was that I knew that two weeks before, when one of the children of Robert Kennedy had been threatened, Ethel Kennedy had called Clint Hill at Secret Service, and he had sent a slew of agents to Boston where the child was. Robert Kennedy had been dead for six years and had never even been President. You could say Secret Service has always had a soft spot for the Kennedys. A fact that wasn't lost on Johnson.

"And Johnson, being Johnson, didn't just let things pass. One of his favorite games on the ranch was Let's Lose Secret Service. He loved to drive fast, and it was all his agents could do to keep up with him at the best of times, but when he got playful, Secret Service was in trouble. One time when he was streaking ahead of the follow car he pointed back and said, 'Look at those bastards back there. They're supposed to be Secret Service, but they look like a bunch of goddamn Mexican generals: all you can see is elbows and asses.'

"And there was the time he gave away their car and left them stranded in the middle of a dusty street in Texas. For reasons nobody knows, Johnson started making friends with the local clergy near the ranch. He took the Catholic priest on *Air Force One* to Adenauer's funeral, and he invited one of the Protestant ministers and his wife to a State Dinner at the White House. Then, in the fall of 1968, he found he was left with another Protestant, a Lutheran minister; he hadn't done anything for him yet.

" 'What kind of a car do you have, Preacher?' Johnson asked him after services one Sunday. When the minister pointed to a Chevy nine or ten years old, Johnson said, 'Well, you ought to have a better car than that. I'm going to give you that new station wagon there,' said the President, pointing to the Secret Service follow car. He then ordered the agents out of the automobile, handed the keys to the minister, and roared off in his white convertible."

Johnson not only enjoyed secrecy and the power it gave him; he felt he had an absolute right to it, Gulley says. "Basically, Johnson felt he could do anything he wanted to, that it was nobody's business but his, and that if you worked for him it was your job to protect his privacy—keep his secrets. It was understood, of course, that if you didn't you were a dead man. All the same, the size of some of his secrets was impressive.

"Like the fact that he had 110,000 acres of land in Chihuahua, Mexico, and used to make clandestine trips to visit it while he was President.

"I don't know the exact date he acquired the land—it was going to be his second ranch—but the first time he visited it that I was aware of was in early 1967. The property was 30 miles northwest of Carmago, and there was nothing there but a 4,600-foot airstrip. He made four trips down to Chihuahua from the LBJ Ranch in Texas while he was still in office, and we were nervous about every one of them.

"These trips had to violate a whole bunch of laws, probably including some about Presidents secretly leaving the country. In addition, American and Mexican customs and immigration laws were broken, FAA regulations were ignored, and certainly we were violating Mexican airspace. There was no clearance for the plane to fly into or over Mexico or to land on Mexican soil. But breaking the law wasn't what worried us. What worried us was the plane we had to use to get Johnson in there.

"The landing strip was so short the pilot couldn't land a jet safely, so we had to get hold of a propeller plane, a Convair. Then we had to make up a reason for taking it down to the ranch and find people to fly it. None of our *Air Force One* pilots were checked out in Convairs, so we had to use other Air Force officers from Andrews, skilled pilots who Jim Cross knew would immediately erase the incident from their minds at the end of the trip.

"Once they got the plane to the ranch, they'd file a phony flight plan, get the President on board without anyone knowing, and fly him into Mexico.

"The first time our guys took him to Chihuahua they didn't have any details about where they were going and what they would find there, with the result that they were outside the United States with hopelessly inadequate communications. The President of the United States was in this godforsaken place, where he had no business being, without anything like sufficient communications.

"In fact, on that first trip the only way to keep *any* communications going in the Convair was to keep one engine running while it was on the ground. This kept power flowing to the radio, but the whole thing was a seat-of-the-pants operation.

"After that, when they got him home safely, and before the next trip, we got a Convair and modified it so there would be reliable communications. Now, if anything happened to the President, or the world, while he was secretly out of the country, at least he wouldn't be almost totally isolated.

"The only part the Military Office played in this Mexican venture was to fly Johnson in and out. He made his own arrangements with the Department of Defense for improving the property after he left office. I was surprised to find he had made arrangements with the Tactical Air Command at Langley Field, Virginia, to get a C-130 transport aircraft to haul pipes and heavy equipment out to this land in Mexico, at DOD expense. He had tentacles everywhere.''

But if it was all right for Johnson to have secrets, this right began and ended with him. Johnson made everyone else's business his own, Gulley says. Mostly out of fear that information would be leaked to the Press or to the Kennedys, he soon demanded that all White House staffers' telephone calls, not just those with the Press, be logged. Whom a staff member spoke to and the subject of the conversation were noted, and the logs were picked up and scrutinized at irregular but frequent intervals. And then there was his taping system.

Johnson had recording devices everywhere, secretly committing to tape thousands of conversations. ''Johnson had an extensive, really extensive taping system,'' Gulley says, ''one that made the Nixon system look like the shabby job it was. Johnson had it installed by the White House Communications Agency, which is under the Military Office, and even though it was put in before I got there, I have the schematic drawings for it. It was a very professional job because it was put in and maintained by communications experts.

''It was an elaborate, sophisticated setup with two systems in his office to pick up conversations, 'Big' and 'Little.' 'Big' covered the Cabinet Room, 'Little' his 'lounge,' or private office. Room microphones are called 'bugs,' telephone taps are 'Charlie Browns,' or C.B.s. In addition to his bugs, all Johnson's telephone conversations were recorded—those at the ranch, in the Oval Office, in the family quarters, at Camp David, even on the road. Tapping devices were also attached to the telephones of his chief staff aides, and Marvin Watson planned to install a bug system in his own office.

''Years later, when I told him about Johnson's systems, Nixon asked me the big question: 'How did he manage to keep it quiet?'

''You had to see Johnson in action to understand how skillful he was at secrecy, and it was a difficult question to answer. But part of the reason no one knew about his taste for taping conversations was that he got professionals from the military to install his system, and only a few people on Marvin Wat-

WHITE HOUSE COMMUNICATIONS AGENCY
THE WHITE HOUSE
WASHINGTON, D.C. 20500

WHCA-A   11 December 1967

MEMORANDUM FOR RECORD

SUBJECT: Recording

On 8 December 1967, Mr. W. Marvin Watson informed me that he desired to discuss with me means by which the Cabinet Room and the President's Lounge could be bugged.

In a discussion with him on 11 December 1967, Mr. Watson informed me that he desired full coverage of the Cabinet Room with multiple microphones but with a control button connected to the large desk which would activate a recording system. He desired this system to be established over a period of the next few months, with a limited distribution of information to personnel within the White House and to be a permanent system. In the President's Lounge he felt that two microphones would be adequate because of the small size of the room but he desired a control button on the President's writing table immediately below the three TVs mounted on the wall. This also is to be a permanent system.

Preliminary discussions have been held with LTC Dalton, LTC Rubley, Captain Swift and Mr. Des Autels concerning this subject. Planning is proceeding based on the guidelines given above.

JACK A. ALBRIGHT
Colonel,   USA
Commanding

78

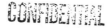

WHITE HOUSE COMMUNICATIONS AGENCY
THE WHITE HOUSE
WASHINGTON, D.C. 20500

WHCA-A   22 January 1968

MEMORANDUM FOR RECORD

SUBJECT: Charlie Brown

On 16 December 1967, Mr. W. Marvin Watson instructed me
to install microphones in the Cabinet Room and the President's
Lounge in order to record conversations taking place in those
rooms. Recording equipment was to be located away from that
area, with a control button at the President's position in the Cabinet
Room and underneath the three TVs in the President's Lounge.

I was instructed that a minimum number of personnel were to
know of this operation and that tapes collected each day were to be
delivered to Mr. Watson's office only.

Installation was completed on 19 January 1968 and a demonstration was given to Mr. Watson on 22 January 1968.

Recording equipment is located in the office of LTC Adams,
Commanding Officer, DCOU. It is concealed from sight in a
locked cabinet. Keys to this cabinet are held by the Crypto Maint-
enance Section of DCOU (Duty Officer) and Commanding Officer,
DCAU. Installation was made by SFC Joseph B. Wilson. LTC
Dalton, LTC Rubley and Mrs. Burson are aware of this installation.

Installation is extremely sensitive in pickup but produces a high
quality recording of all movements and conversations within the two
rooms concerned.

JACK A. ALBRIGHT
Colonel,   USA
Commanding

79

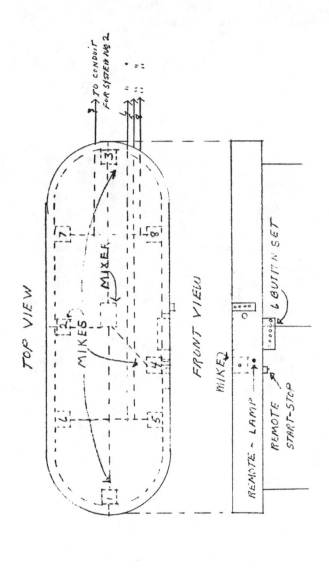

CABINET ROOM TABLE – SYSTEM NO. 1

TOP VIEW

FRONT VIEW

MIKES

MIXER

TO CONDUIT
FOR SYSTEM No 2

MIKE

REMOTE – LAMP

REMOTE
START-STOP

6 BUTTON SET

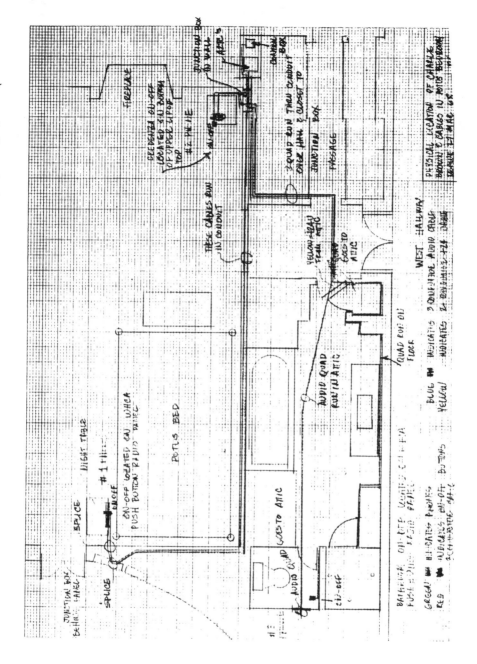

POTUS BEDROOM

81

WHITE HOUSE COMMUNICATIONS AGENCY
THE WHITE HOUSE
WASHINGTON, D.C. 20500

WHCA-A   4 April 1967

MEMORANDUM FOR RECORD

SUBJECT: Portable Transcription Equipment

     Reference is made to conversation with Mrs. Mary Jo Cook on 30 March 1967. Mrs. Cook requested that we provide a portable 24 hour tape recording capability to be used for play-back.

     Equipment was installed in a special carrying case, together with a play-back pedal, and was delivered and demonstrated to Mrs. Cook on 3 April 1967. On 4 April 1967, Mrs. Cook requested that the records be modified in such a way that there would be no indication that this equipment had been provided to her and the accountability on the equipment be dropped.

     Colonel Rubley was informed to take steps to drop accountability for this equipment this date.

JACK A. ALBRIGHT
Colonel,   USA
Commanding

82

WHITE HOUSE COMMUNICATIONS AGENCY
THE WHITE HOUSE
WASHINGTON, D.C. 20500

WHCA-A

4 December 1967

MEMORANDUM FOR RECORD

SUBJECT: Charlie Brown

Reference is made to Memorandums for Record, subject as above, dated 9 and 21 February 1967.

On this date I was instructed by Mr. W. Marvin Watson to install a Charlie Brown capability in his office, with control from his desk and the secretary's desk.

Instructions have been issued for the installation of this equipment this date after the close of office hours.

Charlie Brown capability now exists in the following locations:

        President's Bedroom (Mansion)
        Situation Room
        Mr. Watson's Office
        LBJ Ranch (Office)
        Federal Office Building, Austin
        Communications Center (Duty Officer's Office)

JACK A. ALBRIGHT
Colonel,   USA
Commanding

83

WHITE HOUSE COMMUNICATIONS AGENCY
THE WHITE HOUSE
WASHINGTON, D.C. 20500

MEMORANDUM FOR RECORD

SUBJECT: Charlie Brown

On 28 December in furtherance of instructions issued on 17 December, Jim Jones instructed me to remove all Charlie Brown installations in the POTUS bedroom, POTUS office, Jim Jones' office, Cabinet Room, and lounge during the weekend of 28-29 December.

I informed Jim that an effort to remove this facility in the President's office on 27 December met with disagreement by Mrs. Juanita Roberts. Jim told me to disregard Mrs. Roberts' instructions and remove all facilities.

I called Mrs. Roberts and discussed this matter with her and informed her of my instructions. She disagreed with the instructions, however indicated she would interpose no further objections.

Facilities were removed on 28 and 29 December. Facilities will remain in the White House Situation Room, WHCA Duty Officer's office, and a travel capability. Facilities at Camp David were removed from the POTUS area, but remain in the classified location.

No action will be taken concerning Charlie Brown at the Ranch pending further instructions from Jim Jones.

JACK A. ALBRIGHT
Brigadier General, USA
Commanding

son's staff, the ones who transcribed the tapes, knew about it.

"A couple of hundred of Johnson's tapes were sent to me, and I had them in my safe for months, until early December 1968, when Dorothy Torreto, one of the Keepers of the Secrets for LBJ, called and said some people were coming to my office to take the whole safe away, presumably to ship it to Austin with Johnson's papers.

"An investigator from the Ervin Committee asked me about the Johnson tapes during Watergate. I said they'd been hauled away, but he told me the Johnson people swore they'd looked high and low but hadn't been able to find the safe or the tapes."

PRESIDENT UNDER FIRE

By 1968 the pressures were building up intolerably. Johnson saw his political base eroding; his health wasn't good; the Great Society was foundering; the war in Vietnam was spiraling; everywhere he looked, the land was mined. He lashed out at his critics more and more bitterly and was clearly showing signs of strain, but no one was prepared for the move he made on March 31.

"March 30 was a warm Saturday," Gulley recalls. "I was in the office when Ben Wattenberg, the writer, came in to see Liz Carpenter. Her office was right across from mine, and while she was out of her room he came across and sat and talked with an aide and me. He said, 'The President is going to meet with the Press in the Rose Garden at twelve o'clock' —it was about eleven forty-five then—'and he's going to drop a bomb at the briefing.' That's all he would say. But he was one of the President's speech writers, and one of the people who usually knew what he was talking about, so after he left, the aide and I were trying to figure out what was happening.

"We decided to go over to the Rose Garden and see for ourselves. It was pretty hot, and it was Saturday, so there was only a handful of Press there when the President came out. He made a statement, all in generalities about Vietnam, and there weren't many questions. The President answered the ones there were, and the press conference was over. No big bomb had been dropped.

"None of the questions from the Press indicated they were expecting some big announcement, either. So the aide and I thought Wattenberg just got it wrong." Wattenberg denies now he ever knew or claimed to know Johnson was going to make a big announcement, but in view of what happened he's willing to take credit for being psychic.

"The following night, Sunday, Johnson was scheduled to make a television address from the Oval Office. We had been working on it all day—the military communications people are heavily involved in a thing like that—so I didn't get home until just before the speech went on the air at about nine o'clock.

"I was only partially listening to his speech because I'd read the advance press copies and there wasn't anything earth-shaking in it, but then at the end of the prepared part of the text he announced that he wasn't going to run for reelection. And there was Ben Wattenberg's bombshell.

"The reaction in the White House community was immediate. Right away everybody was calling everybody else, and they were all saying the same thing: does he really mean it?

"The next morning I went into the office, and by six-thirty things had already begun to move. No one really believed what they'd heard, because no one really believed Johnson; if you worked in the White House you learned quickly that what Johnson said and what he did weren't always the same thing. Everyone, all the staff people, believed it was a ruse for whatever purpose. To give him an advantage, or maybe he was putting his toe in the water to see what the temperature was, because at this point the President was getting pummeled by the Press, the demonstrators, everybody.

"But no one believed that Lyndon Johnson would give up the Presidency. The conversation all over the White House consisted of 'Do you believe it?' and 'No, I don't.' Everyone, that is, except Liz Carpenter.

"When Liz came in that morning, it was obvious she had been crying, probably for hours. Her face was puffed up and her eyes were swollen. When Liz got into a mood or was upset, she had a tendency to withdraw, pull into herself, and that's how she was this morning. She kept coming into our office for cups of coffee, but she was very quiet.

"Finally I followed her back to her office. She got very emotional then and said the President had to be talked out of this, that the country couldn't manage without Lyndon Johnson, that it was a terrible thing. I don't think there was one person, outside of Liz, who believed what Lyndon Johnson had said. And in retrospect I think we were all right. I don't believe he did mean what he said. I think he said it for a purpose, and it eventually backfired on him.

"A number of moves Johnson made right after his speech convinced me I was right in suspecting he had a devious purpose. For one thing, he appointed Marvin Watson Postmaster General, and that, I thought, was the most significant thing he did.

"Postmaster General has often been a highly political position, and it told me Johnson was really thinking of running for reelection. Looking back on it, Jim Farley and Larry O'Brien, the real political pros who masterminded previous Presidential elections, had both been in the Postmaster General slot. And now it was Marvin Watson.

"As soon as Humphrey started campaigning, it became clear Johnson wasn't enthusiastic about supporting him. Humphrey's staff would ask for things—airplanes, cars, communications, the list of support items a President and Vice President usually get—and the answer would always come back from the Oval Office, 'No.' They were all things the President would certainly have if he was running for office, but Johnson turned them all down for Humphrey.

"It was obvious to our office he wasn't going to do anything to make it easier for Humphrey, and the speculation grew that LBJ was waiting for a draft from the Democratic Convention. Marvin Watson was out in Chicago, things were in a state of upheaval, and it appeared to us that Johnson, by holding back support from Humphrey, was brightening his own chances at getting the nod from the convention.

"As it got to the finish line in Chicago, Johnson was out at the ranch, and he was constantly in touch with Marvin. Marvin was at the convention, controlling the whole thing, and there was a room in a nearby hotel where an advance man and two Secret Service agents were waiting. There's no doubt in my mind they were waiting for Lyndon Johnson to move into it if Marvin's manipulations worked out and there was a last minute draft-Johnson move.

"To top it all off, Johnson had told his military aide it might be necessary for him to make a trip to Chicago from the ranch, and to have things ready.

"About three or four in the afternoon of the day before Humphrey was formally nominated, Johnson was in the pool when he got a call from Marvin. He had a floating telephone and the call was transferred there. The President didn't stay on the line for more than a couple of minutes; then he took the telephone and he threw it across the pool. He got out of the water, went into the house, and didn't come out again that day.

"I have no doubt that was the moment when Marvin gave him the news that there was no way—there wasn't going to be any draft. The scheme had backfired."

"Immediately after Johnson had made his speech saying he wasn't going to seek reelection, the next morning, in fact, I had a call from the Marine Corps. They said, almost in these words, 'Start packing, Sergeant Major—on January 21 you go to Vietnam.' And they weren't smiling when they said it.

"One thing about the military is they don't like anybody of lower rank giving them orders. They don't like it at all; officers, especially, don't like an enlisted man telling them what to do. Which is what I had been doing since I got to the White House. So when they heard Johnson wasn't running, I moved right to the top of their list of Most Likely to Go to Vietnam. It became clear to me my future in the Marine Corps was murky.

"A number of people around Washington had spoken to me about jobs since I'd gone to the White House, and one of the offers was to join a small business consulting firm in Washington at $17,000 a year. At this point I was the highest paid enlisted man in the Marine Corps, and my base pay was $5,000 a year. So $17,000 was riches. In May of 1968 I made up my mind, so I wrote President Johnson and told him I had decided to resign from the Marine Corps and join this consulting firm. The firm was known to him.

"Almost at once my letter came back with a big 'No' written at the bottom of it. When I got that 'No' I called Marvin Watson, and he told me the President didn't want me to leave. He said that he, Marvin, was arranging for me to go on the Post Office payroll but stay where I was, in the Military Office, as a civilian. It was all settled. So I stayed."

"It was after Johnson's announcement, when he started preparing for his retirement, that we really got into abusing military assets—wholesale, you might say. He started moving people and equipment around so that by the time he got to Texas he was going to be very comfortable. It was all kept very quiet, and only a few people knew anything about it.

"Immediately after Johnson's speech, Cross was called over to see the President, and it was decided he was to be replaced right away by General Robert Ginzberg. Like everything else Johnson did, there was a purpose to it. Cross, of course, was a pilot, and Johnson wanted him at Bergstrom Air Force Base near the ranch, where, if the worst should happen and he should not run or not be elected, Johnson would have Cross a mere sixty miles away with all the assets and manpower of the military available to him.

"In order to be able to put Cross in charge of things at Bergstrom, he would have to be promoted to general, so Johnson set about doing that. He arranged for him to go to Vietnam long enough to get in his missions, and by replacing him in the Military Office with a general, he could claim Cross was qualified for the same rank.

"Bob Ginzberg, who was a fine gent, was on the National Security Council staff and was completely innocent of all these goings-on. Marvin Watson called me before Ginzberg came into the office and said, 'Just tell that general what he needs to know. Keep it to a minimum, and don't volunteer anything.'

"Having got Cross started on his way to becoming a general, we settled down to work. We began by sending the big stuff down to Texas. Two planes were assigned from Andrews to Bergstrom—a Convair that seated thirty-two, which Johnson wanted specially configured, and a T-39, a small jet, which we also modified to suit him. And we sent down the air crews to go with the planes.

"We put two boats on Lake LBJ, ostensibly so Secret Service could follow him on the water, and we put a naval officer down there with them, full time. He operated whichever boat Johnson was using, and he stayed at the ranch, at government expense, until LBJ died.

"We transferred his favorite stewards, who acted as valets, and his favorite chili-cooker. We made arrangements so he could use certain military services: he wanted the barber from Bergstrom to continue to come to the ranch and cut his hair; he wanted to use the commissary and the PX; and we stationed a heart specialist at Brooke Army Hospital nearby.

"GSA fixed up several offices for him in Austin; then we put a helicopter at Bergstrom to take him between Austin and the ranch and provided a crew for that. Tom Mills, the Navy chief who gave the President and Mrs. Johnson rubdowns, was promoted to lieutenant and transferred down there, where he doubled as a ranch hand. In 1976, three years after LBJ *died,* Tom was still on the ranch, and on the Navy payroll. He's a lieutenant commander now.

"At the same time all this was going on, we were sending big transport planes, C-141s, out of Andrews with truckloads of stuff for Texas. Marvin Watson told me to have trucks manned with people I could trust go to the State Department underground garage after dark and load the trucks with boxes and crates. We took them out to Andrews and put them, together with more boxes and crates from the Executive Office Building, onto the aircraft and flew them to Bergstrom. There they were unloaded, before daylight, and stored in space rented by GSA.

"I don't know what was in each crate, of course, but I do

know there were thousands of little gifts State bought for Johnson to give out when he traveled abroad. There were watches with Lyndon Baines Johnson on them, and all sizes of busts of him, the smallest about twelve inches high. There were tie clips and ladies' perfume dispensers and gold chains with the Presidential seal on them. We even loaded up some crates of toilet paper, but I've got to believe that was a mistake.

"Why Johnson wanted these things I don't know, but I do know he wanted them bad enough to get us to mount a big, secret operation. Johnson never did distinguish what was his from what belonged to the government—it was all his.

"In addition to handling his duties as President, and assuring himself of a comfortable ex-Presidency, Johnson found time to raise money for his library and the Lyndon Baines Johnson School of Foreign Affairs at the University of Texas. Knowing he'd lose most of his clout the minute he left office, he intensified his program of inviting millionaires, movie stars and other assorted Big Names to the ranch.

"One time, Johnson, who met all aircraft arriving at his ranch, was in his station wagon with a military aide, Mrs. Johnson, a member of her staff, and the valet, who was in the back seat with a bar over his legs, mixing bourbon and branch water and passing it up to the President, who was in the driver's seat.

"The plane was late. It was raining. The car overheated, so the engine, and with it the air conditioning, had to be turned off. The scene was set for Johnson to erupt.

"First he jumped on the military aide. 'You incompetent bastard. Why can't you do a simple thing like have these planes land on time?' Next it was Mrs. Johnson's assistant's turn: 'I want to tell you something. In your invitations to these people, you tell them I'm sick and tired of having them get off their airplanes and pissing at my house. You tell them, from now on they piss on their airplanes.'

"With these words ringing through the car, the plane landed, and unfortunately the first thing that happened when Mr. and Mrs. —— got off was that Mrs. —— asked Mrs. Johnson if she could powder her nose before driving on to visit the Boyhood Home. That meant stopping at the ranch house, and of course Mrs. Johnson had no choice but to say 'of course.'

"The President's neck turned bright red as he pulled up in front of the ranch house, and the inevitable happened: Mr. ——— also decided to visit the bathroom. The minute they were out of the car, the President turned on the aide and Mrs. Johnson's assistant and roared: 'Do you know *why* I didn't want to stop? Do you know *why* I wanted them to piss on their airplane? He's got a crooked dick, that's why. Everytime he comes here he pisses all over my bathroom.' "

"Johnson wasn't a movie watcher in the Richard Nixon class, but he enjoyed a film from time to time, and Lynda was crazy about them. The trouble was there was no place on the ranch to watch movies except in the airplane hangar, which, like every place else down there, got unpleasantly hot in the summer. To overcome that difficulty, Johnson informed our office that since we had military personnel permanently stationed on the ranch and it was necessary for them to receive continuing education in the form of training films, we would have to convert part of the hangar into a suitable location for the showing of films.

"The 'suitable location' ended up being supplied with a 35 mm projector and a guy to operate it, a huge screen, rows of comfortable chairs and central air-conditioning. The 'military personnel' who had to keep up with their training were two Army baggage handlers who were there only when the President was.

"As with so much else we did on the ranch, the money to convert the hangar into an air-conditioned movie theater came out of the Military Office Secret Fund.

"Another major demand Johnson made for the ranch was for communications equipment. Former Presidents are allowed switchboards at government expense for six months after they're out of office, but LBJ had a switchboard—and twelve men from the White House Communications Agency —down at the ranch until six months after he *died*. They were at the ranch all that time, four and a half years.

"Johnson wanting communications was something I could

understand. When I got to the White House I had never even *seen* a telephone with buttons on it for different lines. The damn things scared the hell out of me lighting up and flashing. In fact, what worried me most about working there was fear I would never figure out how to work them. But by the time I'd been in the White House awhile I had a console with fifteen lines and was a goddamn expert on the thing; I was an acknowledged virtuoso of the telephone.

"So it was an area where I could understand how Johnson felt; cutting off his telephone communications would have been like cutting off his supply of oxygen. Of course, I've got to think that even with the head start he had on me, and more practice, I was technically better at the telephone than he was. He never really grasped the subtleties of how it worked.

"Dolores Stacks, who was Johnson's secretary when he was Vice President, told me about a time he asked her to get Senator Kerr from Oklahoma on the telephone. He had been trying to get the senator on the phone all afternoon, and by now he thought there was a goddamn conspiracy by the office staff to keep him from talking to Kerr.

"What you have to remember is that when Johnson picked up the telephone, the minute he picked it up, a red light went on, and everybody in his offices knew not to buzz him. That he was on the telephone. If he got a call then, the secretary immediately said, 'The Vice President is on the telephone, and will return your call.' She didn't keep the caller waiting, and she didn't buzz Johnson.

"Well, Johnson was so sure that they were trying to keep him from talking to Senator Kerr, for reasons no one knows, that he picked up the phone, dialed 9, which put him into the commercial service, and then dialed the White House. He got the White House switchboard and said, 'Give me the Vice President's office.' So they gave him the Vice President's office, but his red light was on.

"The phone rang, Dolores Stacks picked it up and said, 'Vice President Johnson's office.' Johnson muffled his voice and said, 'This is Senator Kerr and I'd like to speak to the Vice President.' Dolores said, 'Sir, the Vice President's line is busy. He does want to talk to you, and I'm sure he'll return your call.'

"With that, Johnson came out of his chair, yanked open his door—and there was Dolores talking into the telephone. She couldn't figure out why Johnson was there, glaring at her. His red light was still on, and she didn't know what to do, so she said into the telephone, 'Just a moment, Senator,' then she said to the Vice President, 'Senator Kerr wants you. . . .'

"But Johnson exploded, 'Goddamn you, that's not Senator Kerr! Goddamn you, you told him I was busy. I wasn't busy, goddamn it, I wasn't busy at all.'

"Dolores got so upset she started crying, and he was standing there, hollering at her. . . . It used to just drive him completely wild not to be able to get hold of somebody on the telephone."

"While Johnson was busy positioning himself for a comfortable retirement in case things didn't work out at the convention, Bob Ginzberg in the Military Office was getting nervous. He started to wonder what was going on. One morning he called me in and said, 'I realize there are some things going on here that I'm not privy to. I don't know what your instructions are, if you have any, but I do know I'm supposedly in charge here. I'm aware that you and Marvin Watson are constantly in touch, and I want to know what's going on.'

"I said, 'I understand your position perfectly, and I think we should discuss it. Can I come back in half an hour after I finish up a couple of things?'

"So I went back to my office and right away called Marvin. I said, 'This guy is beginning to ask questions, and he has a right to ask questions. What do we do? Do I tell him, or do I not tell him?'

"Marvin said, 'Don't do anything, and I'll get back to you.'

"A few minutes later there was a call for the general asking him to go over to the West Wing of the White House. He was gone about fifteen minutes, and when he came back he called me into his office. 'I'm being replaced by someone,' Ginzberg told me. 'Probably Haywood Smith, although I'm not sure.'

"Ginzberg seemed to speak with an air of relief, and I believe he was happy to get out from under the responsibility of the Military Office. I think he was relieved to be getting off the griddle; he could see that he might be left holding the bag for a lot of stuff that he didn't even know was going on. Six weeks after he came into the Military Office he went back to his job at the National Security Council, and he never did know what had been happening.

"But Johnson sure as hell knew, and he got a scare after Nixon was elected and was announcing the names of his Cabinet members. One morning during that time an aide was standing outside the bedroom waiting to see the President about something, and the newspapers said Nixon had appointed Melvin Laird to be Secretary of Defense.

"Melvin Laird, then a Republican congressman from Wisconsin, had been after Johnson the whole time he was President; he was a real antagonist. Laird was always chasing after LBJ, especially about excesses, like his use of airplanes and things like that.

"When Johnson saw the announcement in the morning paper he said, 'Melvin Laird! Goddamn it, that son of a bitch'll lock us all up. We're all going to jail now,' and I know he was thinking about all the military hardware he had down at the ranch.

"The funny thing is that after Johnson left office and the newsies were beginning to snipe at him about his planes and this and that, Laird issued a confidential memorandum to all Defense Department offices instructing them that no one was to say anything to the news media about Lyndon Johnson without first clearing it with him. Melvin Laird turned out to be Lyndon Johnson's best friend. Of course, it also turned out that Melvin Laird had a heavy hand himself when it came to perks, when it came to using military assets to make life comfortable for himself.

"The White House has never recovered from the example Johnson set for aspiring elephants."

FAMILY

While Johnson was struggling and scheming to transform America into a Great Society, and at the same time pulling himself and the country deeper and deeper into the quicksand

95

of Vietnam, LBJ dog stories and stories of his reactions to his daughters' romances also grabbed the attention of the people. But some of the most revealing incidents between Johnson and his family never reached the newspapers.

Three of our recent Presidents have had brothers who were embarrassments to them. Carter has his Billy, Nixon his Don, and Johnson had his Sam. Ford and Kennedy escaped this fate. Ford was the only child of his mother's first marriage, and the one brother who might have proved embarrassing to Kennedy is now a leading contender for the Presidency himself.

"I had been at the White House only a few weeks," Gulley says, "when in walked this man with one leg shorter than the other, using a cane and wearing a Texas hat. He stopped at my desk and said, 'Is Jim Cross around?' When I said yes, he headed right for Cross's office. 'Hey, wait a minute,' I called. 'Who are you?' He turned around and said, 'I'm the President's brother, Sam Johnson.'

"I had no idea the President had a brother, so I didn't know what to make of this guy, and asked him to wait while I went into Cross's office. 'Let him in, let him in,' Cross said when I told him who was there; then he jumped up, opened the door and said, 'Good morning, Mr. Sam. Come in, come in.'

"I would never have guessed from looking at him that first time that this was Lyndon Johnson's brother, but once you got to know him, and saw his mannerisms, you couldn't miss it. Cross and Sam Johnson talked for a while, and as Johnson was leaving, Cross introduced us, saying, 'Mr. Sam, if you ever want anything, you just call Bill.'

"Later, Cross said, 'I'm going to tell you something about Sam Houston Johnson. He's a hell raiser and a drinker. Sometimes the President will kill you if he finds you responding to him—giving him a car or anything. Other times Johnson will get madder than hell and say, "Goddamn it, I'm the President of the United States and this is my brother. What do you mean by not giving him a car?" You have to play this by ear, but the biggest problem is that he drinks the whole goddamn day.'

"The next time I saw Mr. Sam he was in Cross's office pouring gin into a coffee cup and chatting, when all of a sudden he said to Cross, 'What do you think? Is that company I told you about going to get the reupholstering contract?'

"Cross said, 'I spoke to the Air Force about it, but they want to know, does the President know?' Mr. Sam said, 'Oh, yeah. The President knows about it. He'd like to see these people get the work. They need the work.' So Cross said, 'Okay, Mr. Sam. I'll see they get the contract.'

"Some of the things you hear around the White House you forget you heard because you aren't going to last otherwise, and I was all set to forget that, but after Mr. Sam left, Cross said, 'You know what that's all about? Old Sam, he's screwing that contractor's wife. So you might say he has a personal interest in seeing her husband's company get the contract for reupholstering our Jet Stars.'

"Not long after that, when I'd been at the White House several months, I had my first real exposure to Mr. Sam. At four o'clock on a Sunday morning my signal phone rang—it's directly connected to the White House switchboard—and the operator said, 'Mr. Sam Houston Johnson, the President's brother, would like to talk to you.' Mr. Sam got on the phone and said, 'Hey, Bill. I'm up here in New York, we're having a party, and we've got a yacht up here that we want to go out on.'

"I had no idea what he was getting at, so I said, 'Oh?'

"He said, 'Yeah. We want to go out on the river, but there aren't any lights on in the harbor. We can't see to navigate.' I said again, 'Oh?' Then he said, 'Bill, I want you to get them to put the harbor lights on so we can get out. You see to that, will you?'

"I said, 'Why certainly, Mr. Sam. I'll take care of it right away,' and hung up. I didn't have the faintest idea of what to do, but the first thing I thought of was to call the Coast Guard. I got the Coast Guard duty officer, told him I was calling from the Military Office at the White House, and we needed to have the lights turned on in New York harbor for navigational purposes.

"He explained the harbor was under the control of the New

York Port Authority, but the Coast Guard did have access to it, so I told him to do whatever he had to do, but that we needed those lights on right away. He said, 'Yes, sir. I'll get right back to you, sir,' not knowing who he was talking to but having heard the magic words 'White House.'

"He called back saying, 'The harbor navigational lights will be turned on no later than ten minutes to five, and will be on until it's light enough to see without them.'

"I thanked him and didn't hear anything more. At nine I went to Mass, and while I was there my beeper went off. It was Cross calling from Texas, where he was with the President. 'What in the name of Jesus Christ have you done?' he asked, and I answered, 'What are you talking about?' He said, 'What the hell did you think you were doing this morning? Do you realize you cleared a boat to leave that was under impoundment in New York harbor? How the hell did you get involved in this thing?'

"I said, 'What are you talking about?' to which Cross replied, 'O.K., let me tell you what I'm talking about. The New York Port Authority and the New York City police are looking for a guy named Gulley at the White House who ordered the Coast Guard to turn on the lights of New York harbor so that a boat could leave, and that boat happened to be under impoundment by order of a New York State Court.' Mr. Sam hadn't told me that part of the story.

"The immediate result of the incident was that it made Mr. Sam and me buddies, so the next time he was in the Presidential doghouse, I got involved. Mr. Sam had got himself in trouble in Europe, where, among other things, he'd had dinner with Princess Grace of Monaco and asked her, in the President's name, to come to a fair in San Antonio. The President wanted Mr. Sam back before he did any more damage.

"The trouble was, Mr. Sam wouldn't come without his English girl friend, Lady ———, a woman who was divorced from some Lord but had kept her title, and Lyndon Johnson couldn't abide her.

"A Secret Service agent, Mike Howard, went over and got Mr. Sam as far as New York, but Lady ——— had come along, too. When the President heard his brother was in New

98

York, he called our office at nine in the morning and told us to get Mr. Sam to Washington in time to fly to the ranch with him on *Air Force One* at one o'clock that afternoon. His closing instructions were, 'If that woman's with him, I want you to leave her right there on the ramp.'

"With the help of the Secret Service field office in New York, we got Mr. Sam to Washington National Airport and had him met by a car, but then he balked. Lady —— was with him, and he wouldn't get in the car without her. The driver called me and asked, 'What am I supposed to do now?'

"At this point it was after twelve and I was worried, so I asked the Army aide, Hugh Robinson, to handle it. I told him, 'I don't care if you have to put him in the goddamn car bodily, just put him in it and get him to *Air Force One* without the Lady!'

"Hugh's a big man, six feet two or three, and two hundred and ten or fifteen pounds. He's big. He went up to Mr. Sam, who was still having a scene with the White House driver, and said, 'Mr. Sam, please get in the car.' When Mr. Sam still refused, Hugh said, 'I don't want to embarrass you, Mr. Sam, but my instructions are that if you won't get in the car, I am to put you in it.' With that Sam stopped objecting and thought it over.

"Finally he said, 'Will you see that Lady —— gets to the Watergate Hotel?' Hugh said, 'I certainly will,' so Mr. Sam and Hugh got in the car and drove right onto the tarmac beside *Air Force One,* where Mr. Sam got out with Hugh right behind him.

"At the bottom of the steps to the plane there was a telephone and with Hugh standing right there, Mr. Sam called me at the Military Office and said, 'Bill, you're just like the rest of those goddamn sons of bitches down there at the White House that work for Lyndon. You get the biggest, blackest nigger you can find and you get him to threaten me with bodily harm. You're no friend of mine.'

"With that he slammed down the phone and climbed on board *Air Force One*.

"The last time I heard from Mr. Sam was on the nineteenth of January, 1969, and Johnson wasn't going to be President after noon the next day. I was sitting in a meeting with the incoming Nixon people and the outgoing Johnson people when the telephone rang.

"Mr. Sam just wanted to chat. I asked him, 'Where are you calling from?' and he said, 'I'm down here in Mexico. And Bill, I want to ask you to do me a last favor.' I said, 'Anything I can do, you know I will.' He said, 'Send me a case of those White House cigarettes, the ones in those gold packages with the President's seal on them. Would you do that?'

"I said of course I would, and he said, 'Goddamn it, Bill, you can trade those things for anything down here. I mean, you can trade them for ass.' "

Lyndon Johnson wanted to run everything—the White House, the Congress, the war, the country—and his family was no exception. He felt sure that if people would just have the good sense to leave matters to him, everything would work out right. "Everything" included his daughter Lynda's love life.

"Johnson couldn't stand George Hamilton," Gulley says. "He was a movie actor who captivated Lynda and had a considerable influence on her. Through him she met a lot of Hollywood and jet-set types, which was a new world to her, and she picked up some pointers from them. She changed her hair style, learned how to use makeup and smartened up her wardrobe.

"Lynda partied with Hamilton and his friends here, there and everywhere, getting her picture in the paper and causing comment about her new glamorous image. It was clear Lynda was having a whale of a time, and just as clear that Johnson was irritated. He didn't begrudge Lynda a good time; he just couldn't understand what she saw in this actor who, to say the least, was not his sort.

"George Hamilton was slender, slick, smooth, a sophisticated Rudolph Valentino type. The exact opposite, you might say, of Lyndon Johnson. But the thing that bothered Johnson most, I think, was that Hamilton had a 3-A draft deferment and didn't have to go into the service. He was deferred on the ground that he was the sole support of his mother, Ann Stevens Potter Hamilton Hunt Spaulding, who was living in his thirty-nine-room mansion, Greyhall, in Los Angeles.

"It irritated the hell out of Johnson that boys were being killed every day in Vietnam and here this healthy George Hamilton was safe at home squiring his daughter around.

"I don't know this for a fact, but knowing what I do about Johnson, I don't think he kept his criticism of Hamilton to himself. My guess is that Lynda was left in no doubt about her father's view of a strong, healthy, young American man who got himself deferred for whatever reason. If, as I suspect, that is the case, it explains what Lynda did.

"Lynda came over to our office and told us that George wanted to volunteer, that he had decided to end his deferment and enlist. She asked us if we could do something about it right away, and we said we'd look right into it and get back to her.

"We asked General Hershey, the old boy who was head of the Selective Service, if he would come over, and when he got to our office we all sat down and debated how we were going to go about enlisting George Hamilton. Hershey pointed out that since he was the one with the deferment, he would have to volunteer to give it up; so it was decided the first thing we had to do was get a statement from Hamilton.

"We sent him a letter to that effect, and the next thing we knew, instead of our getting a statement from him at the Military Office, the White House florist got an order for three hundred and sixty-five roses with instructions to have one laid on Lynda's pillow every morning of the year.

"That was the last we saw of George Hamilton. I can only suppose that when Lynda decided to volunteer him, Hamilton stopped just long enough to buy her some flowers before getting out of town.

"Not long after the end of George Hamilton, Lynda came to my office and said she wanted to know about the condition of a Captain Paul Dresser. She had gone to school with him at the University of Texas, they had been semi-engaged, and now she had heard from somewhere that he'd been wounded. She wanted to know more.

"I called the Pentagon for information, and we got pretty

rapid service, but even so, it took a little time to track down one guy among millions; so two hours later when Lynda came back to my office and asked what I'd found out, I said, 'Nothing. They haven't gotten back to me.'

"Lynda went into a tantrum right there at my desk. She stamped her foot; big tears rolled down her cheeks, and she said, 'He may be dead. He may be lying somewhere and no one knows. I want to know what's happened. Right now.'

"Shortly after she left, the Pentagon called. Dresser had shrapnel in his legs and some ear damage from a blast, but he was in a military hospital and doing fine. I passed the information on, and for a time, that was that.

"A while later, when LBJ was down at the ranch for a weekend, I got a call asking me to make arrangements with the Army to have Paul Dresser released from Brooke Army Hospital in Texas and transferred to Walter Reed Hospital in Washington. They were bringing him back on *Air Force One*.

"When he was well enough to be discharged from the hospital, LBJ appointed him assistant Army aide in the White House, a job Johnson just made up, and Dresser came to our office. He was a nice young man, and it was crystal clear the old man was promoting a romance. He ate dinner a lot with the family, and they'd take him down to the ranch with them.

"But two weeks after Paul Dresser came to the White House he met a girl on the National Security staff—and three months after that he suddenly up and married her. When he heard that, Lyndon Johnson decided he didn't need Dresser's services anymore. He called Cross and said, 'That ungrateful son of a bitch. You can send him anywhere you want; just get him out of here.'

"Lynda's search for true love finally ended—in our office. There are military social aides attached to our staff who help out at White House social events and act as escorts when needed. The Military Office keeps a book with photographs and biographies of these aides, and when Lynda needed someone to go with her to Rehoboth Beach for some kind of do, we sent the book over to her. She looked through it and picked Chuck Robb; that's how the romance began.

"On the day of their wedding, our office was asked to get a

bus for the guests the President was taking to Texas with him after the reception. They had to get out to Andrews, to *Air Force One,* and the President said he particularly did not want a bus with 'U.S. Army' written all over the sides—that this was a wedding; he wasn't taking them on maneuvers.

"Whatever was done, I knew it would be pretty damn obvious from the color what it was—a big, old Army bus—but I asked LeRoy Borden in the White House garage to get a bus, some cans of spray paint, and do what he could. It was ready and sitting outside the door to the Diplomatic Reception Room before the guests came out.

"Now you know all the money in Texas was at that wedding, all of it. I said to Cliff Sharrock, who was with me, that there was no way in the world those people were going to get on that Army bus, but just then John Connally and his wife came out. Cliff Sharrock said, 'I know how we'll get them on the bus and have 'em love it.'

" 'Governor,' Cliff said to Connally, 'would you and Mrs. Connally please get on this bus here? It'll take you out to *Air Force One.*' When the others saw John Connally get on that bus, they just jumped on board, one after another, like sheep.

"That left the family, who were going on the helicopter. The President got on carrying Luci's baby, and he was obviously very tired. He'd had a long day, and he was grouchy. The helicopter started to turn its rotors, when all of a sudden they stopped, the door opened, and out came Jim Jones saying, 'Where's Yuki? You forgot Yuki.'

"Yuki was a dog that had jumped into Luci's car when she was stopped at a gas station one day down in Texas, and he came to be one of the legitimate characters around the LBJ White House.

"Yuki, unlike the President's beagle, Him, was one smart animal. The President took a liking to the dog, and it didn't take Yuki long to figure out whose dog he was. When he would go out to the helicopter, so help me God, he'd stop and wait for the aide to salute before he'd go up the steps. But not this time.

"The dog handler immediately opened the kennel and let Yuki out, but somehow the dog got away from him, and Yuki wanted to play—he was not about to get on the helicopter. So all the White House police, all the military, all the Secret Service, were chasing this damn dog, because they knew there was going to be an explosion on that helicopter.

"I went into the Diplomatic Reception Room to telephone for more outside lights so we could see what the hell we were doing trying to catch this dog, which was running through the gardens—he was a little, tiny dog—when Zephyr came in.

"Zephyr, the family cook, was a huge, huge black woman, and she was standing in the middle of the Diplomatic Reception Room in a tremendous light chocolate-brown dress, which made her look even more huge. I was on the telephone and couldn't see the helicopter, but I heard her say, 'Somebody better get that dog, because here come the Man.'

"And sure enough, Johnson was leaving the helicopter, yelling and cursing, 'You sons of bitches, you get my dog. Goddamn it! You bunch of incompetent bastards, you can't even get my dog.' He was striding around the lawn while everybody in the White House was calling, 'Here, Yuki. Here, Yuki,' looking under trees and literally beating the bushes.''

LYNDON JOHNSON IN RETIREMENT

"During the transition," Gulley says, "the Nixon and Johnson people worked together all right, but they more or less kept their distance from each other. There wasn't a hell of a lot of trust between them, but Johnson told everyone to cooperate with the people coming in. He was busy getting his own little world comfortable, but he was helpful. Of course he insisted he be made personally aware of any requests Nixon made, and that he be the only approving authority.

"One of the first requests from Nixon to the Military Office concerned what he wanted done immediately after his inauguration. 'I would like *Air Force One* offered to President Johnson to take him to Texas. I would also like an airplane given to Vice President Humphrey, if he wants one, to take

104

him home.' He said, 'When I left office as Vice President, when I left the Capitol on Kennedy's inauguration day, I had to find my own car and drive it. I don't want anything like that to happen at my inauguration.' So airplanes were provided.

"As soon as Nixon was inaugurated, of course, Johnson became a former President, and along with all the other plans he made for a pleasant period of retirement, he'd decided it would be useful to have a specific guy he would call on in the White House.

"Before he left office, Johnson suggested to former President Eisenhower that since the number of former Presidents was growing, it would be a good idea to have one person in the White House designated as a liaison with them, and Ike agreed. Then Johnson suggested Ike might like to talk to President Nixon about it.

"Eisenhower asked Nixon to find a job for Bob Schultz, who was then a retired Army brigadier general and had been the head of Ike's Military Office, and suggested this post as liaison might be suitable. Nixon agreed immediately—as Johnson had known he would to any request from Ike—so Schultz came into the White House in the brand new formal position of Liaison to Former Presidents.

"Being an ex-general, Schultz immediately surrounded himself with a staff three times as big as he needed, with a colonel as chief of staff, secretaries, an elaborate office, and chauffeur-driven limousine—the whole thing. On his first trip to see LBJ on the ranch, Schultz took eleven people with him, and as a result of that visit I got my start as Liaison, to one former President, anyway.

"As soon as Schultz and his entourage left the ranch, LBJ called me at the White House and said, 'You can tell Dick Nixon this guy Schultz isn't coming to my ranch again, because I don't want to see him and that army that travels along with him again. Anything I've got, I'll deal with you. They can keep him on in that job if they want to, just so long as I don't have to deal with him.'

"Nixon had told Ike he'd hire Schultz, so he kept him on, although they cut his staff down to a colonel and one secretary, but LBJ had meant what he said, and from then on whenever he had any requests or whatnot, he called me. Schultz stayed until the end of Nixon's first term, and when he left, I officially replaced him.''

Johnson and Gulley used to talk on the telephone a lot after the President retired, mostly swapping Country Boy stories and gossiping. Johnson was at his most comfortable with people who shared his rural background.

"Johnson used to call up, and pretty soon we were into storytelling,'' Gulley says. "I'd tell him stories about my childhood. How we had this big iron kettle, heated over a wood fire, that my mother used to boil water and wash the clothing in, with a washboard. This big iron pot sat outside and was used for everything—washing clothes, making soap, cooking tomatoes or the peaches that she canned. Inside we had one heating stove that stood in the middle of the three rooms, and sometimes in the dark of night we'd steal coal from the railway cars and burn it in with the wood.'' Despite his essentially middle-class background, Gulley says, Johnson would laugh and say: "I know. I know just what you mean.''

"Johnson would really respond when I'd tell him how things were when I was a boy. I told him about how, in the summertime, to get cash flow my mother and my sisters and I would pick strawberries for two cents a quart. My mother picked pretty good, and she could pick something like a hundred quarts a day. The rest of us would pick, depending on our age, maybe twenty-five or fifty quarts.

"They paid us by giving us tickets in the shed where we turned in the quarts we'd picked, and then we'd turn the tickets in for cash on Saturday.

"One Saturday we picked until noon, and when we turned in our tickets it was decided we'd have frankfurters for dinner —and that was unusual. We lived three miles from the store, so my mother gave me half a dollar, and I was legging it into town when the half a dollar flew out of my hand and went into some weeds.

"After a couple of hours I finally gave up looking for it and went home. Then my father, my mother, everyone in the family came back along the road, and we looked for that half a dollar until dark. We never did find it. Consequently we

106

never got the frankfurters. But I'll never forget how important that half a dollar was.

"Everybody was in the same boat. There were no rich kids. The lunch we'd take to school in our lunch pails was a half-inch of lard spread on a thick slice of bread." Johnson, Gulley says, would urge him on to tell more and more stories. "All that was missing was the cracker barrel."

Lyndon Johnson in retirement was a mellower man than Lyndon Johnson, President, but the old bite was still there. William Safire tells a story about a trip Henry Kissinger made to see Johnson on the ranch after the former President had left office.

When the visit was over, Kissinger said, Lady Bird Johnson, who was driving him back to his plane, asked him how he thought Johnson seemed. Kissinger said, "I mumbled something about 'serenity in retirement,' and she almost drove off the road. I suppose flattery has to be related to reality, however vaguely."

Johnson still tormented his Secret Service agents, created new projects and oversaw each detail of them, and craved news and gossip from Washington.

"For the most part," Gulley says, "being Liaison to LBJ wasn't complicated. We ran a plane down to the ranch every Thursday that took his weekly briefing papers from President Nixon, and the people he wanted to see. They'd spend the day with him, former staff people, members of the family, whoever.

"Sometimes on the return trips, in addition to his returning visitors, there would be a few dozen eggs or a few quarts of his Texas chili that he wanted delivered to people around town. And at New Year's he'd send me ten pounds of his barbecue, with sauce.

"I talked a lot with Tom Johnson, no relation, who was LBJ's number one guy down on the ranch when he left office. He was a bright young man in the press office under Johnson; he now has the top job at the Los Angeles *Times*—and he went with the President to Texas as his administrative assistant.

"The first week in January 1973, I got a call from Tom saying LBJ would like a conference call with me and Billy Wright. This had to be Bill Wright who worked in the White House travel office, and I was trying to figure out why the President wanted to talk to him. Anyhow, he got on the telephone with us, and his voice had grown hoarse. In retrospect I see he was getting near the end, but in this hoarse, low voice he said, 'Bill?'

"I said, 'Yes, sir.'

"He said, 'Billy Wright?'

"Billy said, 'Yes, sir.'

"Then the President said, 'Bill, you don't know Billy Wright, but he's going to replace Tom Johnson. Tom's going to go be a newspaperman down in Dallas. Now, Billy, he graduated from my school,' the Lyndon Baines Johnson School of Foreign Affairs at the University of Texas, 'number one in his class. But he doesn't know a hell of a lot. He's too young to know a hell of a lot.

" 'Now, I want him to know who you are, and I want you to know who he is. I want him to know you're a can-do man, and I want him to do things just like you do. So sometime if he calls you and says I want something, and you don't think it's right, why you just call and check with me. You got that, Billy Wright?'

"Billy said, 'Yes, sir,' and Johnson said, 'Then get off the phone.'

"The President then said to me, 'Do you understand what I'm saying?' I said, 'Yes, sir. I understand.' He said, 'All right. But I don't know him well enough to know if I can trust him. He might be throwing my name around. So if you see this guy go over the fence and out of the pasture, you let me know.'

"As it turned out, that was the last time I ever talked to Lyndon Johnson.

"Two weeks later, on January 22, at about three in the afternoon, four years almost to the day after Johnson left office, I got a call from our switchboard at the ranch. A voice said, 'Mr. Gulley, I think the President just died.' I said, 'What the hell do you mean you *think?*' He said, 'Well, I helped put him on an airplane to take him to Brooke Army Hospital, but I really think he's dead.'

"I was shaken. Johnson had always been more alive than other people, and it didn't seem possible he was dead.

"I knew the first thing I had to do was notify Haldeman, but if you knew anything about Haldeman you knew you didn't tell him anything you *thought,* so I called Bill Lukash, the White House doctor, and asked him to find out what he could. When he called me back he said, 'That's right, Bill. Big Ears is dead.'

"I arranged planes to get the people who needed to be there to the ranch, and when they arrived, there was a family conference, which included John Connally by telephone, about plans for the funeral.

"At the White House all Presidents have a funeral plan. And they're never followed. While he's alive the President makes the plans, and his wife isn't involved. Then as soon as he dies she changes everything. There are plans that say what's to be done on what hour of which day. It even gets down to how many and which people will carry the casket, how many feet it is to the airplane, how many feet it is to the door—and none of the plans are ever followed. John Kennedy had a funeral plan, but as everybody knows, Jackie Kennedy made hers up as she went along.

"Anyway, Mrs. Johnson pretty well knew what she wanted done. They decided to bring Johnson's body to Washington to lie in the Rotunda at the Capitol so the nation could pay its respects, but that wasn't enough for the politicians, who were all trying to get on the plane to go back to Texas after the lying-in-state.

"Having worked with the Johnsons, I knew you didn't do something like that without checking, and sure enough, when I called Blair House, where Mrs. Johnson was staying, and talked to Jim Cross, he said, 'Mrs. Johnson said she'll give you a manifest, and no one else is to be allowed on that airplane. And, Bill, Mrs. Johnson also said that no one is to be given permission to land at the ranch in any other airplane, either.'

"Only Bebe Rebozo, who represented President Nixon,

and Anita Bryant, who sang 'The Battle Hymn of the Republic' at the graveside, were allowed to land at the ranch. I sent an unmarked Jet Star to Miami and picked up Rebozo and Anita Bryant and her husband—a guy named Green—and flew them in to the ranch together.

"Mike Mansfield was very upset at not being officially included. So upset that he requested his own airplane from Andrews. He was actually sitting on this Jet Star at Andrews when he told the pilot the destination: 'I want you to take me to the LBJ Ranch.'

"At that point the pilot said, 'I'm sorry, sir, but I can't do that without clearance from Bill Gulley at the White House,' but Mansfield said, 'I don't care who you say you've got to go to, we're going to the ranch.'

"The pilot called me right away, and of course I couldn't give him an O.K. on Mansfield, because Mrs. Johnson had been very definite in what she wanted, and she didn't want Mansfield. The pilot went back to Mansfield and tried to explain the situation, but the senator got so angry he stormed off the airplane. In the end, the only politician that was allowed on the plane with the family was Jake Pickle, a congressman from down there in Texas.

"At about nine o'clock the night of the funeral I got a call from the signal board at the ranch telling me Mrs. Johnson wanted to talk to me, but before she did Smith and Cross would like a word. I asked the operator where they were. Mrs. Johnson was in her bedroom; Smith and Cross were in President Johnson's office.

"Smith got on the phone and he thanked me for helping him out with the airplanes and the details that had to be handled here in Washington. Then he said Cross wanted to talk to me, but he'd left the room. 'Jim and I,' Smith said, 'we've been sitting here in the Old Man's office and we've been drinking his Scotch, talking about him. All of a sudden Jim began to worry. He started saying we shouldn't be doing this, we shouldn't be sitting here in his office and drinking his Scotch. He got so worked up worrying about the Old Man that he's run down to see if he's really still where he's supposed to be.' If you knew how frightened people were of Lyndon Johnson, you'd understand.

"I talked to Mrs. Johnson and the girls and their husbands. They just wanted to say thank you.

"The family was expecting several thousand people to come to the ranch over the weekend to pay their respects at the President's grave, and naturally they wanted everything to look right. But the day Johnson was buried there was a hard rain, and the day after that there were high winds. There's a Presidential wreath, a wreath of a special design that has a card on it saying it's from the President of the United States, and it's appropriate for leaving for public officials on their death. There was one on Johnson's grave, but the wind and the rain had just played hell with it.

"I called Rose Woods and told her we'd need another one, that the President's wreath had been destroyed. She said, 'Why, Bill. That's terrible. Who destroyed it?' I said, 'You must have known Lyndon Johnson wasn't going to stay down there more than three days—the wreath got crushed when the stone was rolled back.'

"That wasn't the end of it for me, yet. About two weeks after the funeral Mansfield had a meeting with President Nixon, in the Cabinet Room, and he complained about me. He told the President I'd kept him from going to the ranch for Johnson's funeral, handed him a letter giving him the details, and asked that I be fired.

"Tom Korologos, one of the liaisons to the Hill from the White House, overheard part of this conversation and immediately called me. He told me I was in desperate straits because the Majority Leader of the United States Senate was after me, that he was demanding that the President fire me.

"Nixon flew down to Florida that evening, and that night I got a call from Haldeman. He wanted me to give him a complete rundown on how come Mike Mansfield was not permitted to ride on Johnson's plane and then wasn't permitted to land in his own plane on the ranch. I explained what happened, and I didn't hear anything more about it, officially.

"Later, Rose Woods told me the President got a letter from Mrs. Johnson telling him how helpful I'd been, after her husband's death, and over the years, and that another had gone to Haldeman. Years later when I was in San Clemente with Nixon after he was out of office, he remembered the incident and said I must live a charmed life—I'd even survived Mike Mansfield.

"Looking at what happened after Johnson left office," Gulley says, "the What If's come bubbling up. If, as he hoped until the last moment, Johnson had been nominated and then reelected, could he have coped? Could he have dealt effectively with Vietnam? Would he have retained a hold on Congress? Would the lies *he* had told have caught up with him and cost him *his* office? Finally, would he have lived?

"One thing is certain, wherever he is now he gathers every evening with Franklin Roosevelt, Everett Dirksen, Sam Rayburn, and the other giants he admired, for bourbon and branch water. In this great bipartisan council in the sky, they sip and shake their heads over what has happened to their parties now that the elephants are gone."

III
CHAPTER

Richard Nixon

IN A TELEVISED CONVERSATION with Dick Cavett in October 1978, some time after John Ehrlichman's release from prison, Nixon's former aide said, "The first allegiance in the White House must be to the President. If what you're asked to do runs cross-grain to your sense of ethics or whatever, then you should get out. Right then." This echoes what Gulley has said repeatedly: "In the White House you never worry about the law, it never enters your mind . . . if the President says it's right, it's right."

Ehrlichman and Gulley seem to be reflecting the values and attitudes not only of the Nixon Administration; apparently they held true for the Johnson White House as well. Johnson created in the White House an atmosphere of deviousness and distrust where ends were all-important, and a man was judged by his ability to achieve them quickly and out of sight of the Press and the public. He created a White House administration, built a machine that would get him what he wanted without interference from outside. It was a legacy Nixon, with his own lack of trust and passion for secrecy, was uniquely qualified to appreciate.

As Gulley says, when the Nixon people came in, there was the train, ready to roll. They modified it, streamlined it, and drove it to the point where it ultimately brought disgrace to them and the Presidency itself.

THE LONER

"My son, John," Gulley says, "was being married August 10, 1974, the day after Nixon's resignation. Having safely got the ex-President out of the White House and into California, I wanted to give all my attention to my family, for the next few hours at least. Before I went to church I left word with the White House switchboard not to call until they heard from me, which would be immediately after the ceremony. In about forty-five minutes.

"It didn't happen that way. Three times during the short service my beeper went off, and three times I had to leave the front pew of the church, go down the length of the aisle and into an office in the back where there was a phone.

"Each time it was General Alexander Haig or Jack Marsh or both of them. They'd been handling the transition, Haig for Nixon, Marsh for Ford, and now they were dithering, working themselves and each other up about should I go or should I not go to San Clemente right away.

"The huge military installation out there with hundreds of thousands of dollars' worth of equipment, dozens of personnel and elaborate communications systems had to be dismantled, and it was up to me to have it done. In addition, I was Liaison to Former Presidents, of which Nixon was suddenly one. So there were good reasons for me to get right out there.

"On the other hand, they fussed, how would it look to the Press for the Ford Administration to have *any* official contact, no matter how urgent, with the disgraced Nixon? Looking back on the amount of covert contact the Ford people were to have with Nixon starting just a few months later, and the risk they ran of exposure, all this original delicacy seems a little excessive. In any case, after the third call I told them I'd call them back. Which I finally did. From San Clemente, the next day.

"I had been out to the Nixon compound dozens of times while he had been President, and I would go dozens of times more—although I didn't know that then—but on this trip I

114

felt I was heading for strange territory, and I was apprehensive. I would have been even more apprehensive if I'd known how that first encounter with ex-President Nixon was going to go.

"I wasn't to see him until the next morning, so after I arrived on Sunday I spent the evening with Jack Brennan and Steve Bull, who had flown out on *Air Force One* with the Nixons on Friday. Brennan was Nixon's military aide, Bull was his former appointments secretary, and they were both still in a state of shock, still trying to figure out what had happened. I could see the shape they were in, but they didn't give me a clue as to what I'd find the next day.

"Driving into the Nixon compound that Monday morning was an eerie experience. For years this had been a direct extension of the White House, with the same aura of importance, of powerful things happening. Now it was like a ship that has been abandoned. There was no guard at the gate. The parking lot, which had never had less than forty cars in it, had only two. Everything was empty and quiet.

"I drove in, parked the car and walked over to the building where the President's office was. I hadn't been ready for the sight of a desolated compound, but I was even less ready for what I met when I went in to see Nixon.

"He was tense, strung-out, demanding and combative. He looked as though he hadn't slept; his eyes looked as though he hadn't rested in days—and I don't think he had his head together. He was wearing a suit and tie, of course; he stood up when I came in and we shook hands, but he showed no friendliness.

"He was obviously having trouble with his leg. During his last Middle Eastern trip he had had serious problems with phlebitis, and now he was limping, supporting himself by putting his hand on his desk. But in spite of that he didn't sit down, so, naturally, I didn't either.

"When he spoke he was curt and direct, and he was mainly concerned with getting his 'entitlements.' 'Look,' he said, 'I'm entitled to anything that any other former President is entitled to. Goddamn, you know what I did for Johnson, and you know I did things for Ike and Truman, and, goddamn it,

I expect to be treated the same way. When I travel I expect military aircraft; I expect the same support I provided. I expect communications and medical personnel, everything they had. And, goddamn it, you tell Ford I expect it.' He was distraught, demanding.

"Nixon was concerned about getting his papers and records, too. This was before there was a court order impounding them, but I have no doubt he saw it coming. 'Do you know what their plans are?' he asked, and I said no, that I'd arrived in California the day before and they weren't sure of anything yet back at the White House. I told him the only thing I did know was that as Liaison to Former Presidents I would be the link between them.

"He said, 'Well, you tell those bastards that I'm going to keep my mouth shut. I'm not going to be talking to the Press. I'm not going to be making comments about Ford or the administration, but, goddamn it, I want them to know I'm here. And I want them to know there are certain things I expect from them. Briefing papers. Certain treatment.' At this point he was an angry man.

"I realized this was only three days after the resignation, but I was very surprised. I really expected him to take a tack of: Look, there are some things I know Ford will not be able to do for me, and I understand that. I think I was expecting a Richard Nixon of that type. What I found was exactly opposite.

"That whole first meeting only lasted about fifteen minutes, and in spite of the obvious difficulty Nixon was having with his leg, we stood up the whole time.

"Before I left he said, very coldly, 'Is it going to present a problem for you, working with me?' Since it seemed we were being direct with each other, I said, 'I'm not here to pass moral judgments. I'm here to do a job. No, it won't be any problem for me.'

"We shook hands again briefly; he thanked me in a very stiff, formal manner for coming; and I walked out of there feeling a little off balance. I was really surprised by the way he had taken me on when I went in there. I felt as if I'd been dealing with a gladiator who didn't know he was beat.

"There was certainly no clue that day to the way our relationship would develop over my many visits to him, or to how Richard Nixon would change during the next few years.

"All I felt as I headed back to Washington in the Jet Star was that I was in a very difficult position. I was shaken."

His many hours of talk alone with Nixon in the seclusion of San Clemente have given Gulley an insight into Nixon's character which is unique. This period was the lowest point in Nixon's life—he was a shamed, bitter, exhausted and sick man who was the object of perhaps the greatest outpouring of hatred in the nation's history. He was, by Gulley's account: tense, strung-out, demanding, and combative; he didn't have his head together.

"Since then," Gulley says, "it's been like watching someone recover from a serious illness."

In the course of the recuperation, Gulley saw an unguarded Nixon to whom Gulley was both an unthreatening companion and his single remaining tangible link to the White House and all it represented to him.

Nixon's defenses were down, and what he revealed of himself in those years of self-imposed exile shed light not only on Nixon the man but on Nixon the President. To the question that will probably always be asked about Nixon's fall, "How did it happen?," Gulley provides at least a partial answer by helping to explain the enigmatic character of Richard Nixon.

"I didn't have many direct dealings with Nixon while he was in office," Gulley says. "Unlike the Johnson White House, where the President seemed to be everywhere, Haldeman organized the Nixon White House to keep the President's contacts with his staff to a minimum. His ideal, which he actually tried to achieve, was to limit the number of people who had access to Nixon to one: himself.

"Now that I was seeing him every other week, I began to put some of the puzzle of the Nixon personality together.

"For one thing, Nixon is comfortable being alone. As President, he didn't need people the way Johnson and Ford did, and he doesn't need them now. Going beyond that, even with the people he had around him most, there wasn't a close personal relationship. A lot has been said and written about Nixon's friendship for Haldeman, Ehrlichman and Ziegler, but whatever he felt about them professionally, he kept them at arm's length personally.

"When Nixon went to Camp David, for example, he would choose to eat alone. He never asked Haldeman or the others to join him for dinner; they would eat their meals separately. None of the camaraderie existed among them that you might have expected. Nixon told me one time that he didn't believe in socializing with his staff, and he meant it.

"The most important exception was Rose Mary Woods. He was always close to Rose, and if she was at Camp David, she was always asked to dinner with Nixon. So, on a couple of occasions, were two other women secretaries, Pat McKee and Nell Yates. Which was surprising, in a way, because Nixon was never really at ease with women. He's shy with them, and I have a feeling that when he greets them he'd like to stop and bow."

"Nixon likes things to be orderly, organized and well structured, and I think he saw in Haldeman a guy who could provide him with that kind of White House. Where Johnson would never delegate authority to anybody if he could help it, Nixon, having decided Haldeman could and would set up and run the White House the way he wanted, turned the job over to him.

"I had to have some doubts about Nixon in seeing him let Haldeman assemble the kind of people he did. Where Johnson surrounded himself with political pros, Nixon allowed the White House to be staffed with amateurs from ad agencies. It didn't square with Nixon's admiration for hardball players. Because there is within Nixon a mechanism that causes him to respect a person he sees as being tough and competent. He considers himself one, and he doesn't have time for weak people. He despises having them around, and it's ironic that he had so many of them on his staff.

"The reason, I think, was that Nixon didn't think of the Higbys and the others as his people. He thought of them as Haldeman's people, and Haldeman, who *was* Nixon's man, was tough and competent—along with a lot of other things. Nixon dealt with Haldeman; the rest was up to him. So Nixon allowed Haldeman to pack the White House with pissants he knew would do anything they were told.

"There's no doubt Nixon had no use for weakness. We had an aide, an Army colonel, who allowed himself to be put upon by Ron Ziegler, Nixon's press secretary, one time when they were on the helicopter. Ziegler wanted to get past the aide, who was standing in the aisle bracing himself against a seat with his arm. Ziegler simply came along and took this colonel's arm, knocked it down, and walked right past him into the cockpit of the helicopter.

"When the aide came back and told me this story, I told him: 'You made a big mistake. You should have grabbed Ziegler right by the throat.' He said, 'But the President was right there. . . .' I said, 'Right in front of the President. You should have grabbed him by the throat right then.'

"It wasn't three weeks before word came over that the President would like to have a different aide than that guy. He lost respect for him for allowing Ziegler to do that. There's no doubt in my mind he saw it as a sign of weakness. Richard Nixon had respect for a colonel in the Army, and when he saw him accept a thing like that from a guy like Ziegler, who'd avoided the draft, that was a sign of weakness.

"This admiration Nixon has for toughness hooks into his admiration for the military, and his interest in sports, I think. Whenever we hit a sensitive area in our conversations and I saw Nixon getting upset or angry, I could divert him by switching the talk to sports, especially baseball or football. But the fact that he's interested in sports doesn't mean he's athletic himself; he's not. And he does some odd things when it comes to participating in games.

"Paul Presley, who owns the San Clemente Inn, told me that the first time he played golf in a foursome with Nixon, they got out there on the first tee and Nixon pointed to each player in turn and said, 'O.K. Now you and you will be partners, and you and I will be partners, and we'll play winter rules.' Then he said, 'And these will be our handicaps,' and proceeded to assign a handicap to each guy.

"Presley said to me, 'I've been playing golf for thirty-five years, and I wouldn't let any son of a bitch stand there in a foursome and get away with that. But what the hell are you going to do?' He also said that Nixon didn't crack a smile. He was very serious about the whole thing. If he gets a laugh out of something like that, he keeps it to himself.

"So it's not that Nixon's any kind of an athlete; it's the competitive aspect of sports that fascinates him. Richard Nixon is a *highly* competitive guy, and it's all related to what he considers to be strength in a man.

"Nixon's got a tremendous respect for the military, and he's interested in military history. He was appalled when Carter had Major General Singlaub brought back from Korea and reprimanded him in public for saying we should stay in Korea. Nixon said, 'You know, the one who suffers here is Carter, not the general. Number one,' he said, 'the President never talks to the number three guy. If it's necessary to fire the guy, you talk to his boss, who's the Secretary of Defense, and you let him do the firing.

" 'A President can never win this kind of argument,' Nixon said. 'There's no way. The general's not a partisan guy, he's not political; so there's no way you can win by doing that.'

"In one of our conversations, I told Nixon that Carter had sent a memo to Secretary of Defense Brown saying he wanted the number of generals and admirals reduced. That there were too many of them. Nixon said, 'That's not how you do it. The way you do it—the only reason you reduce the armed forces is because you're getting pressure from the tax base because of the cost of supporting them.

" 'What you do,' Nixon said, 'is you say O.K. We're going to cut back by 10,000, and you take 10,000 privates and you eliminate them. They don't want to be in the service, and their folks don't want them in the service, anyway. So now if you can only afford to send those generals and admirals to school for half a day and they play golf the other half, let them.

" 'There has to be some kind of education going on; there have got to be guys who understand the logistics of supplying armies in other parts of the world and all the other complex

120

things that have to be learned. Who gives a damn how many generals and admirals there are anyway?

" 'When a war breaks out, right here in San Diego the Marines have got a training facility that you damn well know about. They can turn out killers every ninety days. But it's no use turning out killers if you haven't educated the generals and admirals to see the big picture and understand what has to be done.'

"Then he said, 'You think I'm pretty goddamn smart, don't you? Well, I'm not. That's what the Germans did when we stripped them after World War One. We told them they could only have X number of people in the army, but we didn't tell them what they could be. So they made them all generals and sent them all to school. That's how you got the Generals' Corps.'

"Nixon was excited and engrossed while he was telling me this theory, and he'd obviously given it a lot of thought. Strategy always interests him, especially political strategy, whether it's on the world level or the local precinct level. He feels sure of himself in the political area—I don't think he does when it comes to the social. He's a great political strategist and manipulator, but I don't think he understands or cares very much about the personal side of life. And this, ironically, leads to his being manipulated by other people.

"I think it was this, partially, that kept Nixon from realizing just how deep his trouble ran during Watergate. Nobody in the White House ever gives the President the bad news, and Haldeman was the last guy to want Nixon to see how things really stood—assuming he knew himself, which I think he did. But I also think he believed, and let Nixon believe, that the President was big enough to sweep the whole thing away. Somehow.

"Lyndon Johnson admired strength and competence in men, too, but there were differences in what those words meant to him and to Nixon. Johnson admired a 'can-do-guy,' somebody who'd do exactly what the President wanted, the way he wanted it done, down to the last detail.

"Nixon admired a 'Guy with Balls,' the tough, hard-nosed game-player, and he'd give him the authority to carry out whatever it was. Unlike Johnson, how the job was done, the means, didn't interest Nixon—and it cost him dearly.''

THE HALDEMAN FACTOR

Of the historians who write about Nixon and his Presidency, probably only the most meticulous will give H. R. Haldeman much more than a footnote. He deserves more, because virtually every contemporary account, Gulley's included, has stressed the importance of Haldeman's influence on the shape and fate of the Nixon White House.

Jeb Stuart Magruder, in his book *An American Life: One Man's Road to Watergate,* says, ''The one figure who was absolutely central to the Nixon White House is of course Bob Haldeman. . . . Almost everyone in the Administration was working, directly or indirectly, for Haldeman, because that was how *his* boss, the President, wanted it.

'' 'Every President needs a son of a bitch,' Haldeman used to say, 'and I'm Nixon's. I'm his buffer and his bastard. I get done what he wants done and I take the heat instead of him. . . .' I never doubted he was doing exactly what Nixon wanted done.'' Gulley amplifies:

''An administration,'' he says, ''is supposed to take its cue from the character of the President. It's supposed that he's the one who sets the tone, the level, the standards. That the ethical buck stops in the Oval Office. That's basically true, and even though it sounds simple and straightforward, sometimes it is and sometimes it isn't.

''With LBJ it was clear-cut. He was so completely in charge of things, so on top of every little thing that happened, it would have been unthinkable for Marvin Watson to issue an order Johnson had not authorized personally. LBJ was never a delegator; he didn't know how to do it. He was a one-man band.

''With Richard Nixon it was different. He delegated wholesale. It was a different approach: Lyndon Johnson wanted to do it all; Richard Nixon wanted to concentrate on the big issues, especially foreign policy.'' The result for the Nixon Administration was that Haldeman, as chief of staff, had enormous power, and the right to speak for the President.

"What we in the White House got," Gulley says, "and the American people got was an administration that took its tone and character from Richard Nixon, as interpreted by Bob Haldeman. LBJ would say, 'Get it done. How you going to do it?' Then put his stamp on every phase of the operation. Nixon would say, 'Get it done.' Period. The rest was up to Haldeman, and he put his stamp on it.

"One time out in San Clemente, months after Nixon resigned, he said to me, 'You know, if I had it to do over again I would never let a guy position himself between me and the staff people the way I permitted Bob to do. I have nobody to blame for that but myself, because I allowed him to isolate me.' It was the only critical thing I ever heard him say about Haldeman, but I also never heard him express any sympathy or sorrow for him, as he did for John Mitchell. Of course, it doesn't let Nixon off the hook, since, as he said himself, he permitted Haldeman to do what he did.

"There's no question Haldeman had the authority of the President behind him right from the start. On one of our first trips to Key Biscayne after his inauguration, early in February 1969, Nixon was out on the lawn in the sunshine with Haldeman when a call came from Agnew. Vern Coffee, the military aide on duty, brought an extension phone out to the President.

"When the President looked up, Vern said, 'Mr. President, the Vice President is on the line,' and held out the telephone. Haldeman, without consulting the President, immediately said to Vern, 'Take that back and tell the Vice President that the President is occupied.' Nixon said nothing.

"Right then we knew two things. One, the relationship between Agnew and Nixon wasn't going to be any different from that between Humphrey and Johnson. And, two, Nixon was going to allow Haldeman to speak for him. And that's a thing Johnson never allowed *anybody* to do.

"In LBJ's Administration there had been only one elephant and a lot of pissants. Johnson had a Goodyear Blimp of an ego—beside his, everybody else's looked like a kid's helium balloon. In the Nixon White House it wasn't like that. You couldn't even see Richard Nixon's ego beside the likes of Kissinger, Haldeman, Haig and, later, Schlesinger.

"Haldeman started sowing discord the minute he came into the White House. There were two groups Nixon brought with him. People like Bob Finch, Rose Mary Woods, Herb Klein and Don Hughes, the new director of the Military Office—those who had been with him in his Vice President days. And there was the Haldeman group. Ehrlichman, Chapin, Higby —the cast of Watergate.

"From the start Haldeman did all he could to cut Nixon's ties to his old staff members, and he succeeded pretty well, with the exception of Rose Mary Woods. As far as I know, every time Haldeman met Rose head-on, Rose won. He tried to get her offices moved out of the White House and over to the Executive Office Building. He tried to isolate her from the President on *Air Force One* by assigning her a seat away from him. He even tried to arrange it so that no one, not even Rose, could telephone the President direct. Each time he failed.

"When you'd been in the White House under LBJ, trying now to isolate the President was a change that amounted to being revolutionary. Johnson would have had a direct telephone line to every guy on the Hill, let alone in the White House, if he could have fitted them on his console. And no one, ever, could have positioned himself between Lyndon Johnson and his staff."

"The day after Nixon's inaugural I was in the President's office with Nell Yates, Dwight Chapin and Haldeman—it was the first time I'd met him. We were discussing the placement of flags around the President's desk. Haldeman wasn't satisfied with them and wanted them changed. We kicked the thing around for half an hour.

"You might have thought the President's chief of staff would have better things to do his first day on the job, but Haldeman had no sense of proportion. It was ridiculous. He gave equal weight to everything.

"On August 17, 1970, for example, Haldeman took the time to write a two-page memorandum dealing with such earth-

124

shaking matters as the size of the cakes of soap at Camp David and the supply of towels by the swimming pool. This happened to be the day Kissinger and Nixon were meeting the Israeli ambassador, Rabin, to discuss violations of the rickety peace treaty between Israel and Egypt that had gone into effect ten days before. Haldeman was not a guy who put first things first.

"At our first meeting, Haldeman had been very friendly. He could be charming when it suited him to be, but basically he was a petty guy, demanding and nasty about little things. He'd raise hell if the radio in the car that picked him up wasn't tuned to the right station. His morning paper had to be on the seat, the news brief had to be next to it, and woe to the driver who was thirty seconds late to pick him up, no matter what the reason.

"That's where he really shone. In making life miserable for anyone who was in a position where he couldn't fight back.

"When it came to Haldeman's self-interest he would stoop to any depth. Each morning the Military Office compiled a weather report and had it delivered to various people around the White House. The weather is reported for whatever areas of the country interest each President. With Carter it shows the weather in Plains, Georgia. When LBJ was President it showed the weather at the ranch so he knew how much rain he was getting, and so forth.

"With Nixon we always reported the weather at San Clemente and Key Biscayne, and the water temperatures in both places because he liked to get out into the ocean. Early one morning Nixon asked Manolo, his valet, 'What's the weather going to be this weekend?' Manolo said, 'Oh, it's going to be great at Key Biscayne.'

"A little while later the President went down to his office and said to Haldeman, 'I want to go to Key Biscayne this weekend.' Haldeman said, 'The weather's going to be terrible there this weekend.' So the President said, 'But Manolo told me just now that the weather was going to be great.' And Haldeman said, 'Well, it's not. As usual, Manolo's screwed it up. He doesn't know what he's talking about. It's going to be terrible in Key Biscayne.'

MEMORANDUM

(

CDR. LARSON

Per our discussion.
No particular problem.
Item #5 may get
expensive.
JRB

THE WHITE HOUSE
WASHINGTON

August 17, 1970

MEMORANDUM FOR :   COMMANDER DETTBARN
Camp David

You asked a couple of trips ago for any thoughts any of us might
have regarding improvements here and there about the Camp and
I thought it might be helpful to list a few, none of which is vitally
important, but each of which would indeed be an improvement.

1. It would be very helpful to have a big outdoor clock up by the
pool so that one could readily see what time it is. This might be
put at the end of the dressing room facing the pool.

2. There never seem to be a supply of towels in the pool dressing
rooms or in the lounge area by the pool. This too would be very
helpful.

3. It would sure help to have a couple of coat hooks in the closet
area of each of the cabins to hang up things that don't readily lend
themselves to hangers.

4. The phones on long cords at the swimming pool are extremely
helpful so that people can get a phone by them when they are spending
a lot of time on a number of calls.

5. As we've mentioned before, we badly need better reading light
in the cabins and someday, hopefully, more comfortable reading
chairs.

6. While there now seem to be a lot of bikes at Camp David, all
of which are racked up in front of Laurel when we arrive, they
rapidly disappear and there are frequently bike shortages for the
guests. This seems to be due to the fact that the stewards and others
latch on to the bikes and they disappear.

126

7. While I guess it's not an important matter, it seems horribly wasteful to use those big bars of soap in the bathrooms at a place like this where you have guests who stay only one or two nights usually. Couldn't you get the small bars of soap that hotels usually supply? Also, I would think that since most of your guests are men, it would be more suitable to use Dial soap or something of that sort instead of Dove which you are presently using.

8. It would be most helpful to have a call bell or a buzzer of some kind in the dining room at Laurel since the galley is so far away and it's very hard to get a steward roused when you want one at the table.

None of the above is to in any way imply any dissatisfaction with the facilities or the operation of Camp David both of which we all feel are superb.

H. R. HALDEMAN

"The next thing was that Haldeman called me and said, 'From now on you will under no circumstances provide Manolo with a weather report.' "

"Plenty of absurd things happened there, but the Nixon White House was not noted for its humor, and as far as I could detect, Haldeman was totally deficient in that area. How else can you explain this memorandum to Hughes asking him to see to Mrs. Nixon's and Tricia's bowling requirements?

"At the time of *this* memorandum the Administration was starting its program of Vietnamization, withdrawing our troops and training the South Vietnamese; dismantling Johnson's Great Society and drawing up the Family Assistance Plan; and authorizing telephone taps to find the source of leaks in the wake of disclosure of the secret bombing of Cambodia.

"Partly it was Haldeman's pomposity that made him ab-

May 26, 1969

MEMORANDUM FOR: COLONEL HUGHES

The President would like to have the bowling ball man come
in and fit Mrs. Nixon and Tricia for balls as soon as possible.
Could arrangements be made for this immediately, please.

H. R. HALDEMAN

cc:
Mr. Chapin

surd. He enjoyed ordering people around, and he did it in the way a schoolyard bully does it. There was always an implied threat about what would happen to you if you didn't do what you were told, and everyone had to obey his rules, except him.

"Not long after Nixon took office, Haldeman started sending us nasty little memos that the White House staff was not showing enough respect for the flag at public ceremonies. Presumably since we were the Military Office we were supposed to do something about this disgraceful state of affairs, as Haldeman's memo points out. (July 17, 1970, incidentally, was three days after Nixon approved the Huston Plan for increased domestic surveillance, and eleven days before he rescinded it, under pressure from J. Edgar Hoover.)

"We got out a little primer on correct Patriotic Behavior at White House Functions and sent it around to everybody on the staff. There was just one thing we overlooked. The President. It didn't matter if we had every member of the staff, and the dogs, holding their hands over their hearts at the playing of the National Anthem if the President forgot.

"There started an endless series of meetings to discuss what we were to do to get the President to put his hand over his heart at the appropriate times. We decided that whenever possible the aide would lean over and prompt the President. Sometimes it worked and sometimes it didn't, but short of having the aide physically take Richard Nixon's hand and slap it across his chest, there wasn't anything more we could do.

"Of course it was true that whenever the President was photographed or appeared on television without having his hand in the right place while they played The Star-Spangled Banner, there'd be a small torrent of letters. And we, in turn, would get flack from Haldeman.

"One of the ironies of the thing was that all the time we were being taxed by Haldeman that it was our duty to make everyone display outward signs of patriotism and no one was exempt, he exempted himself. The massed bands could be playing the National Anthem, but Haldeman would be running around the lawn with his movie camera taking pictures of the President, the crowd, the President, the troops and the

MEMORANDUM

THE WHITE HOUSE
WASHINGTON

July 17, 1970

MEMORANDUM FOR: GENERAL HUGHES

After much discussion, the President agreed to salute when
our National Anthem is played. As you know, he did this
and also sang the Anthem at the All Star Game. It was
great, and your idea was a good one except for the problem
that half of the rest of the people in the Official Party
failed to salute or sing.

We need continually to remind the staff, and all those who
attend public events with the President, what the proper
protocol is at such events. For example, at the ballgame
what the President did Bowie Kuhn did also, but Taft did
not. Taft should have been briefed beforehand as to what
the proper procedure was, as should have other members
of the staff who did not salute.

Now that we have the President saluting, I hope that we can
institute appropriate procedures to inform people what the
proper protocol is and, more importantly, to show the
basic respect for the Flag and the National Anthem of our
country.

H. R. HALDEMAN

cc: Mr. Chapin
    Mr. Butterfield

130

President. Incidentally, Haldeman's little hobby cost the taxpayer more than $15,000 in film and equipment from the Navy photo lab.

"Rose Woods, whose loyalty to Nixon could never be questioned, said from the start that Haldeman's big show of dedication to the President was just that. A big show. She said to us, and she said to Richard Nixon, that Haldeman was a bad guy, that he was primarily interested in Haldeman and didn't have the President's cause at heart.

"It was easy for people who didn't know Rose to write this off as jealousy. Anyone who knew her knew better than that. Above everything else, what mattered to her was the welfare of Richard Nixon, and starting immediately after the inauguration in 1969, she began telling him that Haldeman was lying to him, doing things behind his back, alienating people he would need, that Haldeman would be the ruination of him.

"Rose put in some really miserable years there trying to convince the President and not being able to get through to him. It always turned out that Haldeman could smooth things over or lie his way out of a situation. Naturally, this didn't improve relations between Rose and Haldeman; it just made him that much more determined to put distance between Nixon and his old crowd.

"It wasn't very long before he even started putting distance between Nixon and the guy most people believe was closest to Haldeman—John Ehrlichman. I saw a lot of Ehrlichman during those days when he was running the Domestic Disturbances operation, and he never appeared to the East Wing anything like the way he was portrayed in the newspapers.

"Like Siamese twins, Haldeman and Ehrlichman always seem to be linked in the popular mind. My feeling is that the creature Haldeman-Ehrlichman was invented by the media, because I dealt with both of them for years, and I found them to be very different from each other.

"In my dealings with Ehrlichman he was never brusque, he never showed temper, he never demanded. And that was reflected in the caliber of a lot of his staff as opposed to the Haldeman staff. Ehrlichman had people like John Whitaker, Jana Hruska, Todd Hullen, Ken Cole—likable, hard-working people. He just never came over as being the Germanic, overbearing type he was made out to be.

"You can tell a lot about people at the White House as soon as they get there. If they're in a position where they're allowed the use of cars, planes, the yacht and Camp David, they can get very demanding very quickly. Ehrlichman never was. I'm not saying he wasn't a tough guy when the Oval Office door was closed, but for the most part he and his staff were quiet, low-key types who worked long hours and never offended people. Unlike the Haldeman crowd.

"One of the things that used to worry Bob Finch, a counselor to Nixon, was the way the Haldeman people went around offending everybody. Guys on the Hill, mayors of cities, everybody. Finch used to get calls saying, 'What the hell are you people at the White House doing? You're alienating more Republicans here than you're gaining.' You never heard things like that about the Ehrlichman staff.

"I, for one, was surprised that Ehrlichman was so deeply implicated in Watergate, because, for instance, I don't believe he knew about the taping system—he wasn't trusted by Haldeman to know. And Haldeman ruled the place with an iron hand.

"There was bad blood between the Haldeman and Ehrlichman staffs after a short time. The Ehrlichman people were quickly put in the position, by Haldeman's errand boy, Larry Higby, where they had to ask for everything, and were never allowed to go anywhere with their boss—not to Camp David, not on any trips. In time, the same thing happened to Ehrlichman himself. He'd have to call our office to ask to be added to a helicopter manifest or something of that sort because he'd been excluded by Haldeman."

Haldeman, secure in his position as the voice of the President, didn't hesitate to push people around and aside. The exception was Henry Kissinger. "He was always careful with Kissinger," Gulley says. "He knew Nixon's feeling about Henry, and although Haldeman kept a close eye on what he was doing, he stepped very softly where Kissinger was concerned.

"It was Haldeman's style to bully his way straight to what

he wanted, but with Kissinger he made a point of avoiding confrontations. For tactical reasons, since Henry wanted stage center, Haldeman let him have it without a struggle."

HENRY KISSINGER: TRAVELS AND EGO TRIPS

"Kissinger's opinion of Kissinger was awesome," Gulley says. "He just couldn't get over himself. One time after the resignation, Nixon said to me, 'Ford has just got to realize there are times Henry has to be kicked right in the nuts. It's the only way he can be controlled, because sometimes Henry starts to think *he's* the President. But at other times you have to pet Henry and treat him like a child.'

"From where I sat there was no need to coddle Henry; he took care of that himself, and there weren't many opportunities to kick him in the nuts. It was clear very soon after he came into the White House that among equals Kissinger was going to be the most equal. Right away we began getting requests: for Jet Stars to take him on weekend jaunts, and so forth.

"We put up some resistance at first in memorandums to the President, pointing out that we were running the risk of bad publicity if the Press got hold of it, but this got us nowhere. The battle was finally joined when we sent him to Europe in a converted cargo plane. It was his first overseas trip, and he had requested a luxury 707. We gave him this one instead. It's basically the same plane, but less luxurious—admittedly it doesn't have windows—but it's about one-third cheaper to operate than a 707, and Kissinger didn't need a military plane anyway. He should have been flying commercial. At this point, early 1969, the feeling around our office, and all around the White House, for that matter, was: Who does Henry Kissinger think he is? Little did we know.

"When he came back, Kissinger was boiling. It was the one and only time we ever got Henry on a plane without windows.

133

"Kissinger was good at getting what he wanted. Almost at once he started pushing for Secret Service protection. That had never happened before. There had never been anybody at the White House outside of the First Family who had Secret Service protection. He went about getting it from a sideways angle, by asking for military guards.

"As far as anybody knew, and Henry would have let us know, there was no particular reason for guards—no threats had been made or anything like that. I'm sure that Henry was on an ego trip, and that he also saw all the goodies that official protection would bring with it. If he had a Secret Service detail he'd have them provide a car and driver, there would be guards at his house, there would be baby-sitters for his children when he was out of town. And he would almost certainly have to fly in military aircraft rather than go commercial. Everyone at the White House loved the luxury of flying military.

"As usually happens, a guy's staff reflects the kind of person he is. Kissinger was arrogant, demanding and brusque, and he assembled a crowd like that to work for him. They'd lick his boots but then try to throw their weight around where they thought they could make a little splash.

"He had one guy, Winston Lord, who I thought was really a demanding ass of a guy. Always complaining. The food in the Mess was always bad. The driver didn't comb his hair right. They had the wrong music on the radio in the car. And he was complaining on his own account, nothing to do with Kissinger. One of his secretaries, Sally Dollar, would ask for a car so she could go and pick up Henry's shirts at the laundry. His self-importance just seemed to infect everybody who worked for him. Even his barber.

"Kissinger used the same barber Nixon used, Milton Pitts, and it was just too much for Milton. I think it was cutting Henry's hair, not Nixon's, that affected his ego. It was catching.

"This guy's barbershop—or by that time it was probably a 'salon'—was in the Sheraton-Carlton Hotel, across Lafayette Park on Sixteenth Street, not more than a six- or seven-minute walk from the White House. But by this time he was

July 6, 1970

MEMORANDUM FOR BOB HALDEMAN

As you requested, I have looked into the matter of the military providing personal security to Henry Kissinger. As a practical matter, this could be done by direction of the President.

Although there are some minor complications and possible legal questions, the military has provided such protection on occasions in the past and there probably would be no serious problem.

However, the use of military agents within the White House and in proximity to the President would undoubtedly cause serious friction with the Secret Service. Therefore, I recommend that the President, by executive direction, have the Secret Service provide this protection if it is decided that Henry Requires it.

With regard to the need for Henry to receive full time protection, I believe that this should be looked at thoroughly by a knowledgable group which would include the Attorney General and the Director of the Secret Service. It would appear to me that there are certain political overtones which should be considered as well. In my mind, there is no doubt that Henry is vulnerable, but I believe that there are others in the Administration who are also quite vulnerable. Therefore, I do not believe that Henry's case can be looked at in isolation.

GENERAL JAMES D. HUGHES

135

no ordinary barber. He'd get word from Kissinger's office that Henry would be in the White House barbershop in fifteen minutes, and he would say to Bonnie Andrews, Henry's secretary, 'I'd be happy to come and cut Dr. Kissinger's hair, but a White House car will have to be sent for me.'

"Bonnie, who was Kissinger's personal secretary and a truly lovely girl, would call and ask me to send a car, and I'd do it. It turned out to be a terrible mistake, because of course I'd established a pattern and it got so Milton would demand a car even if he'd been given two hours' notice.

"Finally I got tired of it, and the next time I got a call from Bonnie I said no. I told her I didn't have a car available and suggested she might tell him to walk across the Square or find his own transportation. Bonnie said, 'Oh, dear. Isn't there *something* you can do?' I said I'd see if I couldn't dig something up, just this once.

"I had the garage send a panel truck. The driver said he'd never seen anything like what happened to that barber's face when he walked out of his shop to get into a White House limousine and saw a panel truck waiting for him instead. Everybody in the hotel lobby was looking out to see Milton's moment of glory, of course. That's the last request I got from him. I suppose he decided it was better to walk to the White House and be seen going through the gates than to drive up in a truck."

"Over the years our office did a lot of business with Kissinger. He was engaged in any number of secret undertakings, and he had an obsession about security anyhow. To preserve the secrecy of what he was doing, he often came over to the East Wing of the White House and used our office.

"The Press isn't allowed in the East Wing. They're restricted to one area of the West Wing—if they're going to see a staff member in some other part of the White House they have to be escorted—and we were off the beaten path. This made it perfect for Henry. He used to meet with representatives of the Chinese and the Russians, and occasionally with the Israeli ambassador, Rabin, in our office.

"Later on, when Kissinger became Secretary of State, he

decided he didn't trust the State Department communicators, so we continued to supply him with communications people from our office at the White House.

"But the bulk of our business with Kissinger came as a result of his travels to negotiate peace with the North Vietnamese, SALT with the Russians, his shuttle diplomacy in the Middle East and Nixon's visit to Peking. Most of Kissinger's trips, except for those having to do with the Middle East, were secret, and most went off without a hitch.

"The worst scare we had came at the start of a covert trip to Moscow by Kissinger and Soviet Ambassador Anatoly Dobrynin in April of 1972. The Administration didn't want the American people to know it was negotiating a SALT treaty with the Russians for fear it would raise the hackles of the political Right and jeopardize an agreement. So they did it secretly.

"The preliminary work had been done by General Brent Scowcroft and his team of national security experts in Moscow. Now the time had come for Kissinger to go for the final negotiating, and he took Dobrynin with him.

"Kissinger was so paranoid about leaks that he hadn't even told the staff of our embassy in Moscow what was happening, which meant he had no communications base, and of course it was essential that he stay in touch with the President, so we had to provide one. The only one that was completely secure was the plane, so we put extra radiomen aboard, and a couple of guys to run messages back and forth between Kissinger and the aircraft.

"In keeping with the secrecy that covered the whole mission, the plane was scheduled to leave Andrews for Moscow in the early hours of the morning, but first we had to pick up Dobrynin. A White House station wagon was to meet him on a street corner in Georgetown at midnight and whisk him out to the plane, where Kissinger would be waiting.

"The driver got Dobrynin, all right, but after a block or two he realized he was being followed. He immediately called the signal board, and the dispatcher told him to do whatever he could to lose whoever was following him.

"By going down alleys, cutting through parking lots, doubling back on his tracks, and doing all those neat things he always dreamed but never believed he'd do at the White House, the driver lost his tail.

"About noon the next day we heard from the CIA. In those days the White House license plates were confidential, and the D.C. police weren't authorized to release the numbers to anyone. But when the CIA put some muscle into their request to the D.C. government to find out who had the registration for the station wagon that had picked up Dobrynin from a Georgetown street corner at midnight, they discovered it was the White House.

"The CIA immediately got in touch with the FBI and the Secret Service, and in asking them what the hell was going on, they were also telling them what had happened. Secret Service got all bent out of shape, although it was no business of theirs, but no one in our office told anybody anything. Dobrynin and Kissinger flew off to Moscow for their secret negotiations, and no one was the wiser.

"The whole incident caused the CIA no end of chagrin, and our White House driver no end of satisfaction, you may be sure."

"The mechanics of keeping Kissinger's trips secret were as intricate as the inside of his head. It wasn't just a matter of getting a plane ready and putting Henry on it. We had to be sure that the pilot and crew wouldn't talk; file international flight plans and comply with immigration and transportation regulations but maintain secrecy; and reach an understanding with customs.

"Our White House Communications Center had to keep in contact with his plane so the President could talk to Kissinger, and there had to be a backup aircraft in case of mechanical difficulties. No manifest was kept for the plane, and we made sure there was no way to identify the car or its passenger. Henry would put on a hat, jump into the car, and avert his face as he drove through the gates. The landing area would be clear when the car drove up to the plane.

"Kissinger met with the North Vietnamese outside Paris, and Colonel George Guay, the Department of Defense guy at our embassy there, coordinated our operation with the French. We'd fly Henry to an old airfield at Avord, a hundred and twenty miles south of Paris, where he'd be met by a French plane with a French crew, which would fly him to Le Bourget Airport on the outskirts of Paris. A car would meet him there and take him to a safe house, where he would rendezvous with the North Vietnamese.

"The return trip was the same, except that when he'd land at Andrews I'd sometimes have a Jet Star meet him and take him to New York, where he'd be seen by the Press wining and dining some beautiful woman.

"I kept a list of things to check off on each trip, and the last item on it always was: What happens if we get caught? We did all we could to ensure there wouldn't be any leaks; for a long time even the Secretary of Defense, Melvin Laird, didn't know what Kissinger was doing, and only once did we get seriously worried.

"There'd been what looked to us like ominous speculation in the press, so we had a meeting chaired by Alexander Haig, and Vernon Walters was there. He was an interpreter used by Johnson and Nixon; he was headquartered in Paris and doing spook work with the CIA, the Department of Defense Intelligence and the French.

"Walters, as far as I am concerned, had an ego as big as his ass, and he was a big, fat-assed guy. At this meeting, when he sat down at the table next to me, the first thing he did was take off his wristwatch. That was O.K., until he put it down on the table in front of him, facedown. The reason he did this was so everyone in the room would be sure to see that he was wearing a watch that was engraved to him from Lyndon Baines Johnson.

"What we finally decided to do on the next trip was to throw anyone off the scent by sending two planes, one with Kissinger aboard and one without. The empty plane went to the field at Avord, where a car met it and picked up a dummy package, went on to London to refuel, and came back to Andrews. Kissinger in the meantime had landed at another airfield in France.

"I don't know whether our concern about the secrecy of

that particular trip was well founded or not, since it went off smoothly and no one in the Press suggested that Kissinger was up to anything, or out of the country.

"As a footnote to this period, I was in my car one day and heard over the radio a news report that it had just been revealed that over a period of many months Kissinger had been making clandestine trips into France to meet with the North Vietnamese. I damn near drove off the road.

"All I could think of was that we'd better come up with a hell of a good story and do it right away, because we were going to get blamed for letting the secret slip. I was all set to defend our position to the last when I found out it was Kissinger himself who had finally decided to tell all. Kissinger was one of the biggest leaks in the White House, so there was a certain fitness to his blowing his own cover."

"It's no exaggeration to say that Henry's travels were followed with the liveliest interest at the highest levels in the White House. One evening, a Friday, I had just gotten home from the office at about nine o'clock when I had a call from the White House operator saying Haig wanted to talk to me right away. I said fine, put him on.

"Haig got on the line, and I could tell the moment he started talking that he'd probably had a couple of martinis. I certainly couldn't blame him for that, having to put up with Kissinger and his temperament. Be that as it may, Haig had not been left unscathed by his encounter with the gin bottle that evening.

"I knew, of course, that Kissinger was on his way back from Europe after one of his secret missions to France, but at the time I'd left the office, about an hour before, there hadn't been anything untoward going on—if there had been, somebody would have let me know, wherever I was.

"But Haig said the President, who was at Camp David, and he, Haig, were both very worried because they'd been out of radio contact with Kissinger's plane for the last thirty minutes. He wanted me to check on it and let him know.

"I called the communications center at the White House Communications Agency and asked the sergeant who was the

expert on messages coming in from Henry's aircraft to give
me a rundown on the problem.

"The sergeant said an atmospheric condition was causing
trouble for a radio relay station in Turkey. Kissinger's aircraft
communicated through that station, he said, and it wasn't at
all unusual for an airplane that many hours off the coast of
Europe to encounter this problem. Then he said, 'It'll clear
up in between twenty and thirty minutes.'

"I called Haig, who by this time, I suspected, had had
another martini, and told him exactly what the sergeant had
told me. He asked me where I'd gotten my information, and
I told him from a sergeant at the White House Communications Agency. Haig just fell apart. He said, 'Do you mean to
tell me that in this situation, when Henry Kissinger's plane
may be down at sea, when the President of the United States
is personally concerned about his welfare, that you are relying
on the word of some sergeant? Do you seriously expect me to
go to the President and tell him some *sergeant* says it's an
atmospheric condition and not to worry?'

"At that point Haig wasn't the only one mad. I said, 'General, just back off a minute. This sergeant is an experienced
man. He's been handling aircraft communications for the
White House Communications Agency for eight or nine years,
so just cool it. Calm down. This guy knows what he's doing,
and I'd sure as hell rather talk to a sergeant who knows his
job than to some colonel who's going to have to take the time
to call the sergeant so that he can tell me so that I can tell you
so that you can tell the President.'

"With that, Haig hung up on me.

"I called the sergeant back and told him to let me know the
minute communications with Kissinger's aircraft were re-
established. Sure enough, right on the button the plane flew
out of the area where the trouble had been and Kissinger was
once again keeping the operators busy putting him through to
Camp David.

"The next morning, Saturday, I went in to the White
House, and as I did every Saturday, I took my little grand-
daughter with me. She was about two and a half years old,
and the first thing we did was go to the Staff Mess to get some

breakfast. When we walked in, Al Haig was there, and when he saw me he looked a little sheepish.

"He said, 'Bill, I wish you'd call that sergeant and thank him for the information he gave us last night. I passed it on to the President, who was reassured, and of course it turned out just as he said it would.' "

"I watched Haig's phenomenal rise from colonel to four-star general in four years, inside the White House, and what I saw was an ambitious master-manipulator playing the angles so that he was constantly bettering his own position. As I'll explain later, his bringing Fred Buzhardt in to replace John Dean as counsel to the President only confirmed everything I thought."

THE ASCENT OF AL HAIG

"Haig started his White House career when he was brought in to the periphery of the Kennedy Administration by Joe Califano, who was one of the Whiz Kids of McNamara's band. Haig was a lieutenant colonel and worked for Califano at the Pentagon. Having had no real military experience, Haig managed to get himself to Vietnam for a nine-month tour of duty—the only time he had had command of a brigade—in order to 'get his ticket punched,' that is, see active duty. An absolute necessity for promotion in the military.

"When Haig got back, Califano recommended him for the job of assistant to Henry Kissinger, who had no understanding of the armed services and the Department of Defense, which is obviously crucial to a guy on the National Security Council. This turned out to be Haig's great opportunity. Having sat outside the Secretary of Defense's door in the Kennedy-Johnson years, and having seen from the other end Walt Rostow's operation as the National Security Advisor, he saw that he could be invaluable to Kissinger, and he proceeded to become just that.

142

"Before very long Kissinger, who trusted Haig, made him his deputy, which was a significant step for Haig. It meant he was getting close to that most fertile pasture of all—becoming a Presidential appointee.

"Kissinger's faith in Haig was such that he never worried about his ass being covered while he was off on his secret negotiations, flying all over the skies of the world. He was confident that loyal old Al Haig was back in the White House, passing his messages on to the President and protecting his, Kissinger's, position.

"Meanwhile, what's really going on back at the ranch is that loyal old Al Haig sees the golden gates will open for *him,* now. Suddenly, because Henry Kissinger wants, and Richard Nixon insists, the President must be kept constantly informed on the progress of the secret negotiations, and Haig is the message bearer. Suddenly, he has Access To The President.

"Kissinger was sending messages, in code, for the President, and it never occurred to him that anything was happening except that Al Haig was shooting them up to Nixon exactly as he received them. But what Haig, who is no dummy, saw was an opportunity to change from a caterpillar to a butterfly. He was going to move from carrying Kissinger's briefcase to playing a substantive role, and his audience was going to be none other than the President of the United States.

"What Haig realized—because not only is he smart, he's shrewd—was that Richard Nixon did not consider himself to be the pupil of Henry Kissinger. He considered himself to be the mentor of Henry Kissinger. So Haig gave Kissinger's messages a tilt. He did a little editing here and a little rephrasing there, making a suggestion that this or that point might fall in line better with the President's view of what should be done, rather than with Kissinger's.

"The result would be messages sent back in code with little changes, from Nixon, changes which in fact had been suggested by Haig purely in order to play up to Nixon's vanity. Al Haig was manipulating both players. On the one hand, he was solidifying his position with Kissinger as being loyal, efficient and discreet. On the other, he was furthering his ambitions with the President by appearing to be an innovative thinker who had his head screwed on right because he saw things just the way Nixon did.

"At the same time, he found a way to make use of Bob Haldeman. He began to tell him little, intimate tidbits of gossip about Kissinger—he's screwing this or that broad in New York, that type of thing. Kissinger was hot copy, and everybody wanted to be let in on the inside story, a story nobody but Haig could give out. So he began to use it as valuable currency, and he bought Haldeman's support with it.

"Before long Nixon had formed such a high opinion of Haig that he decided he shouldn't be deputy to Kissinger, he should be Deputy to the President for National Security. Al Haig had arrived. He was a Presidential appointee. He was the number two guy on National Security Affairs. He had open entree to the Oval Office. No more sitting outside the office cooling his heels.

"In the absence of Kissinger he spoke with the same authority as Kissinger, whereas before in the absence of Kissinger he could only speak if Kissinger said he could, and then he could only say what Henry Kissinger had told him to say.

"At the same time, Haig's stock had taken a giant leap over at Defense. The Pentagon was terrified of Kissinger. They didn't want him telling them what to do with their missiles and their submarines or who should be promoted. That was their department, and they wanted to keep it that way. Kissinger was just National Security Advisor to the President, and his role didn't include disposing of bombs or armies and navies. But he sure as hell had the ear of the Commander in Chief.

"But now they had their own boy in a substantial position over there at the White House. He could jump in his car and brief the Secretary of Defense or a few carefully selected generals on what Kissinger was up to, what the President was up to, what was coming down the road to meet them.

"Haig's eyesight is superb where his own self-interest is concerned, and when Watergate loomed on the horizon, I think he saw what might be coming and started making plans to get the hell away from the politicians and back into the military. Since by then it appeared to him that nothing was out of his grasp, he aimed high—to be either the chief of staff of the Army or the chairman of the Joint Chiefs.

"The problem was he only had two stars, and when the Administration started making moves to put Haig into one of these two jobs, they were met with stiff resistance—there were four-star generals who were going to resign in protest if that happened. You have to remember, it was one thing to have Al Haig as a spy in the bosom of the White House; it was another to have him leapfrogging his way over the heads of senior guys in their own military establishment.

"So the best they could do was get Haig the job of second man in the Army—but it had four stars. So there he was, set for life as a four-star general, and he'd done it in only the four years since he'd gone into politics as a colonel.

"Then Haldeman had to go. Rose Woods tells me that the first choice to replace him was General Brent Scowcroft, who had replaced Kissinger as National Security Advisor to the President, but that Kissinger—who was Secretary of State at this point—said absolutely not. Scowcroft, who is a brilliant man, was too valuable to Kissinger where he was. So Haldeman suggested Al Haig.

"Why not? Haldeman was going to need all the help he could get, continuing access to the President, a friend in high places, and he thought Haig was going to be that friend. Nixon agreed, but consulted Kissinger before appointing Haig. Kissinger, who by this time had begun to find out about some of what had been going on while he was off doing his thing, agreed, but only on the condition that he'd never have to go through his former deputy to see the President—that he would have open access.

"This was agreed, but it also triggered a running battle between the new White House chief of staff and Kissinger, now that Haig's ambition, and along with it his ego, was out in the open. Haig had taken so much bullshit from Kissinger over the years he'd spent in his huge shadow that now he'd become Somebody, he was damn well going to be treated like Somebody. And the Somebody he wanted to be treated like was Kissinger.

"The result was a series of petty struggles that did nothing to raise the stature of either of them, like their infantile squabbles over who was going to get the number two room, next to the President, when they traveled abroad.

"Haig never lost sight of what was good for Haig, or of where he wanted to go. He began to build a power base for himself while treading a very fine line. He had to appear to stay loyal to Nixon while deploring all the things that had gone on in the Nixon Administration. He could never stop sniffing the wind, and when it blew for impeachment, Haig was ready to work with the powers on the Hill, of both parties, to pry Richard Nixon loose from the Oval Office.

"Then he settled down to the final piece of business. To becoming President of the United States.

"Nixon was, and still is, totally sold on Al Haig. When we were talking about the 1980 election, before Haig took himself out of the race, Nixon really took me aback by saying he thought Haig was the next best qualified to John Connally to be President. I pointed out that Haig wasn't a general in the mold of Eisenhower, he wasn't a creator of great victories. That he had made it from colonel to four-star general in the White House, through patronage, if you like. That he had no real experience, not as a general and not in the political arena.

"Nixon was unmoved. He said in his opinion Haig was a pretty highly qualified guy. It's also clear to me that Haig had consulted Nixon about his ambitions, and I'd have to say that Nixon gave him encouragement. Haig has used every stepping-stone and played every angle, and just like Kissinger, he's come a long way—all in that palace on Pennsylvania Avenue."

PERKS AND BEING "PRESIDENTIAL"

Gulley, as Keeper of the Perks, had a ringside seat from which he watched the burgeoning of luxury and a style of life that didn't count the cost. Henry Steele Commager views this development, and the apparent lack of reaction to it by the American people, with dismay.

"We look with indifference . . . ," Commager says, "at the growth of what would once have been regarded as royal attributes in our rulers—the numerous luxurious residences they require, the special jet planes, the fleets of limousines, the vast entourage which accompanies them wherever they go. How odd to remember that when Thomas Jefferson walked back to his boarding house after giving his inaugural address, he could not find a seat available for him at the dinner table, or that a quarter century later President John Quincy Adams should have the same experience on a ship sailing from Baltimore to New York."

It was Lyndon Johnson, Gulley says, who opened the door to this royal style of life, but it was Nixon and his men who marched through it and made it a part of the American Presidency.

"The buzz word around the Nixon White House for projecting the proper image was 'Presidential,' " Gulley says. "If a thing or a place wasn't dignified enough or enough in keeping with somebody's, usually Haldeman's, idea of what was proper, then it wasn't 'Presidential.' And that meant money had to be spent on it.

"After Nixon's first visit to Camp David, Haldeman told us that the place wasn't 'Presidential' and something had to be done about it. The cabins, especially the President's cabin, had to be upgraded.

"LBJ had had plans to do some rebuilding of Camp David, and we had let him know that the money was available from the Secret Fund. Then came his decision not to run, and one of the first things he said was, 'Don't do any work on Camp David. Let the next son of a bitch worry about it.' And the next one did.

"When Nixon came in, of course, he was familiar with Camp David, having been there as Vice President. He knew what Camp David was; he knew the potential it had for his personality and what it could do for him. Not long after the inaugural we went up there—Nixon, Hughes, the commander from the Chesapeake Division, who was an engineer and also handled the Secret Fund, Bebe Rebozo, the commander of Camp David and myself. It was Nixon's first visit as President, and we sat down and discussed, in broad, sweeping terms, what should be done about it.

"It was at that point I think Hughes made a tactical error. When we got back, he told Haldeman how the work could be done without letting it become public knowledge. He explained about the Secret Fund held by the Military Office, that it wouldn't be necessary to go to Congress and ask for a budget, and that only two or three key congressmen would even have to be told about it.

"This piece of information triggered in Haldeman's mind a much larger rehabilitation program than he originally envisioned, I'm sure. Especially when he found out what the size of the fund was. The first sign of his revised thinking came when he reported the President wanted a swimming pool outside Aspen, the President's cabin.

"First, though, we began to get some specific inputs from Bebe Rebozo. We were aware, of course, of who Rebozo was and the clout he carried with the President, so when he began to talk in specifics about Camp David, we knew he was speaking for the President. His first suggestion was, 'Before you go out and get boards and nails, let's sit down and devise a master plan for Camp David.'

"Camp David originally was a cluster of cabins that had been built by the Civilian Conservation Corps, the CCC, during the Depression in the thirties. In fact, the original Aspen was two CCC barracks that had been put together for Roosevelt's use when he was calling the place Shangri-la. The camp had been modified and improved over the years but not really that much; it was makeshift work.

"It quickly became obvious from what Rebozo and Haldeman were telling us that we were going to get into millions of dollars to rebuild the camp the way Nixon wanted. It became clear the project was getting too big for the fund to handle, even at its current two-million-dollar size, so it was decided that Bryce Harlow, who was the congressional liaison, would talk to George Mahon of the Appropriations Committee—the Big Daddy of all appropriations. Harlow told Mahon that the size of the fund would have to be increased in order to do what had to be done at Camp David in the manner the President wanted.

"Mahon said O.K., he'd see to an increase in the fund. In the meantime, the Navy came up with some other money, funds for a construction program that had been canceled. Normally this money wouldn't be allocated, but the Appropriations Committee diverted it to us, along with allocating additional money for the fund.

"The justification for all this hanky-panky was the argument that Camp David is a classified site. The reasoning was supposed to go that money from a classified fund was being used on a classified site; the fact that it was spent above ground, for building and decorating elaborate cabins, and putting in a half-million-dollar swimming pool, wasn't known.

"Once we had the money we went into the details of the work, and we immediately hit an engineering problem. The spot the President picked for the pool was right over the bomb shelter—a tremendous hole in the ground the President would go to directly from Aspen in case of nuclear attack. If we dug there, we'd hit the top of the shelter and go through it halfway to China.

"Eventually the pool cost $550,000 because instead of saying to the President, 'Look, we've got a problem with the exact spot you picked. How about another spot?,' they spent hundreds of thousands of dollars to reinforce the top of the bomb shelter.

"Once the President said, 'That looks like a nice place for a swimming pool,' that was it. No matter what the problems. No matter what the cost. No one wanted to be the one to say, 'Mr. President, you can't do that.'

"In addition to all the individual cabins we were building, it was decided to build one huge lodge where Cabinet meetings and other big gatherings could be held, with a lounge and dining room for all the staff. Laurel alone cost over seven hundred thousand dollars just to build.

"Aspen, the President's cabin, is totally equipped for comfort. It has a 35 millimeter projection booth for movies, a tremendous stereo system, four bedrooms and a glassed-in dining room with a table that seats twelve and has a spectacular view. That cabin is strictly for the family, and when the President goes to Camp David, four people, Filipinos from the Staff Mess at the White House, go along just to serve there.

"As you come in the front door of Aspen there's an elevator immediately on the left that goes down into the bomb shelter. It's much more elaborate than the White House bomb shelter, and much deeper underground. But it has the same basic things: offices, communications, beds, a conference room.

"The whole complex is called Orange One, and at one time it was important because it was an effective bomb shelter. But like the White House shelter, it's basically useless now because it couldn't withstand the blast of the bombs that exist today. Not only that, the communications system is antiquated to the point where it would be blown away with a surface blast, and you would have to depend on the possibility that people could get back outside to set up aerials.

"During Nixon's time, General Lawson, who was director of the Military Office in 1974, looked this underground site over and decided the place needed sprucing up. The result was that he ran up a bill for the Secret Fund of $250,000. He put in new beds, psychedelic pictures, fancy bedspreads, new chairs, redid the President's office, had the corridors painted, and just generally threw money down the hole.

"A new director of the Military Office came in, but Lawson must have left some kind of contagion, because the guy who replaced him was all set to redecorate all over again because he didn't like the color scheme his predecessor had chosen. At this point Ford was President, and I called Dick Cheney, who was chief of staff, and told him somebody had better blow the whistle on this guy or we were going to be in for another quarter of a million dollars.

"While we were rebuilding Camp David, nobody ever asked how much anything cost. In fact, what we got was the opposite of an interest in what anything cost; on almost every visit Haldeman would find fault with something that was being done, and we'd have to start over again.

"With few exceptions, Camp David was designed, and run, to please Haldeman. His sharp eye for any displeasing detail never shut, and there was a steady stream of complaints and

150

demands forwarded to our office through the strutting Higby
—who with no difficulty had earned the nickname 'Worm.'

"When it came to decorating Aspen, Mrs. Nixon did get a
say on what color the walls were to be, and the carpeting.
And we ordered a special mattress from Cincinnati because
Nixon has a back problem. However, it was different when it
came to the other cabins.

"While we were building, Mrs. Nixon said, 'When you get
to that point, I would like very much to be consulted before
the cabins are furnished.' So when we got to that stage we
told Haldeman we'd like to arrange a time for Mrs. Nixon
to meet with an interior decorator from GSA to discuss the
cabins.

"Haldeman said, 'That won't be necessary. I've hired a
man who's coming from New York to advise us on this. Higby
will get in touch with him right away.' And that's what happened. He was there for only one visit but charged us a tremendous sum of money.

"In due course the furniture, the drapes, everything he'd
selected was delivered and put in place. Then Mrs. Nixon
came up for a visit and asked the camp commander, 'When
are we going to get to the furnishing of the cabins?' He told
her Haldeman had had a decorator from New York come
down and the cabins were all done.

"Mrs. Nixon said, 'Oh? I'd like to see them.' So the commander and the military aide went around with her, and she
took violent exception to the furnishings. So did just about
everybody who had a chance to see them. They were atro-
cious. The President became aware that Mrs. Nixon was
upset about this, because she told him she was, and all the
furnishings went out. We redid the whole place, this time with
Mrs. Nixon's approval."

"Mrs. Nixon wasn't very well known by the public as a
First Lady, and that's because her manner was low key. She
struck me as having a professional attitude about being First
Lady, that she took it as a serious, full-time job that was part
of the Presidency.

"There were definitely different styles of entertaining at the

151

)   )

THE WHITE HOUSE
WASHINGTON

May 9, 1972

MEMORANDUM FOR :   RON JACKSON

FROM :   L. HIGBY

Will you please make sure that Camp David no longer serves the
sizzling steak platter. It's really kind of impractical and doesn't
add much to the steaks. The steaks are great, incidentally, it's
just that we could dispense with the platter.

EMORANDUM

THE WHITE HOUSE
WASHINGTON

May 10, 1972

MEMORANDUM FOR LARRY HIGBY

Thank you for your comments regarding sizzling steak platters.
I have directed Camp David to insure that they are no longer used
when serving you and Mr. Haldeman. However, since the preponderance
of individuals expressed satisfaction with that method of serving steaks,
we will still utilize them for other guests when they are at the Camp.

CRAIG S. CAMPBELL

153

THE WHITE HOUSE

WASHINGTON

Problems? fele

December 7, 1972

MEMORANDUM FOR :   COMMANDER DETTBARN

FROM :   L. HIGBY

Will you please get fire tongs similar to the ones Mr. Haldeman
now has in his office for use up here with the Camp David fire-
place? The type that you are using simply isn't suitable.

White House; some of them you can spot by the way White House guests dressed in the various administrations. It was business suits with LBJ, white tie with Nixon, black tie with Ford, and blue jeans with Carter.

"Much depended on the First Lady. Her taste, and the amount of attention she paid to entertaining. For example, in the Fords' time, on July 10, 1976, the Queen of England made a visit. The Fords' idea of how to entertain her was to have the Captain and Tenille do their thing in the Rose Garden, and one of their numbers was about two muskrats screwing. This tasteful interlude was followed by dancing in the East Room, and when the President and the Queen took to the dance floor it was to the tune 'The Lady Is a Tramp.'

"Mrs. Ford just didn't take a close personal interest in these things; there wasn't any supervision from the top. With Mrs. Nixon it was just the opposite. She always took a deep interest in planning for social events, down to the last detail, and she was always very quiet about it.

"Mrs. Nixon supervised the menus, the choice of wines, all the details. Bess Abel did these things for Lady Bird Johnson. Part of this might have been that Lady Bird didn't want to compete with Jackie Kennedy, so she didn't want to get deeply, personally into it. Betty Ford just left the thing in the hands of her staff, which was unfortunate because they were so inept.

"Mrs. Nixon had an unusually close relationship with her staff. It was a personal one that extended to the least important girl there. The girls in her correspondence office, for example, felt she was accessible, and she was. If they had a personal problem, they'd go and talk to her in the living quarters. She'd literally give them tea and sympathy. She worried about how much they were paid, how they were making ends meet at home.

"Mrs. Johnson could be very cold to her staff; Mrs. Ford was removed from hers, largely because she couldn't deal with them as a result of her personal problems. And in my time at the Carter White House, Rosalynn Carter didn't know what direction she was going in, what kind of staff she wanted, or how she was going to treat them. But Mrs. Nixon was the only First Lady in my experience who cared about her people as people.

"Both the Nixons were unusually conscious of the little details of White House ceremonies and social events. There's usually a small ceremony on the South Lawn when a visiting head of state arrives or leaves. The Army detachment at Fort Myer was promoting a new unit they had—a fife and drum corps that was all dressed up in 1775 Colonial uniforms. Nixon thought it sounded colorful and decided to give it a try.

"The Prime Minister of England had been on a state visit, so when we geared up for the leave-taking ceremony, in addition to the cordon of troops, we had the fife and drum corps. Everything went off just as scheduled. The President and the Prime Minister came down onto the South Lawn, past the cordon of troops, and across to the cars that were waiting for the Prime Minister and his party.

"At that point the fife and drum corps came into action, escorting them to the cars, and then preceding the automobiles down the driveway to the gate—at which point they peeled off, still fifing and drumming.

"The minute the cars were out of sight Richard Nixon exploded. The music the fife and drum corps had chosen for the occasion was 'Yankee Doodle,' the most popular song of the American Revolution.

"Nixon let it be known in no uncertain terms that he did not consider that a suitable choice of music with which to serenade the British Prime Minister, and the fife and drum corps was replaced forthwith by the Marine Drum and Bugle Corps.

"Which did not mean that the Marine Corps had fully grasped what was considered to be suitably Presidential music in the Nixon White House, as Haldeman pointed out.

"In addition to financing Camp David and the other facilities run by the military, our office got deeply into the President's houses at Key Biscayne and San Clemente. Key Biscayne was smaller and closer to Washington, so it involved less to adapt into a Vacation White House than San Clemente. Flying time from Washington was two hours and fifteen minutes, so appointments could be run in and back by Jet Star in

MEMORANDUM

THE WHITE HOUSE

WASHINGTON

August 25, 1970

MEMORANDUM FOR GENERAL JAMES D. HUGHES

After listening and watching the Marine Combo, the President has come to the conclusion that they do not play the type of music which he feels is appropriate for the White House. We should either have them change their repertoire, and for that matter, their style, or we should just consider not using them any more. The songs that they play are jazzy and of the night-club type. They use a steel guitar, an amplified accordion (which is the principal offender), and the pianist performs like Dave Brubeck, rather than like Roger Williams whom the President likes.

H. R. HALDEMAN

a day. That, and the fact that Nixon rarely spent more than a few days there, meant that less staff and support were needed.

"Which is not to say that military money wasn't spent, and misspent, on Key Biscayne. The first thing they did was build a helicopter pad out on the edge of the water, at a cost of $418,000. As soon as it was built they realized they couldn't keep a helicopter crew just sitting out on a slab of concrete the whole time the President was there, so it was only used to pick up and deliver Nixon. In the end, the helicopter was kept at Homestead Air Force Base, twenty minutes away.

"Among the other things the military spent money on down there was a shark net at $20,000; major communications equipment for $307,000, $16,000 of that amount for the residence; and recurring communications costs of $1,320,000. We also put a communications system on Abplanalp's island, Grand Cay, at a cost to us of $161,000.

"But Abplanalp was a different story from Rebozo, who also benefited from the military by getting a signal phone, with free worldwide telephone service, put in his home next to the Nixons'. Abplanalp had a helicopter pad built at his own expense, and I never knew him ever to ask for anything from us. We never even hauled him on airplanes, as we did Rebozo, unless he was actually with the President.

"The bottom line for military expenditures at Key Biscayne came close to two million dollars. Then we did it all again, only more so, at San Clemente. A Southern White House and a Western White House, both with all the trimmings, were set and ready to go.

"As soon as the Southern and Western White Houses were set up, we got into the wholesale transportation business. Until Nixon came in as President, *Air Force One* had been reserved for the exclusive use of the President. Now we started hauling wives and kids of staff members on *Air Force One*.

"It reached the ludicrous situation where if we couldn't fit them all on *Air Force One,* we'd have to set up additional aircraft—for the families. Ron Ziegler broke new ground by bringing along a baby-sitter in addition to his family; and later on, Haig's aide, Joulwan, did the same thing.

158

"The wives of Nixon's staff members began to take this so for granted that they took it upon themselves to draw up lists of which wife and family would go on which trip to California, as if it were some kind of vacation excursion we were running, not *Air Force One*.

"On one occasion, to show you how out of hand the whole thing had gotten, the President decided to leave San Clemente early, and rather than leaving after the President, the backup plane left before him. The whole point of a backup is to have a plane in reserve, *behind* the President in case of need. But this time the backup, filled to the brim with wives and children, left *before Air Force One*. The reason? So the children wouldn't get home past their bedtimes."

Lyndon Johnson had prowled the corridors of his White House and pounced on anyone who showed signs of an expanding ego. There were no exceptions. In truly democratic fashion he gleefully deflated the puffed-up wherever he found them, and he could spot a bloated pissant at twenty paces.

In the Nixon White House things were different. Haldeman played favorites, allowing his lieutenants to issue commands in his name, and permitting them to adopt the same hectoring tone. "In that atmosphere," Gulley says, "guys with undernourished egos, who now had the opportunity to feed them, made gluttons of themselves.

"The Military Office holds the White House perks, the status symbols, and staff members, high and low, devote more time and ingenuity to trying to get access to them than they do to high affairs of state. Literally. They impress the hell out of themselves and each other by getting the use of a White House car or a ride on *Air Force One*.

"Ego inflation created a problem for us, because big egos call attention to themselves. It was a pain dealing with status seekers from other offices; it was infuriating having one in our own.

"Two of the things we took a lot of pride in in the Military Office were our professionalism and our low profile; the two go together most of the time. Most of what we had to do was, if not classified, at least not for publication. We were there to

159

do a job as well as possible, not to turn the fact that we worked at the White House into an ego trip.

"Sometimes we'd get a young aide who let the thing go to his head, and we'd either rein him in or get rid of him right away. But then we were presented with the biggest publicity-hound in our experience, and we were stuck with him.

"When Nixon came in he brought a new pilot of *Air Force One* with him—Ralph Albertazzie. Albertazzie was without question the best 707 pilot the Air Force had. He had outstanding skills as a pilot. Unfortunately, in my opinion, he also had an outstanding ego; it was bigger than the airplane.

"This guy had a long-range ambition that I believe never left his mind. He wanted to make a name for himself in the Air Force, retire and then get elected governor of West Virginia, his home state. As I see it, Albertazzie started out right away politicking in the White House and the Department of Defense. He hadn't been there long before he saw the possibilities for new and interesting ways to make friends. He began to insist he needed overseas training flights to keep himself up to date on new navigational procedures and international routings.

"We thought it was all a bunch of bullshit, but Hughes would give his approval anyway, to keep the peace. Albertazzie would get a few Air Force generals and their wives, and a couple of senior White House staffers and their wives, and they'd go off to Germany or France or wherever on a 'Training Mission' for Albertazzie.

"While this was going on back at the White House, he was also busy trying to make a name for himself before a wider audience as the dashing pilot of the glamorous *Air Force One*. He appeared on TV shows and gave interviews to magazines and newspapers. The problem this presented us was that this excess exposure wasn't only lifting Albertazzie's profile, it was lifting the whole military profile at the White House— exactly the thing we'd been trying to avoid since LBJ became President.

"In the end all Albertazzie's self-promotion didn't get him anywhere. He actually did enter the Republican primary in the gubernatorial race in 1976, after he retired from the military, but I'm not sure he got enough votes even to count. Anyway, he's never been heard from politically again.

"Among the major league egos in the Nixon White House, Albertazzie's was bush league, a good example, in my view, of a big ego on a small talent. But he had lots of company; he fitted right in with the other characters from Disneyland."

"There are about two hundred people, a hundred Navy Seabees and a hundred Marine guards, permanently stationed at Camp David. It's an isolated spot, which has led to some problems.

"The commanding officer at Camp David, Commander Dave Miller, called one day in the spring of 1973 and asked if he could come down and see me. He was a highly nervous guy, and when he arrived it was clear he was worried.

"He said he had discovered something irregular that had been going on at Camp David for some time, and he didn't know what to do about it. Miller had a new executive officer, a real charger, as they're known in the trade, who was looking into all aspects of the operation up there. One of the things he found was some kind of fiddle with the fuel.

"Miller said to me, 'You know we buy our fuel oil from a company in Baltimore, and when we pay for it we pay out of appropriated Navy funds. Then we get back a check from the company as reimbursement for state tax which we don't have to pay but which was included in the payment price.

" 'For years,' he said, 'it appears these reimbursement checks have been cashed and the money put into a slush fund. Apparently the money's been used for all manner of things and it can't be accounted for.'

"I told him, 'O.K. Go get your house in order and let's get this operation back in line with regulations.'

"Within a matter of a few days Commander Miller called me again, and again he came down to see me. This time the executive officer had found out that the mess hall at Camp David was claiming to feed more people than it was actually feeding. The idea was that the more mouths you could claim to feed, the more money you could get, and the more food you could buy.

"It's especially easy to do some quicksteps around the truth when you're dealing with itinerants, as you are at Camp David, and you don't know from one weekend to the next how many you'll be catering for.

"It seems that the new executive officer had got one of the old-timers running the mess to admit that for years he'd been providing food for one of the commanding officer's personal use, that the funds hadn't always been spent for food, that rationing regulations weren't being followed, and so on.

"To this day I don't know what that money was used for, and I don't want to know.

"Had this happened on a Navy base, there would have been a number of general court-martials, I'm sure. As it was, thanks to the secrecy that's built into the system, I just put a lid on the thing. We changed the way the money was handled, cleaned the thing up, and no one ever heard about it.

"Later I found out that while they were redoing Camp David some of the furniture and bathroom fixtures went out the back gate and were put to private use. One of the commanding officers even had several sets of Presidential dinnerware in his possession—china, crystal and silver. He went so far as to display it in a breakfront in his dining room.

"I think the root cause of the thing was isolation. Those guys up there, hell—there's just nothing to do."

"The Presidential yacht is gone now, but in Nixon's day we used it a lot, and we secretly diverted Department of Defense funds to pay for its upkeep to keep White House expenses low on the books.

"We created an outfit called the Naval Administration Unit and put it down in the Navy Yard. In order to get Department of Defense funds allocated for this outfit, we used it as the parent unit for the stewards serving the White House Mess; that was the ostensible purpose of this unit, but it was really set up to hide the *Sequoia*. You could look through the Library of Congress for ten years, and you wouldn't find a budget for the yacht. The way we had it set up, it was just a boat that was assigned to the Naval Administration Unit, hidden away anonymously in the Department of Defense budget.

162

"Since this unit was under my direct operational control and I was the only one who knew how the funds were spent, there was no way to find out what the *Sequoia* really cost. It actually cost close to a million dollars a season to run, but when I'd get a question from the Hill about it, I'd just figure what they were after was the cost of operating her, of the fuel. So I'd give them the hourly rate for fuel consumption, which, since she was an old diesel burner, came to about twelve dollars an hour. Very reasonable.

"We did the same thing with the White House helicopters. Money was allocated to a Marine Corps outfit called HMX-1 at Quantico, Virginia. That's a helicopter group down there, and they pad their books enough to include the White House operations so that they don't show up anywhere. It's the same with the fixed-wing aircraft, only that's done through the Air Force.

"The reason the White House gets into this position of hiding the source of its funds is that there's no money to pay honestly for the things they want to do. And there was no one able to check up on what was really going on. I could hardly believe it when I found out how dumb the Government Accounting Office was, and how easy to manipulate. A congressman would ask GAO to look into a White House expenditure, or how much something cost, and the guys they sent were never smart enough to pursue the matter as investigators should. I'd give them a set of Presidential cuff links or a gold pin with the Presidential seal, and they'd be on my side. They'd pretty well write what I wanted them to write.

"If I really got up against it with GAO, there were two more weapons. First I could get hard-nosed with them. I could start threatening them with the President. I'd say, 'O.K. If you guys have got the balls to take on the President . . .' But the final weapon, and the best, was that no one could come in the gate unless he was cleared. I didn't *have* to see anybody, because they couldn't get in unless I let them in.

"I remember when Kissinger gave that goddamn helicopter to Sadat, and no one really knows why he did. Right away there was a request from the House Government Activities Committee to tell them how much it cost. GAO came to me, and in the end I got the figure from the Navy, which had bought the thing sixteen years before.

"A helicopter, you have to remember, like an airplane, does not depreciate in value. Every year it's reworked and gets a new engine, and the way they're maintained, the cost of the helicopter you bought sixteen years ago should be about the same as one you might buy today. But as it turned out, of course, the actual number of dollars that the helicopter cost then was a lot less than the number of dollars you'd have to pay today. So when I gave GAO the figure, the purchase price sixteen years ago, it didn't look bad at all.

"Then Jack Brooks, a congressman from Texas who watched Nixon and the Republicans the way Melvin Laird had watched LBJ and the Democrats, said, 'That can't be right. That helicopter cost more than that. I just saw the price of new helicopters the White House is buying, and they cost five times that.'

"When the GAO guy came back to me and told me my figure was all wrong, I said, 'Now look. There's all this new equipment on these new helicopters. This was an old helicopter. They didn't have all this sophisticated stuff in those days.' Now this guy didn't know a helicopter from a pair of bull's nuts, but he was in my office as a representative of GAO, so he said, 'Oh, I see now. Now I understand. It just didn't have all those gadgets, those new expensive things in it.'

"Of course it *did*. It had all the same equipment. The only difference in the price was the difference in the dollar in sixteen years, but he couldn't figure that out.

"Having disposed of what Kissinger's little gift to Sadat cost the American people, there was still the matter of how to pay for it. The President, or Kissinger as his agent, didn't have the legal right to give military equipment—which the helicopter was—to Egypt. But Sadat had it, Kissinger wasn't about to ask for it back, and *somebody* had to pay the Department of Defense for its missing helicopter.

"The story has a suitably ridiculous ending. Funds that were allocated by Congress to the Agency for International Development specifically to help the poor of Egypt were taken out and given to our Defense Department. Today that

164

helicopter that AID bought for Sadat out of money meant for the poor of his country is being used to haul deposed heads of state around Egypt. In the month of February 1979 alone, it was used by the ex-Shah of Iran and two days later by ex-President Gerald Ford."

DANGEROUS GAMES

TUG-OF-WAR

If the things Kissinger was involved in—secret negotiations with the North Vietnamese, the Russians and the Chinese—were part of the up side of the excitement of the first Nixon Administration, demonstrations against the Vietnam War were the down side.

It's hard to recapture the intensity, the raw emotionalism of those protests. Rage and frustration poured out in waves, and violence was close to the surface. Washington was the center of the demonstrations, and largely unknown to the public, extraordinary measures were taken to protect the White House.

Rarely in our history have events reached the stage where the ugliest of all confrontations have taken place, those between the Army and the people. The memory of the National Guard shooting at, and killing, students at Kent State University stands as a monument to the horror of using armed force against the citizenry.

In the grim days of the Washington protests the potential for even greater horror was there. Troops armed with rifles and light machine guns were hidden in the Executive Office Building and in the bowels of the White House itself. Others from Fort Bragg had been flown in and were waiting at Andrews Air Force Base, and troop carriers were ready to transport Marines from Camp Lejeune.

"In October and November of 1969 we felt seriously threatened by the demonstrations," Gulley says. "To deal with the real possibility of violence, to organize and run an operation to put it down if it did erupt, we set up a control center in the bomb shelter under the East Wing of the White House.

"The bomb shelter, which was built in Truman's time, is completely outfitted for the President, including a paneled office with a big desk flanked by flags, bedrooms for him and his wife, a conference room, working space and cots for twenty-four staff members, and a great deal else. It also happens to be obsolete in my opinion, which gets to be important later in the story.

"John Ehrlichman was in charge of the Domestic Disturbances program, as it was called, and it was a very efficient operation. We had a communications center with direct telephone lines to Jerry Wilson, chief of the D.C. police; the mayor, Walter Washington; the National Guard; the FBI and the Pentagon. A closed-circuit television system was also set up, with monitors in the conference room. Whenever we got word of a demonstration where violence might be expected, the center was manned around the clock.

"The Military Office was involved because we provided military support, which we did our best to keep secret. The White House was trying to keep the lid on the situation, not make it worse, which obvious military presence would do. But it was also felt that armed support had to be available in case any demonstration got out of hand, so we hid some three hundred troops in the Executive Office Building and the White House."

These "domestic disturbances" were passionate cries of protest from young Americans against our armed intervention in Vietnam—which was half a world away. The knowledge that federal troops were secreted in their own White House, and might be used against them, could well have blown the lid off in a highly volatile situation.

"Mayor Walter Washington had control over the police and the National Guard," Gulley says. "It was hoped they would be able to handle the disturbance, but if it reached the point where they couldn't, then Nixon would have called in the federal troops—the ones that were there, and the ones waiting in the wings. The Pentagon had a Domestic Disturbances center of its own; unbeknown to the people, the military was ready to move.

"The White House was isolated at times during the demonstrations, and so was everybody in it. One of the tensest periods was early in May of 1970, after the Kent State killings. Kissinger slept in the President's bedroom in the bomb shelter one night because he literally couldn't get out; demonstrators had the White House surrounded, and it was considered too dangerous for him to try to leave.

"On Friday night, May 8, we had alerted the troops, and I was there all night. We didn't know what might happen, but nobody expected what did happen. Nixon left the White House in the middle of the night, with only Manolo and a Secret Service guy, and went to the Lincoln Memorial to talk to the students who were demonstrating there against the war.

"Everyone was taken by surprise, but things are structured in such a way inside the White House that the President wasn't going to be alone for long. Our office was notified immediately that the President was on the move. We had the military Emergency Actions concern with us always; the Football—the famous black briefcase with our retaliatory information—was our responsibility, and it was imperative that it go with the President wherever he went.

"There was a lot of speculation at the time about what was going on in Nixon's head when he went to the Memorial like that, alone in the middle of the night to talk to the demonstrators. Some suspected he was unbalanced mentally when he did it, especially when it was reported that he had been talking sports to the demonstrators. I think it's simpler than that.

"One thing that's always bothered Nixon is that some students don't appreciate the opportunity they're being given. I think he just can't understand them. It comes from two causes. First, Nixon, like a lot of young people of his generation, had to work like hell to be able to make the money to get an education. College wasn't given to everybody who wanted it or didn't know what else to do with four years.

"Second, I think he had a strong aversion to giving college students military deferments. He accepted it because he couldn't do anything about it. But I think he felt that for them to respond to a deferment from serving in the military by burning their schools and rioting was intolerable.

"The reason he talked sports to the kids who were at the Memorial because of Vietnam, Cambodia and Kent State was that it was, and is, his habit to try to find a common ground with anyone he's talking to before getting down to the matter at hand. He didn't want to talk sports with those kids and wasn't under any illusion that they wanted to talk sports with him. He was looking for a way to open the dialogue—like talking about the weather as somebody else might. I've seen him do this over and over again, even now that he's out of office. He'll look for common ground: geography, where you come from; or sports. Then he'll move right on to whatever you're there to discuss.

"To me the episode wasn't out of character. Nixon did impulsive things. He'd decide on the spur of the moment to go to the Kennedy Center and just leave. Everyone else would have to scramble. Going out to talk to the kids was something he wanted to do, and he knew if he consulted with anybody, they'd give him fifty reasons why he couldn't do it. So he just went.

"The Nixon people maintained from the start that the D.C. police were grossly overestimating the numbers of demonstrators at all the disturbances; they said the police were doing it in order to get more money for cleaning up after the protesters. But what really bothered the White House people was that the police figures might make the whole situation look worse for the Administration than it already was. As Ehrlichman used to say about everything: 'How's it going to play in Peoria?'

"They decided to do their own head count, so at Nixon's direction the Military Office told the Pentagon to send a U-2 type of spy plane over the demonstrations and take aerial photographs of the crowds. The counts they had done from the pictures came to a number considerably lower than the police estimates, and the White House press office began releasing the figures—although they never explained publicly how they arrived at them.''

"The Administration tried to play the demonstrations down, but they were taken very seriously. The protesters were out there chanting and clamoring around the White House. They could be seen and heard, they were real; so the elaborate White House control center was set up and the measures were taken to protect the White House.

"The irony of the situation is that threats far more serious than anything that could come from our own protesters are lying out there, but because they haven't actually rattled the fence, nobody at the White House has paid any attention to them. It could be a very costly oversight."

CAPTURE THE CASTLE

"Imagine this situation," Gulley says. "Three out of four of the most heavily protected Presidential facilities, Camp David, the Presidential yacht and *Air Force One,* all under military control, are simultaneously penetrated by agents and a bomb that could kill the President is planted in each one.

"Impossible? Not only is it not impossible; it's exactly what happened one crisp autumn day in 1970 while Nixon was President.

"At 3:30 A.M. four men in black wet suits slipped into the water from the Virginia bank of the Potomac. They towed two 55-gallon drums under the surface toward their heavily guarded objective moored off the opposite shore. They worked quickly and silently, attaching the barrels beneath the hull of their target, then returned, without being spotted, to the Virginia shore, forty-five minutes after they'd left.

"At 8:10 A.M. the telephone rang on Sally Snyder's desk at the Military Office, where she was a secretary. It was an Avon lady who kept Sally on the line, talking about cosmetics, for over four minutes.

"At 8:15 A.M. Colonel Ralph Albertazzie, pilot of *Air Force One,* who was in the dentist's chair at the Medical Office at Andrews Air Force Base, received a telephone call from a General Carson. He identified himself as a reserve Air Force general, now president of a steel company in Albertazzie's home state of West Virginia. He said he was ending two weeks of active duty in his reserve status and was calling to ask Albertazzie if he would bend the rules and give him a tour of *Air Force One*. Albertazzie agreed.

"At 8:30 A.M. Commander John Dettbarn, the commander of Camp David, answered a call from Sally Snyder. She told him their boss, Don Hughes, the director of the Military Office, had two men on their way up to take some measurements in Aspen, the President's cabin. She gave Dettbarn their names, Martin and Higger, a description of their car and its license plate number, and the time they were expected to arrive. Dettbarn said he'd see they were cleared to enter.

"At 9:45 A.M. Martin and Higger were completing their survey of Aspen. They'd been escorted by two Navy enlisted men, who went with them into each room. After taking measurements in the President's bedroom, Martin went into the adjoining bathroom and closed the door behind him. A minute or so passed. Martin flushed the toilet, ran water in the basin, and then came out. He and his escort rejoined Higger, and shortly thereafter they left Camp David in their rented car.

"At 9:50 A.M. Colonel Ralph Albertazzie and Major General Dwight Carson were finishing their tour of *Air Force One*. The general was sitting in the pilot's seat, getting the feel of what it was like to pilot the most famous plane in the world, when he dropped what looked like a pack of cigarettes. Albertazzie offered to retrieve it, but the general immediately reached under the seat and, after considerable fumbling, announced he'd recovered his cigarettes. A few minutes later they left *Air Force One,* and General Carson drove off.

"Between 11:30 A.M. and 1:30 P.M., explosive devices were detonated under the Presidential yacht *Sequoia* and in the President's bathroom at Camp David. A third was found hidden under the pilot's seat on *Air Force One*."

It had taken Charlie Sither, an Air Force counterintelligence agent and advisor to the Military Office, three months to plan, organize and carry out the operation. Dangerous gaps in security were exposed in the very places it was assumed the President was most safe, and the responsibility fell directly at the feet of the military.

Against a backdrop of riots and protests, Don Hughes, director of the Military Office, called in Sither and told him he wanted security tested at all four sites—*Air Force One*, the yacht, Camp David and the helicopter squadron—and he laid down some ground rules. First, no one outside of Hughes, Sither and Gulley, except the people actually used in the operation, were to know what was planned. Second, they could not use any information, or have access to any material, not available to an outsider bent on penetrating those sites.

Although Hughes, as head of the Military Office, was ultimately answerable for the failures in security, the safety of each site was the responsibility of the officer in charge of it. "So," Gulley says, "Hughes planned a program of Show and Tell for the guys involved. As soon as Sither reported all the 'bombs' were in place, Hughes summoned Commander Dettbarn of Camp David, Albertazzie of *Air Force One*, the commander of the *Sequoia* and the commander of the Marine helicopter squadron and invited them to go on a tour of their installations with him and Sither.

"None of them had any idea what was coming, of course, so when they got to *Air Force One* and Albertazzie saw this guy he thought was Major General Dwight Carson waiting for him in the cockpit of the plane, he became confused. Confusion rapidly converted to rage when 'General Carson' leaned down, pulled something the size of a cigarette pack from under the pilot's seat and showed the assembled company an explosive device, all wired and set to be detonated.

" 'Goddamn it!' Albertazzie screamed. 'I've been sandbagged. You sons of bitches haven't played fair with me.' He really took exception to what was happening.

"Next they went to the Navy Yard, where the *Sequoia* was docked. It was in a secure area, with a high brick wall, a guard tower, and guards patrolling it twenty-four hours a day. After observing activities there over a number of weeks, Sither also knew that before the President went out on her, Secret Service went aboard the yacht and did an electronic sweep.

"Sither decided there was probably no way to get over the gate and on board, and that even if they did plant something

171

inside, it would be found. They'd have to find another way. Which, using frogmen, they did.

"When the tour got to the Navy Yard, Sither asked the commander of the *Sequoia* to describe his security. The commander explained why it just wasn't possible for anyone to get to the yacht. Then the guy who had been in charge of that part of the operation said, 'If you'll all step around here . . . ,' and they all stepped around to where they could see the *Sequoia*. He then pushed a button, and up came this bubbling red stuff, gallons of it, imitating a bomb that could have blown the *Sequoia* into Baltimore.

"Next they went over to Anacostia, where the helicopters were based, and here there was some good news. Sither's man in charge of this phase of the exercise said they'd tried three times that morning to get to the helicopters but the Marines hadn't fallen for it. The commander of the helicopters, who had been sweating, was off the hook.

"The party then took a chopper to their final destination, Camp David. When they got there they walked down the path to Aspen, where they were met by 'Martin' and 'Higger,' went into the cabin, through the President's bedroom, and crowded around the bathroom door. Sither went in, flushed the toilet, and goddamn if there wasn't a *psssst!*, followed by a geyser of water shooting out of the President's john.

"Later, Sither told Dettbarn, who was in shock for several days, that on an earlier attempt his men had actually managed to get over the fence at Camp David and as far as the door of Aspen, but hadn't been able to get into the cabin. That didn't make Dettbarn feel any better."

"After the demonstrations were completed, Hughes brought everybody back to the White House and down to the bomb shelter, where I joined them, to explain how each site had been penetrated.

"We had a tape recorder set up, and when Sither turned it on, Sally Snyder's telephone conversation with Commander Dettbarn was played back. Only it wasn't Sally, of course; it was an agent who had posed as an Avon lady and kept Sally on the phone long enough to be able to mimic her voice. Sither explained to Dettbarn that as a result of his falling for that call, 'Martin' and 'Higger,' using fake IDs from a printing shop on 14th Street, had got into Aspen and planted their bomb.

"It was Albertazzie's turn next, and when Sither played back his conversation from the dentist's office with the phony general, he got bent out of shape all over again. 'Bullshit!' he roared. 'It's all bullshit! I escorted him. I was with him. No goddamn way did he plant that bomb.' Albertazzie was not taking this well.

"Sither completed the explanations by telling the commander of the *Sequoia* how the frogmen had attached simulated explosives to the hull of his ship, and by congratulating the commander of the helicopter squadron on his security. It was nice to see one happy face."

"This was all very closely held," Gulley says, "after it happened as well as before, because we flunked three out of four of the tests and we had been fighting off attempts by Secret Service to get a foot in the door of our operation for years. If they'd ever found out what happened, we'd have had a lot of explaining to do, which we might not have been able to do.

"Our worries that it would leak were probably needless. Who the hell was going to talk? Everybody involved had been threatened with pain and suffering. The only big talker was Albertazzie, and no way was he going to put his handsome neck into the goddamn guillotine. Everyone knew about his political ambitions in West Virginia, and here he'd fallen for a line from some phony president of a corporation out there and jeopardized the President's life. Albertazzie was *never* going to talk."

A number of things came out of this test. An electronic fence and sensors were installed at Camp David, and new procedures were set up to verify a caller's identity. A doubling of the guard and stricter identification checks were ordered for *Air Force One*. And an underwater screen was installed around the *Sequoia,* one that couldn't be penetrated without triggering an alarm system.

Another effect of the test was the impact it had on Gulley.

It marked the start of a campaign he waged over the next seven years to alert the White House and the Department of Defense to the very real dangers of a terrorist attack. "I could never get anybody to listen," Gulley says. "You wouldn't believe—nobody could possibly believe—how vulnerable the White House is.

"It's a case of tunnel vision, channeled thinking. The Secret Service thinks in terms of bodily guarding the President in crowds and on platforms—although as a matter of fact most of them can just barely pass their annual firearms test. And the military thinks only in terms of nuclear warheads, SAC and retaliatory strikes.

"Nobody's thinking of mortars in the bushes around Andrews, where *Air Force One* is parked, or heat-seeking missiles launched from under the cherry blossoms when the chopper lifts off the White House lawn, or a helicopter full of armed guerrillas landing on the lawn—even after they got living proof of how easy it was to do."

The following are excerpts from reports in *The New York Times* and the Washington *Post* of an incident that occurred on February 17, 1974, at about 2:00 A.M.:

A young soldier [Pfc. Robert Kenneth Preston], who flunked out of Army flight school last September, commandeered a helicopter at Fort Meade . . . and landed on the South Lawn of the White House. . . . The ease with which the aircraft penetrated the supposedly restricted air space over the White House raised serious questions among law enforcement officials who said that Preston could have flown right into the building undetected if he had not attracted so much attention by his bizarre antics along the way.

Maryland State Trooper Louis Saffran, who was in a state police helicopter that followed Preston . . . said later the pilot "could have driven right in the front door" of the White House if he had wanted to. . . . "I thought," Saffron recalled, "where is everybody? Why are just we here?"

[Secret Service spokesman] Jack Warner said there is a contingency plan for dealing with an air attack on the White House, but refused to discuss its details or to say whether it was activated yesterday morning. He also refused to discuss the size of the security detachment or to say how many guns were used or whether things would have been different if Mr. Nixon or his family had been there. . . . Asked if the security measures at the White House had been adequate to deal with the incident, the Secret Service official replied: "Apparently they were."

"This guy," Gulley says, "landed on the White House lawn not once but twice that night. Not a shot was fired at him until he had circled the Washington Monument a few times, led a whole flock of D.C. and Maryland police helicopters on a wild chase all over the skies of Washington, and landed on the lawn the *second* time.

"No attempt was made by the Secret Service protective detail to prevent this guy from landing, or from taking off, or doing anything, until after he landed the *second* time. They didn't know what the hell was going on in their own front yard until half the city of Washington knew.

"I was down in Key Biscayne with the President, and I knew more about the goddamn thing than they did sitting in the White House.

"I got a call shortly after two o'clock that morning. It was the board supervisor of the signal board, the military switchboard, and he said, 'An Army pilot has made an unauthorized landing on the South Lawn. The aircraft has been shot at and hit.'

"The guy who was giving me this information was in the basement of the EOB and obviously hadn't seen any of this, and I wanted to get a fuller account, so I called the Command Center at the Pentagon—there'll be more about this later— and asked the duty general what he knew. He told me the helicopter had been stolen from Fort Meade by a guy who had washed out of flight school but had a private pilot's license for fixed-wing aircraft. I asked him for a report as soon as possible; to please call me in Florida as soon as he had it.

"Then I called the Secret Service control office at the White House and asked what they knew about the situation, and they knew less than the operator on the signal board. They didn't know where the helicopter had come from, who'd

175

taken it, even that it had been stolen. Secret Service didn't
know anything.

"Forty-five minutes later the duty general called me back
with a full rundown on what had happened, and I called Secret
Service in the White House. So there I was, in a bedroom in
Key Biscayne, Florida, giving the Secret Service information
about a helicopter that had landed on the White House lawn
right outside their office, right under their noses.

"You would have thought that this might open the eyes of
the people in the White House and in Defense. And, mind
you, terrorists had been killing and kidnapping and maiming
in Italy, Ireland, England, Germany, Holland—all over Europe and the Middle East for years. Here a helicopter lands
on the lawn in front of the President's house and nothing
happens. Six armed guys in that chopper, and the White
House could have been in enemy hands inside of three minutes. Less.

"No wonder the newspapers said Warner wouldn't discuss
the security measures at the White House. He couldn't. There
aren't any worth discussing, and there weren't any fewer in
effect that night than there would have been if the President
had been there. When Warner was asked if the security measures had been adequate to deal with the incident, he said,
'Apparently they were.' The only thing that's apparent is that
the Secret Service and the military were lucky. And the tragic
part of it is they didn't learn a goddamn thing from it.

"The average citizen on the streets of America, if you
asked him, would say, 'Yes indeed. They're planning all the
time over there at the White House, and at the Pentagon, to
protect our President from terrorists, from kidnapping. It may
happen in foreign countries, but there's no way it could happen here.'

"The truth is, there is no system. No plan. The physical
security at the White House is terrible. They go around and
lock up at midnight like any good housewife. They do have a
number of uniformed guards who—with difficulty—qualify
with weapons, but they only look good.

"There is no way you could bring in an armed unit in an
emergency, not as things are now. You could run through the

176

Marine barracks at 8th and I streets, S.E., three miles away; and through the barracks at Fort Myer in northern Virginia; wake them up and hope you'd find enough sober to come out. But then you'd have to find weapons and ammunition. These are ceremonial people, not troops trained to combat terrorists. Besides, by the time they got to the White House, the President would either be dead or the terrorists would be holding him hostage.

"The airspace over the White House is off limits to aircraft, and there's radar coverage from National Airport which will pick up anything that penetrates it—assuming there's anyone watching the screen, which often there isn't. That might deter your tourist flying his two-seater Cessna over Washington, but it sure as hell isn't going to stop a team of trained terrorists.

"In the first place, a skilled pilot could come in undetected under the radar, and in the second place, it wouldn't matter whether he was detected or not, because by the time anybody responded to the signal from the radar unit, it would all be over anyway.

"Take a simple operation. A dedicated bunch of fire-eaters wants to make its point by either killing the President of the United States or holding him hostage. Anybody in the world can find out where the President is at almost any hour of the day by reading the Washington *Post*, and if he's in Washington, he sleeps at the White House. So the terrorists decide to go in at 2:00 A.M.

"They put six guys armed with grenades and automatic weapons into a helicopter, fly up along the Potomac, which is the flight path to National Airport, then peel off at 16th Street. Fifteen seconds later, while the guy manning the radar station —again assuming he's awake and not in the john—is trying to figure out what that blip on the scanner is, the helicopter's on the lawn of the White House, and the handful of sleepy White House guards and Secret Service guys are stumbling around, being mowed down. Sixty seconds after that, the President is either dead or in terrorist hands.

"Not only are there no James Bond–like devices to protect the President at home—no moats with piranhas, or bullet-

177

proof screens that descend at the first footfall in the corridor —which I'm not suggesting there should be; there isn't even an alert security force trained in counterterrorist techniques. Which I'm suggesting should have been tucked into the White House complex years ago.

"Worse than this, the guys at the White House who *are* concerned with the President's security, the Secret Service and the military, not only don't work together; they've got a rivalry going that actually jeopardizes the President's safety. Simple common sense, which is in as short supply around the White House as it is elsewhere in Washington, tells you that what's needed is coordination.

"Somebody should be given the authority, outranking Secret Service, military or any other authority, to pull together an effective, well-equipped, highly trained security operation. That nutty soldier *did* land on the White House lawn, twice, and walked away from it. We've lost ambassadors and businessmen to terrorists all over the world. What does it take?"

FOOTBALL

The weakness in government planning presents threats more grave than the possibility of a terrorist attack on the President, Gulley asserts. There are fallacies and failures throughout the vital Emergency Actions system, which depends on the President in order to be mobilized.

Unlike an attack in time of war, or one of which there has been warning over a period of time, the Emergency Actions Procedures are designed as our response to a sudden, unanticipated military attack. The President would have from a very few minutes to twenty-five minutes to retaliate before the enemy missiles landed. Only a few minutes if they were launched from a submarine, up to twenty-five minutes if they were long-range ICBMs.

Gulley, who was responsible for seeing that the procedures could be implemented, says the system is a shambles.

"We've spent billions building and perfecting a superb military machine, and throughout the world it's believed there's no military threat we couldn't meet if we chose to—no attack, no matter how sudden, that the President couldn't answer with the push of a button,'' he says.

"But, because of a breakdown at the top of this marvelous military pyramid, if the crunch came, nothing would happen. We'd be paralyzed by our lack of realistic planning and foresight.

"It's the responsibility of the Military Office to see that the President is notified of any sudden unexpected military attack; that he's able to communicate immediately with his military advisors, wherever he is; that he's safely and speedily evacuated; and, above all, that he gets the Football—because it's only the President who can issue the order for a retaliatory strike.

"There's a manual called the 'WHEP'—'White House Emergency Procedures' manual—that sets out exactly what's supposed to happen in the event of a sudden attack. The White House and the Pentagon each have a copy, and it spells out in detail the steps the Pentagon is to take to notify the White House and how the White House will respond.

"For a number of years, thanks to personal ambition and military bullshit at its most dangerous, the White House 'WHEP' and the Pentagon 'WHEP', unbeknown to the Pentagon, laid out different procedures—which just about guaranteed that the President wouldn't even know the missiles were on their way until after they'd landed. I'll go into that later, but this gives you a taste of how screwed up the whole process can and does get.

"I coordinated the 'WHEPs' just before becoming director of the Military Office, and since then the Pentagon and the White House have been working from identical ones. This is how the Emergency Actions Procedures are programmed to go, under the best possible conditions for us. Those conditions would be an attack that was launched in the daytime, in good weather, when the President was in the White House, and when the chain of command and all the Presidential successors were in Washington. Already you can see this is fantasy.

"Our radar network signals enemy activity to NORAD

Headquarters, which immediately signals the Command Center at the Pentagon and, simultaneously, signals the National Emergency Airborne Command Post, of which there are now four. NEACP (pronounced 'kneecap') is designed to function as airborne headquarters for the President in such an emergency, and the prime NEACP is stationed at Andrews. When the signal comes in from NORAD a claxon sounds, a light goes on, and NEACP is launched in twelve minutes.

"The Pentagon Command Center, which is responsible for relaying information coming in from NORAD, signals the White House, all Unified Commands around the world, the Secretary of Defense, the Secretary of State and all the Joint Chiefs. It will deliver this message: 'We have an incoming with a high degree of probability,' which means there's a 90 percent chance the missiles are coming. At the same time, people are constantly keeping track of incoming information to determine what the probable target is.

"NEACP by this time is moving down the runway. It will take off shortly after notification of the alert, unless the White House orders it to stay on the runway.

"As soon as the word of the attack comes into the White House military switchboard from the Pentagon, our operator does three things. One. He hits the button that triggers a light and sets off a claxon in the bomb shelter under the East Wing, alerting the warrant officer with the Football, signaling him to go to the President immediately.

"Two. He gets the President, Vice President and the National Security Advisor on the phone and delivers the message. Three. He pushes another button which sounds at the headquarters of the helicopter squadron at Anacostia, sending two helicopters to the White House lawn, ready to evacuate the President, and another to the Vice President's residence to get him.

"While the White House signal board operators have been doing this, the Pentagon operators have been busy getting the President's military advisors on the telephone for a conference call. Assuming everything works right, and we're talking about an alert of just a few minutes as well as a twenty-five-minute one, the warrant officer with the Football is in with the

President when the President gets on the line with his advisors. The warrant officer has opened the Football because he knows the combination and the President doesn't; taken out the Black Book, which has the information in it; turned to the right page, the one with the retaliatory options on it; and put it in front of the President.

"Once on the telephone with the President, his advisors try to tell him as much as possible about what the area of probable impact is, because that's critical to his choice of retaliation: Rare, Medium or Well Done. If the target is a military installation, there's an option—identified by number—to hit a similar installation in Russia. If the missiles are headed for Washington or Chicago, he has an option for Moscow or Leningrad. If they're coming from all directions, he can just push all the buttons at once.

"A second round of calls from the White House signal board goes to the President's chief of staff, members of the Cabinet, the Federal Preparedness Agency, which has responsibility for the Presidential successors, and so on. Of course, if it's a very short countdown, the only message the signal board is likely to deliver at this point is: 'That big goddamn boom you just heard was Baltimore.'

"An agreement has been reached that in such a situation— where missiles would be coming in from a submarine—the President would go to the bomb shelter and the Vice President would go to NEACP by helicopter from his residence. Otherwise, the helicopters would be on the lawn, ready to evacuate the President, and cars would be waiting in case the weather was too bad to fly. Another car would be waiting on the far side of the Treasury Building, where a long underground tunnel from the White House comes out.

"In a twenty-five-minute alert, the President would go out to the lawn of the White House where the helicopters would be waiting. The director of the Military Office would be there with him and would say, 'Mr. President, I advise we go to Cactus,' or one of the other eight sites within twenty-five minutes of the White House by helicopter.

"These classified sites are well known to anybody who's interested, so actually it would be like playing the shell game;

181

the only advantage we'd have over the enemy is they wouldn't know which site had been chosen, and even that advantage has been seriously weakened. There is good reason to believe that through the cooperation of friendly countries, the Russians and some countries friendly to them have radar available to them in Washington which could track the President's helicopter from the minute it leaves the White House lawn, and this information could be sent instantly to wherever the missiles were being launched.

"Instead of heading for one of the secure sites, the decision could be made—if the target was Washington, for example—that the President's helicopter would marry up with NEACP at one of the designated airfields, civilian or military, within a defined radius of D.C.—the limit of range for the helicopters because of fuel capacity. In either case, whether the President reached a Presidential Emergency Site or NEACP, he would now be in a position to communicate with his military leaders and, through the Emergency Broadcast System, with the people.

"That, in a brief outline, is how it's supposed to work. And there's no way in the world that it could.

"The first, most obvious fallacy is the idea that the Russians will launch their attack at our convenience and not when Jimmy Carter and Amy are alone on a raft shooting the rapids in Colorado, the Vice President is campaigning for some Democrat in northern Minnesota, the Secretary of Defense is bird-watching in the marshes of South Carolina, and the chairman of the Joint Chiefs is on a junket to Australia. All of which activities would have been reported in the papers and on television.

"There are provisions built into the Emergency Actions Procedures for dealing with a crisis when the President travels, of course, and seeing that they're carried out is one of the responsibilities of the director of the White House Military Office.

"As has been described, he has to see to it that the aide with the Football is always with the President, that the nearest NEACP is readied for immediate takeoff, that communications with the Pentagon have been arranged, that there is a place for a helicopter to land and evacuate the President, that *Air Force One* is parked in such a manner that it can be airborne in the shortest possible time—and I always had a backup in a different location so we could evacuate the President if *Air Force One* was knocked out for any reason. He also has to locate the nearest PEF—Presidential Emergency Facility.

"These are isolated sites, manned twenty-four hours a day, scattered throughout the world, installations the much-abused Secret Fund was set up to maintain. You want to get the President to one of these sites if possible both for safety and because they are communications centers. Some are operated by ITT, who built them; some by the Federal Preparedness Agency; and some are under military control.

"They're supposed to be top secret, of course, but I don't think there's much doubt the Russians, for one, have a blueprint of where they are. The big thing we have going for us is that they would have no way of knowing which one we had taken the President to. There are scores of them.

"So before the President goes anywhere, in this country or overseas, the director of the Military Office goes to the computer and—let's say the destination is Mule Shoe, Texas—he gets a printout on what sites are available near Mule Shoe. He picks out the site, tells the Secret Service agents going with the President, then tells the helicopter pilot so that he can get his coordinates from where he'd pick up the President.

"All these things are done whenever the President goes anywhere outside Washington. But taking the example of a vacation by President Carter, by the time he and Amy are back on shore the short-warning drill is over, and there isn't a hope in hell that he's going to get on a conference call with his advisors before the mushroom clouds start forming."

"Another area of dangerous weakness lies in the President's lack of familiarity with the procedures and facilities for his own safety in the White House. Only two Presidents in my time at the White House, Johnson and Ford, ever toured the emergency facilities in the White House and went through the tunnel that goes under the Treasury Building and surfaces on the other side. Four people could walk abreast through that tunnel, and it's lined with emergency rations and cots—enough for two hundred people.

"However, like the bomb shelter, it's not nearly strong enough to provide any real protection in a nuclear attack. It couldn't withstand a blast of more than 25 psi—pounds per square inch—which in the context we're talking about is nothing. And I could never get anybody's attention when I tried to talk about it.

"Rockefeller took more interest in the emergency facilities than any President or any other Vice President during my time at the White House. His plan was to dig a hole in the earth more than a mile deep, which would be lined with protective shields. It would be near the White House and would have been the command post from which the President would operate. The idea was that he'd have secure communications and be able to survive. It was impractical, but at least the Vice President was thinking about it.

"What to do with the successors to the President is hopeless. The Military Office used to be responsible for evacuating them, too, but when I became director I unloaded it onto the Federal Preparedness Agency. As it is now, helicopters are supposed to come in from Quantico, Fort Meade and Fort Belvoir, land at sites all over Washington, and pick up the successors.

"The FPA is staffed with retired Air Force colonels who spend their time rewriting old emergency scripts, regardless of new developments they could draw on. There is no way they could get their act together and pick up the successors in under thirty minutes, by which time the missiles have dropped anyway.

"In any case, if they did get that act going, the safest place for the successors to be would be on the ground, even standing in front of the White House, looking up. Because the way the FPA has this structured, the helicopters are going to be bouncing off each other, and there's going to be a sky full of aluminum."

Another critical weakness, Gulley says, is that not once has the human failure factor been taken into account. A failure in notification, a failure in equipment, a failure in the security of our system so that it's been penetrated, a failure to expect the unexpected. "It came as a hell of a shock when Don Rumsfeld, Secretary of Defense under Ford, discovered that the White House and Pentagon copies of the 'White House Emergency Procedures' manual said different things.

"During the *Mayaguez* affair, when Rumsfeld was Ford's chief of staff, he'd been concerned by the confusion in communications between the White House, the Pentagon and the Area Commands. When he took over as Secretary of Defense he told General Brown, chairman of the Joint Chiefs, he wanted to spot-test the Emergency Actions system, and together they went to the Command Center at the Pentagon, where Brown proceeded to explain the system to him.

"Then Brown said, 'If you pick up that telephone there, it will ring directly to the President. It's an emergency line, only used in grave crises.'

"Rumsfeld picked up the phone, and what he got was not the President, it was our operator at the White House signal board. Rumsfeld said, 'This is the Secretary of Defense. Let me speak to the President.' At this point Rumsfeld and the operator part company on exactly what happened. Rumsfeld says he timed it and ten minutes went by before he said anything—the operator says it was three minutes—but they agree that finally Rumsfeld said, 'What the hell are you doing?' to the operator.

"The operator answered, 'I'm trying to find Kollmorgen,' who was director of the Military Office at the time.

"Rumsfeld said, 'What the hell are you trying to find Kollmorgen for? I want to speak to the President.' The operator answered, 'Sir, my instructions are that you cannot speak to the President until you are cleared by the director of the Military Office. And I can't find him.'

"So here you had a situation where the chairman of the Joint Chiefs of Staff, and the duty general in the Pentagon Command Center, believed all along—for many years—that all they had to do in a crisis was pick up that emergency phone and the President would immediately answer it. And it would not have happened.

"This is how the screw-up came about. During President

Kennedy's time, one of my predecessors at the White House Military Office saw there was no clear understanding of what the military Emergency Procedures were as they affected the White House. He decided they should be written down in a manual, the 'WHEP,' to be given to both the Pentagon and the White House—which was a fine idea.

"However, because he was personally ambitious, he thought he'd play to both groups. In the White House 'WHEP' he gave priority of notification, and therefore of importance, to administration people. And, in order to make himself appear to the administration to play a more substantive part in the White House than he did, he wrote himself a big role in the proceedings—a role that was not only unnecessary, but obstructive and potentially dangerous.

"Then, since he knew the Pentagon wouldn't accept his list of key participants and their order of priority, he wrote a second 'WHEP' for *their* consumption. The Pentagon jealously guards their prerogative of advising the President on military matters without interference, so he knew, for example, that the Secretary of Defense would balk at having the National Security Advisor notified of an attack at the same moment he was. So, for the Pentagon, he reversed the order in which individuals were to be alerted.

"He also knew that no Secretary of Defense would stand stili for having an emergency call from him to the President cleared by the director of the Military Office. So, although these were the instructions he put in the White House 'WHEP'—and, as Rumsfeld discovered, our guys faithfully followed them—he simply omitted mentioning that step in the copy of the 'WHEP' that went to the Pentagon.

"In all those years no one had bothered to test the system without alerting everybody ahead of time, and we were damn lucky no foreign power tested it for us.

"Rumsfeld raised the roof, and when it came down, it came down on the Military Office, naturally. Kollmorgen was leaving anyway, but I didn't wait to be made his replacement before I made some changes. I coordinated the 'WHEPs' so that everybody knows who is to be notified and in what order. And I eliminated the unnecessary and dangerously time-consuming step of going through the director of the Military Office to reach the President. Now the operator gets the President as soon as the flash comes in from the Command Center.

"But the problem still exists that we don't have a system to ensure that the President can talk to the guy who has the button under his finger. There are missing links all along the chain of communication. Let's say NEACP has launched, because it launches in twelve minutes or less—unless it's stopped. Who's going to stop it? That's one missing link: nobody's responsible for telling NEACP to stay on the ground and wait for the President or Vice President to arrive.

"Suppose, then, that you get the President onto a helicopter, which is the prime means of evacuation, the first line. NEACP is off in the blue, and the President has decided to marry up with it at one of the designated airfields within helicopter range. To do that he has to communicate with NEACP.

"If communications on the ground, at the White House, are intact, the President can do that. He'll talk from the helicopter to the White House switchboard and through them to NEACP. Alternately, if the White House capability is gone, the President can talk to NEACP—but only as long as it's within fifty miles of the helicopter, in the line of sight. Otherwise, forget it. He couldn't communicate with NEACP or anybody else.

"All these billions have been spent—you've got generals on duty around the clock in the Command Center; there are guys in silos, ready to push buttons at a moment's notice— and one administration after another, including Carter's, has refused to spend the money necessary, about $250,000, to put adequate communications in the President's helicopters so that he can talk to somebody other than the White House.

"The President would literally be isolated in that helicopter, not getting any information, unable to make a rendezvous, not able to talk to the people he *has* to talk to."

The heart of the matter is the Football, and there, Gulley says, lies another area that's full of misunderstandings. "The Football has taken on a kind of mythology because it's supposed to be some ever-ready Answer Box. The truth is that it raises as many questions as it answers. Most people think there's a guy sitting outside the Oval Office, or the President's bedroom, and he has the Football with him at all times. There isn't. There's a warrant officer sitting in the bomb shelter way over under the East Wing, bored out of his skull, a long-distance sprint from the President—who wouldn't know what to do with the Football unless the warrant officer was there to show him.

"No new President in my time ever had more than one briefing on the contents of the Football, and that was before each one took office, when it was one briefing among dozens. Not one President, to my knowledge, and I know because it was in my care, ever got an update on the contents of the Football, although material in it is changed constantly. Not one President could open the Football—only the warrant officers, the military aides and the director of the Military Office have the combination. If the guy with the Football had a heart attack or got shot on the way to the President, they'd have to blow the goddamn thing open.

"First of all, what is the Football? It's a black briefcase with a combination lock on the top, under the handle. The lock is covered with a strip of the same leatherlike material as the rest of the briefcase. It's a perfectly normal briefcase, with a partition inside. The upper part has three compartments that can be used for loose papers; the lower part is for books, or whatever.

"There are four things in the Football. The Black Book containing the retaliatory options, a book listing Classified Site locations, a manila folder with eight or ten pages stapled together giving a description of procedures for the Emergency Broadcast System, and a three-by-five inch card with authentication codes.

"The book with the Classified Site locations is about the same size as the Black Book, and it's black, too. It contains details and locations of all the classified sites all over the country where the President could be taken in the event of an emergency.

"The folder with procedures for emergency broadcast are

there because it's hoped to get the President on the air to the people as soon as possible after a hit, if he survives, to reassure them the government is functioning."

Gulley points out that since the warrant officers sitting in the bomb shelter have nothing to do but read the Black Book, and *Playboy,* in order to stave off mental atrophy, they presumably are fully familiar with its contents. If this sounds like questionable security procedure, consider the situation that existed before Gulley took over the Military Office.

Until that time the combination to the Football was in a sealed envelope locked in a safe in the warrant officers' office, and it was inspected periodically by the director of the Military Office to be sure no one had tampered with it. Excellent intelligence security, but highly impractical.

The President is given only a few minutes to respond to this kind of emergency, an attack alert, and to get out of the Mansion. Even on the dead run, the nimblist of warrant officers could not be expected to complete the course in time. He would have to twirl a combination lock, get out the right envelope, dash over and up to the Mansion, figure out the combination to the Football, open it, thumb through the Black Book until he came to the options page and put it before the President.

Gulley chose to save precious minutes and gamble on the discretion of his men.

"The Black Book is what the exercise is all about," Gulley says. "It's about 9 by 12 inches and a half to three-quarters of an inch thick. It has seventy-five loose-leaf pages in it, printed by a classified printing press in the Pentagon. It's printed in black and red, and on the vital page, the options page, the retaliatory options appear in red.

"In addition to the immediate options in case of unexpected attack, there's a detailed explanation of how many delivery vehicles Russia has and where they are, where the probable targets are, and the time factor from launch to arrival. There's provision to furnish this same information about the Chinese, but they don't yet have the capability to hit us. Probable routes the Chinese missiles would take have been thought out, but as of mid-1979 the Chinese had only a limited arsenal (twelve to fifteen missiles), capable of hitting Russia or Europe.

"There's also an explanation of how many missiles we have, where they are, and which routes they would have to fly to reach their targets—which presents another problem. Depending on where they're launched and where they're heading, our missiles would fly over a number of other countries, some of which might think they were the target. The Black Book explains which governments should be approached before we launch our first missile and what the risk would be if we didn't warn them.

"All this in only a few minutes from the original signal.

"The authentication card has numbers and letters arranged in lines, not unlike a Bingo card. Each person who has a part to play in the Emergency Actions Procedures, including the successors to the Presidency, has a card, and each is numbered—one for the President, two for the Vice President, and so on down the line. Except for the numbers, all the cards are identical, and their purpose is to provide an easy way of verifying that the person you're talking to has a card and therefore is on the list of players involved in the decision-making process.

"Changes in the Black Book and authentication cards are made all the time; there's a guy over at the Pentagon who makes delivery of the changes to everyone concerned on the same day. But when they're made, there's no briefing of the President; he has no idea there's been a change.

"In fact, there were times while I was in the Military Office when changes for the Football have sat in the safe for three months without being made. Nobody bothered to do it. It's a good bet very few of those with authentication cards bother to carry them, either, any more than they leave telephone numbers where they can be reached. If the balloon ever did go up, it would be pure pandemonium."

So far, Gulley has pointed out failures in the Emergency Actions system as it applies to situations that, presumably, have been analyzed. His major worry, however, is about a particularly threatening situation that has not been addressed,

190

and in which the present procedures would be totally inadequate.

"How arrogant can we get?" Gulley asks. "Do we really think the Russians are going to be dumb enough to attack us between nine and five on a weekday when we're all conveniently in town sitting at our desks next to the telephone? And in spite of all the evidence from other countries, do we really think we're immune to terrorism?

"Everyone in the world knows that by law the President is the only one who can push the button for a retaliatory strike. Do we suppose the Russians haven't figured out that if, at the same time they launch their missiles, they knock out the President, Vice President and Secretary of Defense, they'll paralyze us? We've got the world's greatest military machine, and a handful of guys could shut the whole thing down before one missile was launched, or one bomb dropped.

"A coordinated terrorist and missile attack seems obvious to me, and not taking it into consideration is dangerously arrogant negligence," Gulley says. "If the nuclear missiles are going to start flying, whoever launched them is playing for keeps. He'll know what our retaliatory strike capability is, and he'll do everything in his power to prevent us from using it. The best way to do this is to get at the guy who pushes the button, and that—as the whole world knows—is the President.

"The way it's structured now, only the President can make the decision about the degree of retaliation. The Vice President doesn't have the power, and the Secretary of Defense isn't authorized to accept a decision from him unless and until they're absolutely certain the President can no longer function.

"Who's going to make that decision? If communications are gone, who knows whether the President is in the bomb shelter, on the helicopter, where he is, or if he is?

"Attack the White House, knock out communications— some of the antennas are actually still above ground—and you neutralize the President. Get him over in the bomb shelter under the East Wing, and all he's got is a telephone, just like the one in anybody's house. It's hooked up to the military signal board, which is over in the basement of the Executive Office Building, but if you knock that out, which anybody could do by getting at the terminals, the guy's totally isolated.

"In any case, for insurance purposes, whoever has launched this attack is going to take out as many of the chain of command as he can. With our wide open society and free press, he's going to know just where all these people are, too."

Among the great ironies in this situation, the lack of protection against terrorist attack, there are the lengths to which we go to protect the President in other ways. "We are security-conscious in so many other ways," Gulley says. "The President's food is separately prepared and guarded so he won't be poisoned; the fuel for *Air Force One* is under constant watch so it won't be contaminated; bomb locators and disposal personnel check out any place the President is to make an appearance and then maintain tight surveillance over it. Even the air the President breathes is protected.

"One of the people permanently stationed in the White House bomb shelter is a chemical-biological man, an Army sergeant. His primary duty is to maintain and monitor radiation detectors that are located throughout the White House, at Camp David, in the Vice President's residence and at various other strategic places. The detectors are there to prevent any attempt to poison the President or Vice President by the use of radiation, which it's suspected the Russians did to the Czech leader Eduard Benes.

"But where's the protection for the most important things of all? Communications? *Air Force One?* The helicopters? NEACP? *Air Force One* and NEACP are both stationed out at Andrews, and anyone who wants to can find them. The key to it all, however, is communications—a sitting duck.

"The aerials at the White House that are still above ground are vulnerable; the signal board across the street at EOB has terminals that are vulnerable; the alternate White House switchboard is disguised as a water tower out at Camp David, and *it's* vulnerable. It's such a great secret that Khrushchev is reliably reported to have said to President Eisenhower when he was up there visiting over twenty years ago, 'Never before have I seen a water tower with aerials.' Khrushchev laughed; Ike didn't.

"Take out the President's communications in an emergency situation and you've got pandemonium. The President is the linchpin of the entire system, and in order for it to function he has to be able to receive information and issue orders.

"That means," Gulley says, "you've got to have two things. One, a functioning President, and, two, foolproof communications. They are the key ingredients, so they are the things you've got to protect. Instead of which we have a President who's at risk in his own house, and a communications system that's a shambles."

There's a final ironic twist to the Football story. "The risk that the President will get separated from the Football is greater now than it's ever been," Gulley says. "Whenever the President travels anywhere, whenever he sets foot out of the White House, the military aide who accompanies him has the Football with him. That hasn't changed under Carter. What has changed is that now when Carter goes to Plains, for example, the aide and the Football don't stay within a few hundred yards of the President's house as they have in every other administration.

"Now the aide and the Football stay at a hotel in Americus, Georgia, ten miles from Plains. Which makes nonsense of the whole Emergency Actions Procedures."

The physical vulnerability of the White House and the inadequacies of its emergency military procedures, Gulley makes clear, are matters of far less interest to those who inhabit the White House than its political vulnerability.

"In the Nixon Administration, just like all the others, the view was basically narrow," he says. "They all seem to feel that as long as the war wagers over in the Pentagon get what they need to keep us militarily mighty, that's the end of it for them. Forgetting that the political and the military come together at the top—in the White House—where the President of the country and the Commander in Chief of its armed forces are the same guy.

"Like Johnson, Ford and Carter, Nixon was running for

reelection from the time he took office. That was where most of the energy and practical long-range planning went. Putting aside the rhetoric, and using simple expenditure of effort as a measuring rod, as always, getting reelected was top priority.''

CAMPAIGNING

''The Nixon people were running for reelection from the time they took office,'' Gulley says, ''and, like Johnson, Ford and Carter, Nixon was running against the Kennedys as well as everybody else. When Ted Kennedy was up for reelection to the Senate in 1970, the Republicans were having a tough time trying to get somebody to run against him, because of course he was unbeatable in Massachusetts. Hell, it was a job nobody wanted. The party finally persuaded Josiah Spaulding to be the sacrificial lamb, and Nixon and the Administration were grateful to him. Which was one reason Haldeman erupted when he got a call from the hapless Spaulding asking just whose side the United States Navy was on in this campaign.

''It seems Ted Kennedy had conned the Navy into bringing the aircraft carrier *John F. Kennedy* into Boston harbor on August 3, and then letting him take a group of retarded children out on her. When Haldeman heard about it, he got Higby to call me for some answers. We got in touch with the office of the Secretary of the Navy, John Chafee, formerly governor of Rhode Island, later a United States senator. It turned out the Kennedy people had promoted this with Chafee, who, off his own bat, had agreed to let Kennedy use the carrier for his worthy cause.

''In the end all Kennedy's causes benefited. He got national coverage as a fine, powerful, public-spirited man who was able to get this huge aircraft carrier to take a group of poor, retarded children—and newspaper people—out for a day of fun.

''If Chafee knew what was good for him, he hid under his desk for the next couple of weeks.''

Like Johnson, the only Kennedy Nixon ever approached was Jacqueline, but where LBJ failed, Nixon succeeded. There's political irony in this, since the President she agreed to visit was a Republican who had run against her husband, had almost beaten him, and was now President after all. There's human irony in it too, because if Nixon had beaten John Kennedy in 1960, her husband might still be alive.

"Mrs. Kennedy had never returned to the White House from the time she left after the assassination," Gulley says, "but now, in February of 1971, the official portraits of her and of John Kennedy were done and ready to be hung. When the Nixons invited Mrs. Kennedy, Caroline and John to come for dinner and a private viewing of the paintings, she accepted.

"Because every move Jacqueline Kennedy made, and most of the moves the White House made, were watched by a thousand eyes, and Nixon was insistent that the Press was not to know about the visit, we made special efforts to be discreet. By using unmarked cars and planes to bring them down from New York and take them back, we were able to keep the Kennedys' private visit private.

"According to Nixon's account, in spite of the maudlin possibilities it had, the visit was pleasant and lighthearted, and 'Jackie was very bright and talkative.' "

"Along with Ted Kennedy, but in a different way, Nixon also kept an eye on Ronald Reagan. He was careful to stroke him from time to time, and one way he did it in 1969 was by approving a trade mission to the Far East for Reagan and his wife, Nancy. Setting this trip up was my first exposure to the Reagan staff, and they came on as being very professional.

"The Kennedy staff was professional, too, if what you mean is they both got the job done and got their man what he wanted. But where the Kennedy people were abrasive table-pounders who implied all the time that the President, whoever he was, *owed* their man something, the Reagan people were low key. Both groups, Kennedy's and Reagan's, were a bunch of snakes, but where the Kennedy men were rattlers who'd hiss and bite, the Reagan guys were boa constrictors —they'd just sneak up quietly and swallow you.

"Reagan's people knew just what kind of facilities we had for travel abroad, and on my first call from them they came right out and asked for the best: one of our plush 707s. I told them we were sorry but none were available; however, we could fix Reagan up with a less plush but comfortable 135.

"They said, 'Thank you very much. We'll get back to you.' Which, in a way, they did, because a little while later Haldeman called. The President would appreciate it, he said, if we could come up with a 707 for Mr. and Mrs. Reagan.

"The next time I talked to the Reagan guys, they didn't say anything about leapfrogging me to Haldeman; they just said they certainly did appreciate it that we were going to give Reagan a 707. Mrs. Reagan, who, incidentally, was taking along her private hairdresser, Julius Bengtsson, wasn't a good air traveler, it seemed . . . it certainly didn't matter to Reagan personally, his staff said, but he was much concerned about his wife . . . and so on and so on. They were sure I would understand. I did.

"The campaign had picked up speed early in 1972. I went to a meeting about how CREEP was to be set up, and Jeb Magruder, Dwight Chapin and one of the advance team were there. The advance men are the guys who go into a place ahead of the candidate, in this case the President, and make all the arrangements for his appearance. They pick the locations, galvanize the local politicians, get out the drumbeaters. And on occasion, the candidate's interests aren't the only ones they're concerned with.

"One time I was sitting in the bar of the San Clemente Inn with some other people when Omar Brenner, the manager of the inn, came over. He sat down and said, 'You know, I've got a problem, and I don't know what to do about it.' One of the advance men, ———, had just put the arm on him to find a girl for one of Haldeman's top guys.

"Someone I was sitting with said, 'Christ, if he wants a girl, why the hell doesn't he find one himself? Why ask an advance man?' Omar said, '——— says Haldeman's guy told him he was so well known that he couldn't risk being recognized if he went out looking for a girl himself. So he got ——— to do it for him. And now ——— wants *me* to do it for *him*.'

196

"In any case, we were in this meeting, and one of the things that came up was the fact that Haldeman wanted the CREEP people to have White House privileges, even though they were on the CREEP staff, not the White House staff.

"I asked just exactly what they had in mind, and they said they'd expect to use the Mess, White House cars, military planes, and so on. I said, 'No goddamn way will they do that. Those are members of a political committee; they're not members of the White House staff.' I reminded them that they were talking about Department of Defense assets and that we didn't even haul members of the White House staff in a car over to Republican or Democratic headquarters a couple of blocks away. We weren't about to start using military airplanes for guys not even working for the government.

"Chapin got really upset and started telling me Haldeman had promised this to various people to get them to work for CREEP and that it was going to happen. To which I said no it wasn't. It finally got down to Chapin telling me that the President was the Commander in Chief of the Armed Forces and, as Commander in Chief, he could do anything he wanted with them, and if that meant the military was to feed and haul political people who had nothing to do with the government, then that's what they'd do.

"The lines were pretty clearly drawn, and my parting words were, 'If you do this, some of you are going to end up in jail.' That's what I said, and I said it because I was so furious, not because I had any inkling of what they were going to get into before it was all over.

"I may say that later the Ford people seized on the precedent of letting political people use White House facilities and seized on it with gusto. They put their people from the Republican National Committee and the Reelect Ford Committee on the White House Staff Mess list, let them use White House cars, and gave them free rides on government aircraft just the way the Nixon people did. The Carter people have got some of their political types doing it, too, as well as Carter's unofficial advisor, Kirbo. It's all illegal as hell, but it's the usual thing—once a thing gets started it stays in place, legal or illegal. It started under Nixon, and it's been there ever since.

197

"I've got to admit that the Nixon advance people were professional as hell—tough, hard-nosed, well organized and completely ruthless. When they were on the road they'd telephone back to Dwight Chapin when they saw something they didn't like, and they'd get immediate instructions on what to do. Chapin had direct access to Haldeman, so there was no question where the orders were coming from.

"There was a lot of speculation at the time of the campaign and after that the anti-Nixon demonstrations, or some of them, were rigged. Even the one in San Jose where they threw rocks.

"I don't have any evidence that that particular demonstration was rigged, but knowing how the Nixon advance team worked, it's well within the realm of possibility; it was the kind of thing that was often discussed at pre-trip meetings.

"Our office was heavily involved in the planning for all trips, and in the course of discussions, Chapin and Ron Walker would often plan what means they'd use to 'sucker in' the crowd, arouse sympathy for the President, and put the protesters in the worst possible light. It was standard for them to tell Secret Service to let any particularly unsavory-looking characters get close enough to the President so the news media would pick them up.

"An example of this was when they hired people to infiltrate and stir up the crowd lining the route after the inauguration in 1973. The military aide in the motorcade told me that as they passed some particularly rough types, an advance man riding with him said, 'Those guys are ours.'

"This was tough on Secret Service, naturally, because they had to protect the President, and it made their job a lot harder. But there were no lengths, in my opinion, to which the political types wouldn't go to achieve whatever it was they wanted.

"What they wanted in Haldeman's day sometimes meant moving mountains, at government expense. In July of 1969, Nixon was returning from a trip around the world which was code-named Moonglow, because he had stopped to greet the Apollo 11 astronauts on splashdown.

"We planned to fly the President into Hickam Air Force Base in Hawaii for refueling before the final leg of the trip, and there were a dozen reasons, from security to the cost and ease of servicing the aircraft, for doing it there. Haldeman, however, had other notions.

"He wanted the plane to land at Honolulu International Airport. The reason: so the Press would get a shot of the President descending the steps of *Air Force One* with Diamond Head mountain in the background. There were a couple of outstanding reasons why this was a lousy idea—two huge mounds of dirt from an airport construction project, mounds that were big enough to block out the view of Diamond Head.

"Undeterred, because once Haldeman got an idea he stuck with it no matter how ludicrous it was, he instructed us to have the military bring in bulldozers and move the mountains of dirt. Which we did. We also had them moved back again. That was probably the most expensive 'photo opportunity' ever paid for by the American taxpayer.

"Television is one of the areas where the President has such an edge on the other party's candidate that there's no way to even the score. The President can get TV exposure almost any time he wants it, and with *Air Force One*, his fleet of planes, helicopters and cars, his timing can be flawless. A skilled advance team, which Richard Nixon certainly had, could make the media work for their guy, whether they liked him or not. Take Nixon's return from China in February 1972.

"He stayed over in Alaska for nine hours on his way back from Peking, and the main reason was so he would arrive back in Washington in prime television viewing time. The timing was critical because they wanted the arrival to coincide with a station break. Not many things make the citizens angrier than having a politician interfere with their favorite TV program.

"They were looking for two other things in this Alaskan stopover. They wanted a rested-looking President, because ever since his television debates with Kennedy, Nixon has been very conscious of the fact that he photographs badly when he's tired. And they wanted to ease the jet lag.

"It turned out that this quiet Alaskan interlude wasn't so uneventful after all. No sooner had Nixon arrived at the base commander's house, where he was going to stay for those nine hours, than Walter Hickel, the ex-Secretary of the Interior, showed up. Hickel had left the Nixon Administration firing shots over his shoulder as he went, and no one was sure whether Nixon was going to see this guy or not.

"Finally Nixon agreed to greet Hickel—they'd shake hands and say a few words—because there was no point in antagonizing the Alaskans. Then the unexpected happened. Hickel walked in with a guy who had long hair and a guitar.

"Hickel insisted the President listen to a song this guy had composed which was all about the right of students to protest, and the whole bit. Nixon sat through it all, and it went off without incident. Until Hickel and the guitar player left, at which point Nixon exploded, and everyone, Haldeman included, got an extended ass-chewing.

"Nixon left Alaska and made his triumphal return to Washington; *Air Force One* was right on time, which it always is, and Nixon got worldwide television coverage. They were gloating over the points they'd scored, until the next day when Jack Anderson broke the Dita Beard story. She claimed the government had made a favorable settlement in an antitrust suit with ITT in return for a large political contribution, and the Administration was back on the defensive."

"A really interesting figure who came into the Nixon camp in the first administration was John Connally. Here he was, closely tied to Lyndon Johnson, and a leading power in the Democratic party. Then he became closely tied to Nixon and the person Nixon considered the most effective politician in the country. Both LBJ and Nixon relied on him, used him, and had the highest possible respect for him.

"One reason is that Connally has charisma. Johnson was the Crass Cowboy, Connally's the Cowboy with Class.

"Nixon almost always ate alone at Camp David, but if you had put John Connally up there with Richard Nixon, Nixon would never have eaten alone—Connally would have been invited to every meal, breakfast included. He, more than any other political figure I can think of, has the ability to inspire confidence in other politicians.

"One time I heard him address Nixon's senior staff at the

San Clemente Inn. It was early in 1971 and the polls showed Nixon down. The staff was gathered in a party room downstairs, and Connally walked in like the professor addressing the students. It wasn't as if he was talking to the senior advisors to the President of the United States; it was as if these guys had no idea of what being a President was all about.

"And yet he antagonized nobody. He told them, 'If you bastards don't start getting the message out to the American people about what their President's doing for the country, you're going to get him defeated. All you're doing is bickering among yourselves, spending time backbiting and feuding.'

"There they were, the heavies of the Nixon gang—Haldeman, Ehrlichman, all of them—sitting there like a bunch of little boys listening to John Connally chew them out. You could see they were awed by him. He was a goddamn spellbinder.

"When John Connally became Secretary of the Treasury, Nixon told the Military Office, 'I want this guy to have anything he wants. He can use my plane. He can have Camp David. I know his wife isn't fond of Washington, and if the environment of Camp David will help to keep him in this job, then I don't care if we have a helicopter for them that commutes between the South Lawn and Camp David. I want him to have anything he wants.'

"The only person who came close to getting the kind of preferential treatment Nixon showed Connally was Bebe Rebozo, and unlike Rebozo, Connally never took advantage of it. He never went to Camp David except as a guest of the President, and the first time he wanted a plane to take him to Texas, he called me and asked about the different planes and what they cost to operate. I explained that a Convair cost about half what a Jet Star cost, but it took twice as long. Connally said that didn't matter, a Convair was fine for him. It was a memorable response in my experience at the White House.

"As soon as Connally became Secretary of the Treasury he moved in as the resident Heavy. He overshadowed everybody, including Kissinger.

"One time Nixon returned from giving a speech in Miami

at the AFL-CIO convention. It had been a touchy business because George Meany hadn't wanted Nixon to address the group in the first place. A number of labor leaders walked out when Nixon appeared, but in the end it turned out to be a success for Nixon because the ones who stayed cheered him and generally showed their approval. The White House staff decided to mark the occasion by staging a big welcome home for him on the White House lawn.

"All the senior people were assembled, and when the helicopter touched down they cheered. Nixon walked among the admiring and greeted them one by one until he came to Connally. As soon as he saw him, Nixon put his arm on Connally's shoulder, took him right into the White House and up in the elevator to the family quarters.

"The rest of the group had followed behind, and Kissinger was standing right there in the hall in front of the elevator when the President ushered Connally into it—and then shut the door right in Kissinger's face. I was standing a little distance away with Cindy Van den Heuval, Julie and Tricia's secretary, and Kissinger was so furious at being excluded he turned like an enraged bull and barreled out of there so fast he nearly knocked Cindy down."

WATERGATE

There's a line that divides the stormy Nixon Presidency, a line so distinct it's possible to fix the date it was drawn: November 8, 1972, the day after his sweeping reelection victory.

Nixon's first term was tumultuous, as was his abortive second one, but in a different way. His first four years were marked by bold initiatives. Some, like the secret bombing of Cambodia, aroused unprecedented protest among the people. Others, such as Kissinger's covert negotiations with Peking, which led to our recognition of the People's Republic of China, were hailed as masterstrokes.

But by the end of that first term Watergate had gained momentum.

The years 1969–1972, filled as they were with challenge and confrontation, ultimately exhausted the people and drained Nixon. The last of Nixon's strength was sapped by the campaign, which he approached as if he were the underdog, and by his efforts to "contain" Watergate—at least until after the election. When his moment of victory finally came and he won reelection by the largest popular vote in American history, he was unable, by his own account, to savor it:

"A few days [after the election] I described in my diary a curious feeling . . . that muted my enjoyment of this triumphal moment . . . I am at a loss to explain the melancholy that settled over me on that victorious night," Nixon recalls in his memoirs.

Chuck Colson, who spent several hours with Nixon and Haldeman in the President's office that election night, also felt the atmosphere of flat joylessness:

"If someone had peered in on us that night from some imaginary peephole in the ceiling of the President's office, what a curious sight it would have been: a victorious President, grumbling over words he would grudgingly say to his fallen foe; his chief of staff angry, surly and snarling; and the architect of his political strategy sitting in a numbed stupor. Yes, the picture was out of focus. If this was victory, what might these three men have looked like in defeat?"

Nixon says he is unable to understand the feeling of melancholy he experienced then, but he has identified similar reactions at other times and warned against the dangers that lie in them.

Nixon constantly urged his staff to read his book *Six Crises*. On the most notorious of the Watergate tapes, the "smoking gun" conversation with Haldeman on June 23, 1972, he said, "I want you to re-read it, and I want Colson to read it, and anybody else . . . in the campaign. Get copies of the book and give it to each of them. Say I want them to read it and have it in mind. Give it to whoever you can. . . . Actually, the book reads awfully well . . . that *Six Crises* is a damned good book."

It was good advice. It's a book worth reading in many ways, most importantly for the insight it gives into this most

203

complex man. Certainly anyone working with Nixon should have read it, and read it attentively. It's even possible that if Nixon himself had reread it in those first postelection days, and heeded his own words of warning, he might have survived Watergate.

Some people are accident-prone; Richard Nixon is crisis-prone. He loves a challenge, and if it is great enough, and the stakes are high enough, the outcome of that challenge becomes critical. Once challenge is elevated to the status of Crisis, Nixon will meet it with all his skill and energy, which even his most ardent foes admit are formidable.

In *Six Crises* he details the way in which he met and overcame situations which to him were critical, and puts forward a convincing case as an authority on challenge. He would have done well to reread this passage in the aftermath of his victorious struggle for reelection:

> The point of greatest danger for an individual confronted with a crisis is not during the period of preparation for battle, nor fighting the battle itself, but in the period immediately after the battle is over. Then, completely exhausted and drained emotionally, he must watch his decisions most carefully. Then there is an increased possibility of error because he may lack the necessary cushion of emotional and mental reserve which is essential for good judgment.

An argument can be made that if Nixon had taken the time then to regroup physically and psychologically, he might not have made the serious, and finally fatal, errors in judgment he made in the following weeks. Haldeman says that he and Nixon had seriously discussed plans for a sweeping reorganization of the government as early as September 1972, but it was in the weeks immediately following the election that the plans hardened. Had Nixon taken time to reflect on his overall position, he might have handled this delicate political situation differently.

As a first step in the governmental reorganization, which was to feature as its centerpiece the appointment of his own men to the key positions in every department, Nixon demanded written resignations from each member of his staff

204

and Cabinet. The time he chose to make this demand was the very morning after his triumphal victory at the polls. He himself admits he was wrong in the way he did it, if not in what he did.

> The call for resignations included the entire White House staff and all Cabinet members. I see this now as a mistake. I did not take into account the chilling effect this action would have on the morale of people who had worked so hard during the election and who were naturally expecting a chance to savor the tremendous victory instead of suddenly having to worry about keeping their jobs. The situation was compounded by my own isolation at Camp David, where I spent eighteen days in the four weeks after the election, holding more than forty meetings with old and new appointees and making plans for the second term.

If Nixon's judgment was poor on the timing of his demand for staff resignations, it didn't improve under the pressure of those forty-odd meetings. Pressure that, ironically, was self-imposed.

Haldeman, in *The Ends of Power,* advances a theory that the threat of a massive reorganization of the government so frightened and antagonized the entrenched Washington power blocs that they exploited Watergate in a determined effort to bring down Richard Nixon.

The blunder of asking for resignations on the day after winning reelection and threatening greater "house cleaning" throughout the bureaucracy didn't make Nixon any friends in the Washington establishment, and might well have sharpened appetites for anything damaging to him, but it wasn't this that led to Nixon's fall.

In November of 1972 he won reelection by a landslide, and if he still wasn't a popular figure to most Americans, he clearly had their support. As far as Watergate was concerned, it wasn't too late to go "the hang-out route." Indeed, although it might have caused him and his Administration embarrassment, a forthright statement at this point might have put an end to the matter.

It would be simplistic to say that Nixon's emotional let-down after the campaign triggered his fall. He might have made all the same decisions after four weeks of rest and still opted to stonewall. However, it's possible that he sealed his own fate in those feverish weeks between the election and the inauguration.

In 1972, while Watergate was still mostly smoke and little flame, Kissinger is reported to have quipped, "The illegal we do immediately. The unconstitutional takes a little longer."

Like a bad brush-fire, Watergate had begun to spread in the early summer of 1972, during the campaign, but it had been contained successfully enough to allow Nixon to be renominated by a vote of 1,347 to 1 at the Republican National Convention on August 23. And for Nixon and Agnew to be reelected by a landslide—60.8 percent of the popular vote and 97 percent of the electoral vote—losing only one state, Massachusetts.

Stunning as these election figures are, they say more about the people's low opinion of Nixon's Democratic opponent, Senator George McGovern, than they do about Nixon, because at that point in November, Americans didn't think much of the job their President was doing. Just four days before the election, November 3, the Gallup organization released figures showing Nixon had achieved his lowest approval rating to date: 27 percent.

After the election was successfully won, the building of walls in a mood of militant defensiveness began to take the place of initiative. Soon it was hard to tell where Watergate began and ended, who was touched and who was not.

"The whole question of who participated in Watergate and to what extent is bound to get muddy," Gulley says, "because Haldeman ran CREEP and Haldeman ran the White House. I made the Military Office position clear: we weren't doing anything for political people or political purposes. But then they'd just lie to us, or not tell us the real reason behind their requests to us. There's no doubt that we were used, and there was no one to go to about it.

"Watergate spread like mold through cheese, and covering things up was so much a part of life in the White House that after the 1972 election you couldn't say flatly when you were asked to do something, whether it would turn out to be related to Watergate or not. Like two things that happened during Haldeman and Ehrlichman's final days in the White House in April 1973.

"The weekend before they left, Nixon, who was in Key Biscayne, had given Haldeman and Ehrlichman permission to use Camp David one last time. While they were there, Higby asked me to send a Jet Star to Butler Aviation Terminal at Miami International. A package addressed to Haldeman would be delivered to the pilot, who was to take it to Andrews, where he would be met by a White House car, which would take the package to Camp David.

"When I checked to find out if the operation had been completed successfully, the driver said yes, the package had been safely delivered. He also told me what was in it: ten pounds of stone crab from Joe's Crab House in Miami. (Figuring the price of jet fuel alone, the fish for their last supper cost the taxpayer $500 a pound.)

"Higby's last Haldeman request was different. On Sunday, April 29, the day before Haldeman and Ehrlichman's resignation, Higby called the garage and asked the dispatcher to send a truck to pick up some boxes that were being taken out of Haldeman's office. The dispatcher called me to get authorization to do it, and I told him to go ahead.

"The next day, Monday, April 30, the President announced that his aides had resigned. Tuesday, May 1, nine hours after the President's speech and thirty-six hours after the truck had left with Haldeman's boxes, the FBI posted agents outside his and Ehrlichman's office doors."

"As Watergate hotted up, the vulture instinct that's built into all politicians brought so many congressmen and senators down from the Hill that the sky was black with them as they circled over the White House looking for a hunk of meat. Since they were looking for anything they could get, whether it had anything to do with the campaign, or CREEP, or not, the safest thing for anybody inside the White House to do was make sure nothing remotely questionable got outside.

"Or, if it was outside, get it back in a hurry. There was a scramble to bring anything of a dubious nature back inside the stockade where the troops were making their stand. Which is what we did with the transcripts of telephone conversations Henry Kissinger secretly taped while he was the President's National Security Advisor.

"Not long after Haig replaced Haldeman as chief of staff, he called me and asked me to come and see him. When I got there he said he had a highly confidential project he wanted to discuss with me. In a bomb shelter at Pocantico Hills, Nelson Rockefeller's estate in Westchester County, there were some thirty crates of top secret papers Henry Kissinger had put there for 'safekeeping.'

"Even though the Rockefellers are an empire unto themselves, it's doubtful they'd meet the requirements for storing classified government documents, and now with everybody asking a million questions about everything, Haig and Kissinger wanted to get those papers out of there.

"It was imperative the Press not find out about it, because they'd want to know what Kissinger was doing secretly taping conversations in the White House in the first place, and in the second, what the transcripts were doing being stored on private property. So Haig wanted me to come up with a plan for a 'covert mission.' Which I did.

"I arranged for one of our unmarked planes to fly to Westchester County Airport and assigned Sergeant Herb Oldenberg from our office to collect the boxes of papers and bring them back to the White House. As soon as the plane landed, Oldenberg rented a truck and drove to the Rockefeller estate. When he got there he got the crates out of the bomb shelter, put them on the truck, loaded them onto the plane, and flew back to Andrews.

"At Andrews, still working alone, he put the crates in an unmarked White House truck and drove it back to the East Wing, where he put them into a room in the bomb shelter.

"I kept the papers down there for about six months, and every once in a while Kissinger would send someone down to get some of them. I have been told that in anticipation of a possible subpoena, Kissinger was doing a little weeding and pruning, so if they ever see the light of day all the public will get is a sanitized version of his conversations. Finally, after six months, I turned the whole thirty crates over to one of Kissinger's people, and once again they left the White House.

"The irony of the thing is that one of Haig's big worries about the whole situation was that this was classified material that was being stored on private property. And that's probably where they were again, six months later, on somebody's private property."

"Once Watergate really got going, nobody in the White House knew where the next blow was coming from. Leaks were springing all over and going to the Washington *Post* as well as to half the guys on the Hill. We were getting hit from all sides with demands to explain this or that.

"One demand came from the Government Accounting Office, courtesy of Senator Proxmire. Proxmire had received information that the White House Staff Mess, which was controlled by the Military Office, was subsidized. That food for White House staff members was being sold for less there than it was to enlisted men in the Mess at the Pentagon, and that they were selling booze. So GAO demanded an audit.

"Al Haig had just taken over as chief of staff, and he'd come in wearing a white hat. We'd got rid of the Bad Guy, Haldeman, and here was the Good Guy, Haig. Initially there was relief throughout the White House because Haig was seen as a welcome change, a guy who himself had suffered under the Haldeman regime when he was Kissinger's deputy. Little did we know that his personal ambition and ego far outstripped Haldeman's, matching that of Kissinger himself.

"Haig's first reaction to the GAO request to examine the Staff Mess was, 'Why, sure. Let 'em come in and audit. We've got nothing to hide.' So I went to see him and explained we had considerable to hide. After that he changed his tune and said, 'Well, see what you can work out with Fred.'

"Fred was Fred Buzhardt, a friend and 1946 classmate of Haig's from West Point. He had been an aide to Strom Thur-

209

mond, who was his mentor, and now he was one of Nixon's lawyers during Watergate. Anyway, I went over to see him.

"One of the problems we had with the Mess was its membership. It was a violation to have White House staff using a Navy Mess in the first place, but by now we had members of CREEP there, too. Added to that, we were illegally using the Military Office Secret Fund to support it, so we were in a lot deeper than underselling the Pentagon Mess on meatloaf.

"I told Buzhardt all this was going to come out and embarrass everybody if we let GAO near the place. I explained that funneling money from a classified fund alone would get us into a hell of a lot of hot water.

"Buzhardt listened and said, 'I've got the picture. I've got the picture.' Then he told me, 'You know, when I was general counsel for the Defense Department,' which he was in the early 1970s, 'we had that big PX scandal over in Vietnam, and I knew how to handle that. I was getting a lot of pressure, so what I did was I created a dummy audit board and put it in my desk drawer.

" 'A couple of months would pass, and when someone would ask me how things were progressing with our audit, I'd make up a little progress report from this audit board that never existed and show it to them. Then another couple of months would pass, and when they'd press me again, I'd do the same thing.'

"As Buzhardt was telling me this, all I could think of was what trouble Nixon was in having this guy for his lawyer. Watergate was bad enough, but here the President was being represented by a guy who was telling me that he made up dummy auditing boards when he was legal counsel for the Department of Defense. That's what he told me he had done in the middle of a scandal that rocked DOD and resulted in sending a number of people, including one general, to federal penitentiaries.

"Anyway, at the end of our conversation, Buzhardt said he'd take care of stopping GAO. But the people at GAO, although they may be dumb, have been around a long time, so they went to the Navy and said, 'It's your Mess; you audit it.' In the end I did what I did so often at the White House. I said, 'No way. That's classified information, so forget it.' "

"During this period everybody was under a terrific load of pressure, and people reacted to it in different ways," Gulley says. "I didn't see much of Nixon in those days. It wasn't until after he resigned that I saw a lot of him, but when I did he seemed to be handling the pressure as well as or better than the guys around him, outwardly anyway.

"Rose called me one day in the spring of 1974 and asked if there was something I could do about getting Maurice Stans's wife into Walter Reed Army Hospital. When Stans had been Secretary of Commerce, his wife, who had cancer, was admitted to Walter Reed—where she really had had no right to be—and all her records, as well as her doctor, were there.

"Now Stans was no longer in the government, of course, and Watergate was down on him, but his wife was ill again, and he wanted her to go back to Walter Reed. I told Rose there was no way, legally, that we could arrange that, but she said, 'See what you can do, please. The President is personally interested in this.' So I said O.K., I'd look into it.

"In a situation like this I could just call Defense and say do it, and they'd do it. But they'd also probably call the Washington *Post* and *The New York Times*. So I had to lay my groundwork pretty well and have a pretty convincing reason why it had to be done. I talked to the doctor at Walter Reed, and I talked to the people at Defense, and when I thought I had things pretty well set up—although they weren't perfect —I went to see Rose.

"I was sitting in her office when Nixon walked in. He said, 'Oh, excuse me,' and started to back out, but Rose said, 'No, Mr. President, we were just talking about Maury Stans's wife, and Bill says he thinks the Press will probably find out.'

"Nixon said, 'I don't care. This woman is dying of cancer, and I want her comfortable, with the doctor that she knows.' I said, 'I'll take care of it.' Which I did.

"I thought to myself, here's a guy about to be run out of the Presidency, and yet he doesn't mind taking some more flack. Why not desert Maury Stans now? If this guy is the hardened criminal that everyone is making him out to be, if he's a gut fighter who'll stab anyone in the back and doesn't give a damn about people or things, why would he now put another knot in the rope that's around the apple tree waiting for his neck? Why's he doing this when he doesn't have to?''

DEEP THROAT

The drama of Watergate has produced a cast of characters who are oddly two-dimensional. The Nixon of the tapes is a rough-talking political tough. Haldeman-Ehrlichman is a two-headed Germanic monster intent on subverting the course of justice. Woodward and Bernstein are the ink-stained Hardy Boys of a Dynamic, Big-City Newsroom. The things all these people did were of great significance; yet they themselves are curiously bloodless.

Most intriguing of all is the shadowy, and pivotal, figure of Deep Throat, the disillusioned romantic who, eschewing glory for himself, herded the two Boy Reporters along the path that led to the first resignation of a President in American history.

''Deep Throat, I believe, was really two or three sources,'' Gulley says, ''but the main one, in my opinion, was a guy called Scott Armstrong, who was an investigator for the Senate Watergate Committee. I had another candidate, someone in the White House, but on the way to verifying my suspicions about him I stumbled over Armstrong, whose identity Woodward and Bernstein had secreted in the most traditional hiding place of all—right out in the open. On their staff.

''After leaving the government, Armstrong went to work, officially, for them. In an Author's Note in *The Final Days*, Woodward and Bernstein say the contributions of Armstrong and their other associate, Al Kamen, 'were immeasurable . . . we will never be able to thank them enough.' I don't know about Kamen, but from what I now believe about Armstrong, I'm sure their gratitude to him comes from the heart. Armstrong then went on to be coauthor with Woodward of *The Brethren*, about the Supreme Court.

''That an investigator for the Watergate Committee of the

Senate would have access to the widest range of information from every possible source is obvious; and so is the fact that just by having the job he had, he'd be able to scare the hell out of a guy, thereby improving his powers of recollection.

"Another thing Armstrong had going for him was that he had access to what everybody under threat of indictment wants: information about himself, how things look for him.

"Woodward tried a number of times to get me to talk to him. His first approach was through the commander of the *Sequoia*, who had been a fraternity brother. When this guy told me he was a friend of Woodward one mystery was solved: information had been getting to the Press about things going on on the yacht that could only have come from a source on board. At one point even Julie's husband, David Eisenhower, had been suspected of being the inadvertent leak. Now it made sense.

"I didn't talk to Woodward then, and I didn't meet with him when a gal in Mrs. Nixon's press office, Terry Ivey, asked me to. First she suggested setting up a lunch for Woodward and me; then she invited me to her house for dinner with him. Finally I did talk to him on the telephone.

"I opened by telling him I knew he and Bernstein were getting a good portion of their information from the secretarial staff at the White House and I wasn't going to participate in rumormongering. I wouldn't under Lyndon Johnson and I wasn't going to now. Woodward responded in a friendly, confiding way, saying, 'Look, we're both reasonable people. We come from the same background . . . ,' which did nothing to reassure me about the quality of the information he was getting. Yale University didn't play much of a part in my youth, and I doubt a dirt farm in southern Illinois did in his.

"Woodward went on in this vein for a while, but when he saw he wasn't getting anywhere, he changed tactics. He said, 'We have some information about things that are going on in the Military Office, and about you personally, that I'm sure you wouldn't want to come out. We could publish them if we wanted. We have enough to publish.' I told him, 'Publish any goddamn thing you like, I'm not playing your game.'

"One thing our conversation told me was that he did have

information on an internal matter in the Military Office that was not on the level of secretarial gossip. The source had to be someone in the White House who was close to a person with responsibility in our office—probably me—and there weren't many that fitted those shoes. I couldn't figure out who it was, and since it wasn't a big deal, I forgot about it until my search for Deep Throat dusted off my memory.

"In January 1974, Steve Bull and I were in San Clemente with Nixon and shared a house near the compound. Steve was under investigation by the Senate Watergate Committee, and one day while we were in California he had a telephone conversation with Scott Armstrong that lasted close to an hour. It obviously wasn't the first time they'd talked, and what Steve was after was information from Armstrong about his own position, whether he was in serious trouble.

"I felt sure Steve hadn't done anything he shouldn't, but in the climate of those days, I was concerned about his talking to this guy at all, and especially about the loose, rambling way the conversation was going.

"Later, in October of 1974, after Nixon resigned, Steve and I again shared a house in Capistrano Beach, near San Clemente. Steve was still working with Nixon; I was out there on military and Liaison business; and Fred Fielding, who had been on John Dean's staff, stopped by for a visit.

"Haldeman has said he believes Fielding himself was Deep Throat; I think he just provided some of the information—either in a trade-off, direct or implied, with Armstrong, or inadvertently. While he was visiting, Fielding and Steve talked about Steve's legal problems and discussed conversations they'd both had with Scott Armstrong.

"Putting it together now, especially in view of what I believe about the 18½-minute gap on the Watergate tapes, the finger points to Armstrong: (1) Woodward had information about the Military Office which could have come through Steve Bull and not many others—and Bull talked to Armstrong at length; (2) Woodward and Bernstein say Deep Throat told them about the deliberate erasures on the Nixon tapes in the first week of November 1973. As is discussed later, by late September of 1973, I believe Steve Bull probably knew all about the 18½-minute gap.

"Steve refuses to believe Scott Armstrong was a source for Woodward and Bernstein. He says he and Armstrong are friends and it could never have happened.

"I don't know what the law says about an official investigator for a Senate committee passing information on to a newspaperman for publication, but there might be rules about things like that. If there are, they could explain why Armstrong, if he is Deep Throat, has failed to step forward and claim his place as the hero of Watergate."

Revelations about Nixon's tapes were about to break Watergate wide open, but before they did, a not-at-all-two-dimensional figure descended on the beleaguered President. "There were some lighter moments during what was basically a grim time at the White House," Gulley says, "and one of them was provided by the Russians. Nobody closer to home was giving us any comic relief.

"On June 16, 1973, Soviet Premier Brezhnev arrived for a visit, and we were in charge of the arrangements. He and his party first went to Camp David, and everything they had requested was straightforward, with one exception: although it was understood that because of space requirements the Soviet staff would double up, it was specified that the number three stewardess was to have accommodations to herself whenever there was an overnight stop. That meant we had to assign a cabin just to her.

"We couldn't figure it out, until it all became clear a little after midnight the evening they arrived. Two of Brezhnev's KGB men went to the stewardess's cabin and escorted her down the path, past the wondering eyes of half a dozen of our guards, to Brezhnev's cabin. She stayed there until dawn, when the KGB escorted her back to her own cabin.

"After their stay at Camp David, the Soviet party went to San Clemente on June 22. Brezhnev was given Tricia's old room, and Manolo told me this is what happened that night.

"Manolo was getting ready to go to the cottage on the Nixon property where he and his wife stayed when two KGB agents, with the young stewardess between them, came marching down the long hall toward Tricia's room.

"Suddenly, Mrs. Nixon's bedroom door opened, and she stepped out, just as the Russian party was bearing down on her. Manolo stood struck to stone while the scene unfolded. Mrs. Nixon stepped into the hall, paused, then turned and went back to her room, leaving the door open. The three Russians strode past her open bedroom door, looking neither left nor right. Thirty seconds later Mrs. Nixon reemerged and went down the hall in the opposite direction.

"Some people give Mrs. Nixon credit for quick thinking and tremendous tact. Others say it was dumb luck there wasn't an unscheduled meeting in the hall. But everybody agrees it was about time somebody got laid in Tricia's room."

Whatever satisfaction Nixon got out of Brezhnev's visit, it couldn't have lasted long. On the day Brezhnev left, the twenty-fifth of June, two things happened. The House agreed to a Senate bill to cut off funds for the bombing of Cambodia. And John Dean began his testimony before the Ervin Committee.

THE TAPES

"The tapes, of course, were the key to the last act of Watergate," Gulley says. "It's still almost unbelievable to me that in as small and rumor-riddled a place as the White House, only three or four people knew about Nixon's taping system. I didn't know about it until the rest of the world did—although for some time I'd been tripping over clues, but they'd mistakenly led me to believe it was a telephone monitoring system.

"I always liked Alex Butterfield. He was tabbed as a Haldeman man, because he went to school with Haldeman, but my association with him went back to the Johnson years when Alex was an Air Force colonel. He worked over at the Pentagon handling an aircraft support operation that was an extension of the White House Military Office.

"Alex had left the Pentagon and was in Australia on a special project having to do with the F-111, but when Nixon became President, Haldeman wanted him in the White House.

216

He says now that Butterfield approached him, but I doubt that. Haldeman told Hughes, who was head of the Military Office, that Butterfield had agreed to retire from the Air Force in order to join the Administration and for us to expedite it.

"In other words, he said to Hughes, 'Tell Defense to get the guy out of there, bring him back, retire him, and get him in the White House—tomorrow.'

"Butterfield wound up in the office next to the President, which turned out to be a help to me, because I could get straight, reliable information from him. Haldeman was always covering his ass so well you never knew when you got a request from him whether in fact the President knew about it, and some of these requests involved spending hundreds of thousands of dollars—modifying aircraft, for example.

"When it reached the point where Nixon would say, 'Who did that?' or 'Where did that come from?,' we saw that some things we thought he'd directed be done were news to him, so I'd go to Alex and find out what I could. He'd say, 'Bullshit. The President doesn't know anything about that. That's strictly Haldeman.'

"Rose Woods hated Butterfield with a passion and thought he was short on brain power—mainly because he worked for Haldeman. I think Butterfield saw what Haldeman was and lost whatever respect he'd had for him when he got to the White House, but I could never make Rose believe that. She felt he was part of the Haldeman team and, like the rest of them, was against her.

"One of the first times I was in Alex's office, a button on his telephone console lit up, and the minute it did, Alex turned away and pushed the button again. There had been no sound, and he didn't pick up the instrument, so, since it obviously wasn't the telephone, I figured Alex must be controlling some kind of monitoring device or tape system that was recording the President's calls. Haldeman, Ehrlichman, Kissinger, all had telephone taping systems, so I assumed from Alex's button that the President did too.

"They'd been quick off the mark to get taps on their telephones; they'd been in the White House just over two weeks when Ehrlichman asked for his.

"Nobody in our office knew about Nixon's taping system until Butterfield's testimony, and then everyone wondered why he hadn't called in the White House Communications Agency and had the military do it as they had Johnson's, instead of turning it over to Haldeman and some clowns from Secret Service who didn't know what they were doing.

"The reason goes back to a meeting Nixon had with J. Edgar Hoover. Immediately after Nixon was elected they met in New York, and Hoover told Nixon then never to use the signal board, the military switchboard in the White House. Hoover said Johnson had told him that the military monitored and taped telephone conversations.

"And as a matter of fact we did—but only as directed by Johnson himself. Still, until the day he left the White House, Nixon didn't want to use the signal board, and distrusted the military, as did Haldeman. Which explains why he didn't get the military to install his taping system. However, later on Nixon was very curious about Johnson's system.

"On my fifth or sixth visit to him at San Clemente, Nixon and I got around to discussing the Watergate tapes. He said, 'You know, periodically I would recall we had a taping system, but for the most part I was hardly aware that what I was saying was being taped. Except on occasion, particularly in meetings with foreign leaders when they would make statements that were a little surprising to me; then it would cross my mind and I'd think, I hope that tape is picking this up.

" 'But it wasn't on my mind during general conversations,' Nixon said. 'I never really knew just how it worked, and I wasn't aware that it worked if there were just staff people in there with me. You know, it was a damn cheap system; it only cost a couple of thousand dollars. I'm sure Johnson had a much more elaborate system.'

"I said, 'Yes he did.' Nixon said, 'Did you know about it?' I said, 'Yes I did.' Then he said, 'You know, Johnson told me about it, but he never really told me how extensive it was or how it worked. Of course my first reaction,' Nixon said, 'was to get it taken out. I suppose you know what kind of a system it was?' That was Nixon's way—asking without asking.

"So I told him about Johnson's system, and that for a time

6 February 1969

MEMORANDUM FOR RECORD

SUBJECT: Charlie Brown for John Ehrlichman

1. On 6 February 1969, I responded to a call from Bud Krogh, Assistant to Mr. Ehrlichman, to General Albright requesting WHCA assistance regarding installation of a recording capability on Mr. Ehrlichman's office phone lines.

2. In subsequent conversation with both Mr. Krogh and Mr. Ehrlichman, it was agreed that the WHCA would install an IBM recorder in Mr. Ehrlichman's office which would be capable of being electrically connected to any of the several phone lines associated with the call director on Mr. Ehrlichman's desk.

3. The sensitivity of this installation was pointed out to both Mr. Krogh and Mr. Ehrlichman and it was agreed that it would be accomplished during other than normal working hours following Mr. Ehrlichman's departure on 8 February.

4. LTC Gilmore was tasked with the installation and Mr. Wong was apprised of all action this date.

FREDERICK W. SWIFT
Maj, SigC
Deputy Operations Officer

219

WHCA-A   7 February 1969

MEMORANDUM FOR RECORD

SUBJECT: Charlie Brown for Mr. John Ehrlichman

On 6 February 1969, I informed Colonel Hughes of a request received from Mr. John Ehrlichman concerning the installation of telephone recording equipment in his office.

Colonel Hughes, in a subsequent telephone call, informed me he had discussed this matter with John Ehrlichman and Bob Haldeman and that I should proceed as requested.

JACK A. ALBRIGHT
Brigadier General, USA
Commanding

his tapes had been stored in my office. Nixon was interested by that and wanted to know if I'd been questioned about the Johnson tapes during Watergate. I told him I had, and that when I'd told somebody from the Ervin Committee that they'd been hauled away, he said the LBJ people had told him they didn't know what happened to them.

"When I told Nixon I hadn't been asked for the schematics of Johnson's taping system by the Ervin Committee people, and hadn't volunteered them, he said, 'There's nothing to be gained by telling those bastards anything.'

"Nixon has continued to defend his having a taping system in the White House. He told me, 'I'm still convinced that it was the right thing to do, for Johnson and for me. You know, the only continuity you have in sessions with foreign dignitaries is to have on tape what you said and what they said. I still think it was something a President should have, and the American people should have, if it ever came down to that.'

"Unlike Johnson's system, which was sophisticated, and which he controlled manually, Nixon's was activated by sound. This was because Nixon is hopelessly unmechanical. He's not a buttons guy. He could never operate a system like Johnson's.

"The fact that it was triggered by sound made for an interesting situation, that and the fact that almost nobody knew it existed. Lots of times when Nixon would leave the Oval Office for the day, Steve Bull, his appointments secretary, would have the field to himself. Bull was a great mimic, and a very funny guy, and one of the things he did best was imitations of Richard Nixon.

"Steve would get in there in the Oval Office and, unaware at the time of the taping system, he'd start making the kind of speech Nixon was given to making, using the same gestures and phrases. It was uncanny, and uproariously funny. He'd wind up his 'and I want to make one thing perfectly clear' speech, and then he'd go over to the drawer where the souvenirs were kept.

"Steve would pretend to pass out tie clips and cuff links, with appropriate Presidential comments on the worthiness of the recipients, and even though you saw Bull in front of your

221

eyes you couldn't believe it wasn't Nixon.

"When Butterfield told the world about Nixon's taping system, and that it was voice-activated, the first thing I thought of was Steve Bull and his mimicking of the President. It's sure as hell going to screw things up for the historians.

"In the days after he gave his testimony, practically no one was talking to Butterfield, but he and I continued to chat. The first time I talked to him after that I said, 'You know, when I heard you say what you did to the committee, I was sure it was part of a plan to shoot down John Dean.'

"He said, 'Let me tell you, there was no one more surprised than I was at the reaction. I didn't know that the tapes hadn't ever been mentioned to the committee. I got no instructions, no game plan from Haldeman. Before I appeared I asked him where we were, what had been told to the committee and what hadn't. And I was getting no response.'

"Then he said, 'I called Senator Howard Baker on the Sunday before I was going to testify, on July 15, to discuss my appearance with him, and I mentioned the tapes to him. I'd told the committee staff about them a couple of days before and got no reaction from them. I got no reaction from Baker, either. He showed no interest in them. So I had no warning that my comment about the tapes was going to lead to what it led to.

" 'I just assumed,' Butterfield said, 'that other people in the White House who knew about the tapes had discussed them with the committee investigators.'

"I don't believe they were playing a game with Butterfield. I know it's been said since that the committee was playing a deep game with him, but that's just to make them look good, I think. Regardless of Rose Woods's opinion of him, Butterfield is a pretty astute guy and would have recognized any interest in a particular area.

"I think what happened is much simpler. I don't think anyone recognized the significance of what Butterfield had. Of the tapes. I don't think the Haldeman people did, when Butterfield was talking to them before his testimony, and I don't think Howard Baker did when he was talking to Butterfield on the telephone.

222

"It wasn't until it was out there in the committee room and in front of the great American public on television that the penny dropped."

What happened to the missing eighteen and a half minutes of a taped conversation between Nixon and Haldeman has been a source of conjecture since it was revealed on November 21, 1973. Gulley believes the explanation lies in an incident that took place at Camp David late in September that year.

"I spent a weekend in Texas. I'd gone to the LBJ Library in Austin on business and stayed over so that Mrs. Johnson could fly back to Washington on the plane with me. She had committee meetings there the following day.

"In my job I had to stay constantly in touch with the White House and let them know where I was, so the first thing I did after I checked into the motel in San Antonio was call the signal board and give them the necessary information: the name of the place I was staying, my telephone number, how long I expected to be there.

"After I'd done all that, the operator told me the Army aide, Colonel Bill Golden, wanted very badly to talk to me. Golden was the duty aide at Camp David that weekend, so I told them to put me through to him up there, which they did.

"As soon as he got on the line he said, 'Bill, something's happened up here, and I'm not sure just what it was. But I may be in serious trouble. I went over to the cabin Steve Bull and Rose Woods are using for an office, and not realizing Rose was there, I walked in without knocking. I thought Bull was alone.

" 'Steve and Rose were bent over a tape recorder,' Golden said, 'doing something with tapes, and when they realized I was there, they both acted startled. Steve immediately took my arm and walked me out of the cabin. He was obviously irritated with me; he was visibly upset. You know that's not the Steve Bull we're used to.'

"I said to Golden, 'Don't worry about it. If you're in trouble, I'll take care of it when I get back.'

"I didn't hear any more about it until later, after the news broke about Nixon's tapes and the 18½-minute gap. When that revelation was made, Golden says, he was convinced that without realizing it he'd been a witness to that famous erasure. There was the tape recorder, the fact that Bull had a lot of mechanical ability, and his reaction to Golden, which was out of character.

"I've discussed this with Steve Bull recently, and although he admits working with Rose Woods on transcribing the subpoenaed tapes, both at Camp David and Key Biscayne, he denies having made any erasures.

Although a report prepared for Judge John Sirica by an advisory panel of electronics specialists and related testimony produced evidence that admittedly contradicts Gulley's theory about the erasure, based on his experience, Gulley nonetheless has serious doubts about these findings and remains firm in his belief that Bull is clearly the most logical person to have made the erasures.

"There are a couple of things I should say here about the tapes and whoever was involved in erasing them. First, those tapes were readily accessible. That was well known in the White House at the time, and the lack of security over them was discussed in the newspapers later on. As Bull said, he was working on them both in Florida and in Maryland, so access to the tapes really was no problem.

"Second, the feeling in the White House at that time was intensely defensive, and as I've said before, that defensiveness was about the White House itself, about where we worked, not about Richard Nixon. There was a desire to close ranks against whoever was attacking us. In that atmosphere, it's my belief that any number of staff members would have responded to a request from Rose Woods, or several others, to participate in doing whatever was done to the tapes. I know I would have.

"Leon Jaworski has said he thinks Nixon erased the tapes himself, but you will never make me believe that Richard Nixon ever, ever erased a tape. He has trouble making a ballpoint pen work. He would automatically depend on someone else to do it for him.

"Whether Nixon asked Rose and Steve to do this, or

whether they discussed it, no one is ever going to know. No one can say what went on between them and the President. Not Haldeman, no one. Only they and Richard Nixon know, and I don't see any of them telling.

"As a footnote to the tapes, one afternoon Rose called me and said, 'Would you do me a favor? Would you call me here in my office every three or four minutes?' I said sure. She said, 'If the conversation we have doesn't make any sense, I'll explain later.'

"What was happening was that she had an office full of reporters, and she was trying to show them how it was that the 18½-minute gap in the tapes could have come about by accident. Her story was that it could have happened as she leaned over to answer the telephone, and I provided the calls. The result was a memorable photograph of Rose, tied up in knots."

"I never thought Nixon knew about the Watergate break-in when it happened," Gulley says. "But knowing what happens in the White House once a thing is known, I then knew Richard Nixon had to know from A to Z about Watergate.

"What I think happened was that he felt personally involved, that he had friends involved, and that in trying to protect those guys, he figured he was big enough to make it all go away. I think he just kept walking farther and farther out in the water until all of a sudden the water was up to his nose."

One of the many confusing aspects of Watergate is that although the term sprang from a single event in the Nixon Administration, it soon became a generic term that covered a whole line of Administration wrongdoing. It took in the burglary of Daniel Ellsberg's psychiatrist's office, the Huston Plan for Domestic Surveillance and all the convoluted twists and turns of the cover-up.

It became a lawyer's playground: What was at issue? What was relevant? What was admissible? What was privileged? And, interestingly, the central figure was himself a lawyer, one who, once again, failed to follow his own advice.

In *Six Crises*, Nixon says, in discussing the Alger Hiss case:

"Hiss, a lawyer himself, had made the fatal mistake no client should ever make—he had not told his own lawyer the full truth about the facts at issue." As Nixon's humiliated lawyer, James D. St. Clair, was to discover, his client, who knew much better, had done the same to him. And it proved fatal.

RESIGNATION

"I was shocked by Nixon's decision to resign. Even as late as July 1974, I thought he might weather the storm after his two trips, to the Middle East and Moscow. Foreign policy was where he was strongest, and in addition it looked as if Stennis and some of the real giants on the Hill were ready to back him. I also thought his choice of Ford as Vice President was going to help him stay in office.

"Most of all, I knew Richard Nixon was a fighter, and I believed that before he would resign he would go down the impeachment route. So I have to say I was shocked.

"But then, you live a sterile life when you work at the White House. My life consisted of getting there at six-thirty in the morning and staying there at least until eight or nine at night. I'd been doing that for so many years that I, and people like me, lost touch with the public. I really didn't realize the venom that was in people—whether that venom was there rightfully or not—I just didn't realize it was there.

"I think it's clear Nixon didn't realize it was there, either. Or certainly didn't realize the extent of it.

"By the end of July, I finally saw it was just a matter of weeks. There were four things happening in the White House that I felt were particularly significant and pointed to the end of Richard Nixon.

"First, I was sure Haig was no longer fighting to keep Nixon in office. I think he saw he had a pretty goosy mustang on his hands and just wanted to get him out with as little rumpus as possible. Second, Melvin Laird was in and out of the White House all the time, more than usual, and he was strongly pro-Ford.

226

"He was also one of the biggest leakers in the Administration. His aide, Colonel Walker, visited columnists Evans and Novak all the time. In fact, he called it his 'daily run,' and would tell us what Laird was telling them—that Nixon couldn't hold on any longer.

"Third, Haig was giving things to the Ford people they hadn't been given before. All of a sudden the Vice President, instead of being treated like the second-class citizen he'd been all along, was being treated like somebody who mattered. He and his staff were upgraded starting the last week in July.

"Fourth, Kissinger was beginning to take liberties with the Press that he hadn't taken before. He was beginning to speak in the first person, and I took that as a very strong sign that he felt Nixon's days were numbered.

"The thing that shook me most happened one time when I went into the press office. Ron Ziegler had pulled in his horns altogether by then; he wasn't even meeting the Press; and the Administration was clutching at straws. It was about eight in the morning when I got to the press office, and Jerry Warren, who had taken over from Ziegler, was sitting at his desk— crying. He's a very calm, deliberate fellow, so that shook me. He looked up when I walked in, and all he said was, 'I see no way out of this.'

"Most people in the White House knew the end was coming, but I don't think anybody thought it would come so abruptly. It's surprising that word of the resignation didn't spread through the White House faster, but it didn't really get out until about noon of the eighth, when it was announced that the President was making a television broadcast that evening.

"Until then, only the immediate Nixon circle knew about his decision: the family, the photographer Ollie Atkins, Rebozo, Kissinger, Scowcroft, Haig. One reason it was particularly important the news didn't hit the street was that Ford was traveling and didn't know yet about Nixon's decision.

"As soon as Rose told me what was happening, things began to move very fast for me. I started the wheels turning for Nixon's departure and then dealt with the personal things he wanted done at Camp David. It turned out all he wanted was for somebody to collect the family's possessions—a painting, some clothing—and a dozen of his favorite Camp David highball glasses. But since the Press's mouth was watering for any hint of things to come, I arranged for a guy with lockjaw to go up there.

"Handling the details, along with the unreality of the whole situation, kept me from fully taking in what happened, but the next morning, August 9, what had happened was rammed right home. Nixon's farewell in the East Room was painfully emotional; it hurt everyone there, especially Rose Woods.

"She had a tight rein on herself and did very well through the East Room thing. Then she went out on the lawn to see the Nixons onto the helicopter, and did well there, too. But as soon as the chopper left, she collapsed and had to be taken to the doctor's office.

"Rose's life is very entwined with the Nixons'. She was adamant that she never wanted to be known as 'Aunt Rose,' but she was as close as family could be. There were times, for instance, when she would be tired at the end of the day and they'd ask her to join them to watch a movie. Nixon's taste in movies ran to *Gone with the Wind* and other films out of the 1930s, which I'm sure Rose had seen many, many times, but I never knew her to beg off anything—dinners, movies, whatever.

"I don't think that probably even Nixon suffered any more than Rose did through Watergate and that whole period. She fought everyone who was against him and stayed loyal. She still is to this day. Nixon's farewell must have been an agony for her.

"Even before Nixon finished speaking in the East Room, flowers and telegrams began arriving in San Clemente by the truckload. They came in such numbers, I had to assign Don Murray from the Military Office to handle them. It was as if a man of importance had died."

"After I got back to the White House from my first trip to see Nixon in San Clemente, I was getting all kinds of conflicting signals. Yes, Nixon would get briefing papers; then no, he wouldn't. And so on about everything. Jack Marsh by this time had been formally appointed the transition guy for Ford, and it was apparent that either he was hopelessly indecisive or the whole situation was out of control.

"In one meeting we had—Marsh, a guy from the General Services Administration, some lawyers from Phil Buchen's office, and me—the discussion centered on Nixon's papers and whether or not they'd be sent out to him. A final decision hadn't been made, but there was a strong likelihood the court would put a hold on them.

"At the end of the meeting Marsh took me aside and told me that Ford was going to sign an order preventing anything more from going to San Clemente. I asked him what was behind it, and Marsh said Ford was getting pressure from various congressmen and senators, and Buchen was leaning heavily on him.

"Whatever the reason, nothing more was going out there, Marsh said. He also told me there would be no more courier planes, and that the ones I'd sent would have to be paid for by Nixon, as would his use of *Air Force One* the day he resigned.

"I told Jack then that in my opinion a lot of this was never going to happen. The court might freeze Nixon's papers, but for the rest, I didn't see it happening. I said, 'What are we talking about here? Are we talking about a former President? Or are we talking about a criminal? If we're talking about a former President, there are precedents, like giving them an airplane to fly them home when they leave office. Because of the time his resignation became effective, noon, Nixon had been President until he was four miles out of Jefferson City, Missouri. What does he do? Pay for the rest of the flight, from Jefferson City, Missouri? Come on.

" 'If we're talking about a criminal,' I said, 'then maybe we'd better wait until a court says that's what we're talking about.'

"At that point I started shipping stuff out to San Clemente as fast as it fell into my hands, things that weren't yet under lock and key. In addition to papers, there were things of a personal nature—letters, mementos—in warehouses and different places around town. Rose or somebody would tell me where they were, and I'd scoop them up and send them out. I'd have done exactly the same thing for Johnson or Ford.

"I saw Nixon again on August 30. This time things at San Clemente were a little better organized and a couple of secretaries had arrived. When I went in to see Nixon, there was a considerable change in him, too. He was a little calmer. He was less formal, less tough-talking. I told him that the President and Mrs. Ford sent their best wishes to him and Mrs. Nixon, which was a lie. But it had an effect on him. I stressed that the difficulty I was having wasn't with Ford personally but with Jack Marsh and lower-level people. I let him think Ford knew I was shipping stuff out to him, which Ford did not. The only thing Ford ever did was inquire about Nixon's health, but believing my lie helped Nixon's morale considerably.

"This time Nixon and I sat down and had a long conversation. He said he'd been talking to Joe Waggonner and a couple of other congressmen, and they'd told him there was a lot of bitterness. 'I realize there's going to be bitterness,' he said. 'I expect that. But I want to know specifically what their plans are. I want to know when I get my papers. When do I get my personal effects? What are they going to do with my wife's and daughters' things? And Rose's stuff? These are personal items, nothing to do with the Presidency.'

"I didn't have any answers, but I wanted him in no doubt about the seriousness of the situation. 'Your office at EOB,' I said, 'they've put guards on it. Rose is allowed to go in there and work, but she's not allowed to take anything out.' He said he was aware of that but did I think there'd be an improvement in that situation. I said no, I didn't, but I did tell him one thing that had been settled. Ford had decided Nixon was to be sent briefing papers, intelligence evaluations and the like, and that I would be bringing them out every two weeks.

"He asked me if I thought he'd be allowed the use of military aircraft, and I said no, that in fact there was a possibility he might have to pay for the planes that had been used by and for him so far. To that he said, 'Well, if that's what the bastards want, I'll pay.'

"I said then that I really didn't think anything was going to come of it, because the courier planes had been on military business for me, not personal business for him. And that I didn't think anybody in his right mind was going to make him pay for *Air Force One* from Jefferson City, Missouri, where he was at twelve noon on the ninth, when he stopped being President, to El Toro Marine Corps Air Station in California, where it landed, and back to Washington.

"He didn't show any anger at any of this, but he was interested in knowing how much I thought Ford was personally involved in the decisions. He asked me that specifically. I said that it was very hard for me to tell, that I'd been dealing through Jack Marsh, so I really couldn't answer that with any certainty. I think he was asking me that because he was ready to accept any decision Ford made but didn't want a bunch of bureaucrats deciding his future.

"When the meeting was ending he thanked me and said that one thing he had thought about in the last few days was that he was sorry he hadn't had more time to get better acquainted with some of the people who were in the White House and did so much for the President. He said one of the things he would always regret was that he hadn't taken the time to get around the White House more. Then he said, 'I'd like to give you a memento.'

"When Nixon said that I was really surprised. And so was Steve Bull when Nixon asked him to please bring in a watch. Bull knew all about the watches but certainly didn't expect Nixon to give me one. Up until then, he told me later, Nixon had given only one watch, and that was to Gerald Ford when Nixon made him Vice President.

"When he gave me the watch, Nixon said, 'I really appreciate you being available. I'd like you to know that nothing more can hurt me, but associating with me can hurt those who do. You should always keep that in mind, because the media aren't going to let up on me. This is not going to satisfy them; they won't be satisfied until they have me in jail. You should keep that in mind.'

"I knew that at that time the Press was getting a lot of its information from Secret Service agents. The way I knew is that the switchboard in San Clemente was run by the military, and when the calls came in, we knew who they came from and where they went. Secret Service agents were talking to the Press. We didn't monitor the calls, but we kept a log as a normal procedure, so when press reports would say, 'A source inside the compound . . . ,' they were right. About that part of it, anyway.

"They were wrong about a lot of other things, and one of them was about the drinking that went on. There was press speculation that Nixon was drinking heavily, and that Mrs. Nixon was too. I never saw that. I've been with Nixon when he's had a Scotch and water, but he's what I would call a moderate drinker, and it wasn't any different then than it is now."

"As far as my activities were concerned, there was utter confusion from August through December. At one point I had had a truckload of Nixon's personal items all loaded and ready to go to Andrews to be flown out to San Clemente, when Phil Buchen called the White House gate and told them to stop the truck. That was in September.

"As soon as I was told, I called Buchen's office, and he said although the shipment was all personal items, not official material, moving it violated the court's order. That the order pertained to 'personal memorabilia.' Well, it was that, all right. Among other things, there was Nixon's gavel from his years as Vice President and president of the Senate, autographed photographs from world leaders, his pipes and Tricia's wedding dress.

"Things weren't made any easier when Ford granted Nixon a pardon. Ford's an open, honest man in my opinion, and I think he made up his own mind on the pardon. It was just like his bringing his old cronies into his Administration—lots of people criticized him for that. Everybody, for instance, knew that Hartmann was a difficult personality; even Mrs. Ford was against bringing him into the White House, but Ford stuck with Hartmann, and the others. I think it was the same kind of personal decision with the pardon.

"I knew on Saturday, September 7, that he was going to make the announcement at ten o'clock the next morning, Sunday. I'm sure I was told for one purpose—so I could keep Nixon informed, because Ford was still weighing the pros and cons, and the thing wasn't completely nailed down.

"Brent Scowcroft had called and asked me to come over to his office. When I got there he said to come in and close the door. Then he said, 'You ought to know that tomorrow morning at ten, Ford is going to make a statement to the Press that he's going to grant Nixon a full pardon. I'm sure this is going to affect your operation,' and he was right.

"I called Jack Brennan in San Clemente right away, and he said, 'Bill, are you absolutely sure of this? Are you sure of your source?' I told him I was. 'Do you know what the wording is?' he asked, and I said no, only that it was a full pardon.

"The pardon was a very tightly held thing, and although Ford had doubtless thought about it for a long time, when he made the decision, he moved fast. Nixon had very little warning. Nixon had planned to go to Palm Springs on Saturday, the seventh, to visit the Annenbergs. The Secret Service agents were already out there waiting for him, the communications people were there, all the arrangements were made. Even then, Nixon wasn't absolutely sure it was going to happen.

"The next morning, Sunday, at six o'clock California time, Brennan called me at home. He said, 'Look. He,' meaning Nixon, 'is driving me crazy. Can you confirm that this is still going to happen?' I said, 'All I can do is go back to my source' —I didn't tell Jack who that was—'and double check. Then I'll call you back.'

"I called Scowcroft, who was in his office. I was a little worried about security myself at this point, so I said, 'There's some interest on the West Coast in this matter we discussed yesterday. Is it still on?' He said, 'Yes, it is. They're setting up for it right now.' So I called Brennan back, and I'm sure they were warming up the television sets in San Clemente.

"After that last conversation with Brennan, I went right to the office. I was sure there'd be a tremendous reaction, and the White House was going to be flooded with calls and telegrams. Which it was.

"The Administration made no preparations for the inevita-

233

ble reaction to the announcement, for the obvious reason that they didn't want the word to get out ahead of time. Ford didn't want to be lobbied by every guy in Congress, and the Press would have gone crazy. So when the word was spoken, all hell broke loose in the White House, and no one was ready.

"I had to send cars all over town picking up telephone operators to man the switchboard, which was jammed, and telegraph lines were backed up all across America. The country was up in arms.

"As soon as Ford made his announcement, there was a circling of the wagons against the onslaughts the Ford people knew were coming. You could feel their apprehension; it was in the air everywhere. Inside the White House, backs got stiffer as the stream of Press coming up the driveway got bigger.

"The reaction among those in the White House itself was mixed, as was to be expected. The Ford people mostly felt, and said, 'We were against doing this, but O.K. Now it's done, and it's as far as he's going. It's over. Now Nixon's on his own.' They felt Ford had done Nixon a tremendous favor. I was told Marsh and Hartmann were against it.

"The less-partisan staff members felt a sense of relief that the thing was over. There had been apprehension that Nixon might be hauled into court, that Ford would be put on the spot sooner or later to do or say something, that the whole thing would drag on and drag the new President down.

"The pro-Nixon people went the whole way in the other direction. 'Why should he have been pardoned?' they said. 'He didn't do anything in the first place.'

"My own opinion is that there was enough evidence—and it doesn't matter how pro-Nixon you might be—there was enough evidence on September 8, 1974, to send a former President of the United States to jail. And basically—and it doesn't matter how anti-Nixon you might be—basically, jail is no place for a former President of the United States.

"In addition to what you might call the legal questions, there were fears for his life. He was in bad health, as became clear very shortly after the pardon when he landed in the hospital. On that last whirlwind tour of the Middle East and

Russia before he resigned, Dr. Tkach felt that the clot in Nixon's leg was so dangerous it could move at any time and kill him. Tkach told him that, but Nixon still insisted on going on. It was almost as if he hoped it would happen.

"Those in the White House who had some sympathy for Nixon felt that he would get mental and physical relief from the pardon, and that it was what Ford should have done. But there was no outpouring of emotion, no reaction that a beloved President had been spared the ultimate humiliation. People didn't feel that way about Nixon. He didn't inspire devotion. But there's no doubt he's a hell of an interesting man."

IN SECLUSION

"I've seen a side of Nixon that most people, even people who were in the White House during the years he was President, haven't seen," Gulley says. "Nobody's all one-sided. Nobody's all the suave sophisticate that Henry Kissinger's supposed to be. Or the sweet Southern Belle, as Rosalynn Carter's painted. Or the hardball-playing tough guy that Nixon's made out to be.

"I'm not saying there aren't those sides to those people. It's just that there's more to it than that. More to them. And I saw another side of Nixon. In my job you also get close to the people closest to the President—to Luci Baines Johnson, to Julie Eisenhower—and it colors your viewpoint. You see a softer side than the people do who just deal in issues and carry out orders.

"I've never defended what Nixon did. One reason is that I'm not sure I know what he did, or that anybody really knows. If he did some of the things he's supposed to have done, then I couldn't defend him, nobody could. But as I said to Nixon that first time I saw him after the resignation, I'm not in the judgment business. And I'm not.

"I've heard it said that Nixon feels he has to demonstrate

that he's one of the boys because he really feels he isn't. And that this shows itself in his conversation. That he curses a lot and throws his weight around and generally talks tough-guy talk. Maybe that's true, but if so, I never saw it. Maybe what I saw was unusual, but it's there. What's on the Watergate tapes is there, too. Nobody's all one thing, not even Richard Nixon.

"What I saw was a guy who, once he feels comfortable with you, once he knows you, doesn't feel he has to prove anything. There's just an easy give-and-take. I never saw him acting tough or trying to impress by cursing or making extravagant statements.

"What he really liked was to talk about issues. Get into them. Part of it undoubtedly was that once he was out of office he had time to do this, to think about things and to reflect out loud on them. He liked to get into a subject and then show you how it fitted in with other areas, with a current situation, for example, and then how different people affected that situation.

"He enjoyed talking about people. He'd discuss some guy's strong points and weak points, but always holding them at a distance, not in a personal way. He'd evaluate someone's abilities, even people he knew very well, in a detached way. And in the end, whatever or whoever we were discussing, the subject would come back to politics."

Gulley and Nixon met in Nixon's office at the compound. At their earliest meetings Gulley felt that Nixon's attitude to their relationship was that he, a former President of the United States and a world leader, was dealing with a minor civil servant.

"When he talked to me the first time, I think he saw himself as a hated elder statesman, but still an elder statesman with the prerogatives that go with having been President. He was telling me what he expected.

"Then he began to come to grips with the way it was going to be."

When this happened, Nixon began to relax with Gulley, and except for the period when their conversation was entirely preoccupied with the political advice Nixon was sending back to Gerald Ford during his campaign for the Presidency, their talk was far-ranging.

"I wasn't always sure what I was going to meet when I'd visit Nixon. I wouldn't really call him moody, but he can get upset by things, so you can't be sure he's going to be the same every time you see him. I'd go into his office, and maybe something from an earlier appointment, or a telephone call, bothered him, and I could tell right away.

"Anger is defined in him. When he's mad, he's mad. You're left in no doubt.

"When Nixon talks to you, he looks directly at you, he never turns aside. It's disconcerting. He also talks very fast, especially when he's talking about something that has a special interest for him, and his hands are constantly in motion. He interjects 'Don't you think so?' and 'What do you think?' into whatever he's saying.

"Most of the time he doesn't expect you to come back with anything, so he goes right on. Then he'll say, 'Maybe I'm wrong' or 'Maybe that's not your feeling,' and he'll pause again.

"When you do have something to say, when you do answer, he listens carefully. He's very intent. But he doesn't laugh a lot, which doesn't mean he isn't enjoying himself.

"When he does laugh, he literally slaps his thigh. When I told him right after Carter came into office that despite the image he was trying to create of this God-fearing preacher man who didn't touch the demon rum, Carter and Rosalynn both climbed into the bottle from time to time, Nixon laughed and said, 'Carter drinks? You mean to say he *drinks?* Goddamn!' and he slapped his thigh with his open hand.

"We talk about people a lot, but it's not very personal, it's not earthy as it was with LBJ. Johnson would lead you into that kind of thing and ask for it in return. I don't think there's ever been a dirty story told between Nixon and me. But the gossiping's pretty good. He likes to hear political gossip, especially, but there's never been speculation about the sexual activities of anyone we're talking about.

"Nixon's interested in whether some guy's decided he's not going to run, or he'll ask, 'What do you think? Did he really take money from that Korean?' And he's interested in what goes on at the White House. He was concerned about the speculation in the press about the Ford children, about them and marijuana. He didn't believe it, number one, but what really bothered him was that a story like that was being circulated by what he always called The Goddamnpress.

"But he's never showed interest, and I never discuss with him who's screwing who, which goes on all the time at the White House. I never volunteer it, and he never asks.

"One time Nixon said, 'Did you see that Susan Ford is marrying a Secret Service guy?' I said yes, I knew about that, and then I told him a little background. 'You know,' I told him, 'Susan was pretty wild while she was at the White House. She was only seventeen when she came there, of course, but the Fords had problems managing her. There were two or three times when they were really concerned about whether they were going to be able to keep the Press from knowing about her escapades.'

"Nixon said, 'Well, as far as her marrying a Secret Service agent goes, it should not have got that far. You can't permit that. I never get familiar with the Secret Service. They've got a job, I've got a job. The minute you start getting familiar with people, they start taking advantage. I always hold those guys at arm's length. I think they're great guys and do a fine job, but I don't believe in letting your staff move into the quarters.'

"Nixon repeated several times that he shouldn't have let Haldeman isolate him the way he did. 'I didn't realize I was being isolated,' he said. 'You do have to have somebody who can protect your time. You've got to have that, a tough son of a bitch who'll stand up to senators and congressmen and whoever. Who'll stand up to them and say no.' But it hadn't occurred to him at the time, he said, that it cut him off from everyday life at the White House, too.

"He asked me what his staff had been up to that he didn't know about. He said, 'About the Ford children smoking pot at the White House, did you ever know of anything like that going on, of anybody doing that kind of thing, while I was at the White House?'

238

"I told him I'd never heard of anything of that kind. Then he said, 'Well, what do you *think?* Hell, you knew everything that was going on. Do you *think* the staff was smoking pot and doing things like that?' I told him I hadn't run into anything at the White House, but I did tell him about the kids stationed at Camp David and on the yacht that I'd had to have transferred for smoking pot.

"Then I told him about the lad at Camp David who had been found smoking marijuana after Carter took office. He was told he was going to be transferred as a result, but he came right back and said if we tried to transfer him he'd go to the Press. The camp commander asked him what he was going to tell the Press, that he'd been breaking the law smoking marijuana, on a naval base at that? The kid said no. What he'd tell the Press was who he'd been smoking pot *with*.

"Nixon said, 'Who *had* he been smoking pot with?' and I told him. Jeff and Annette Carter. The end of the story was that when the commander consulted me, I told him just to give the boy the facts: that he'd accept his transfer and keep his mouth shut or we'd see to it the Navy threw the book at him, which would mean many, many unpleasant and uncomfortable years. The military doesn't take kindly to blackmail.

"That story led Nixon to think out loud about Carter. He said, 'What is it about Carter? Is he intentionally misleading the American public? First he gives everybody the idea he's against drinking, and it turns out he drinks. Then he says he doesn't remember anything about clearing the way for somebody to talk to the Justice Department on Robert Vesco's behalf—and when a memo turns up from Carter to the Attorney General doing just that, everybody's forgotten all about it. Let me tell you,' Nixon said, 'when the Attorney General gets a memo from the President, he doesn't forget. He shits in his pants.'

"There's no pattern to our talk," Gulley says. "Sometimes it'll take off from some event of the day. We talked about Vietnam in the beginning, and he started to be preoccupied about South Africa very early in 1975. He talked a lot about the CIA and the overthrow of the Allende Government.

"About that he said, 'They aren't going to find anything

there. Hell, what was done in Chile had to be done, and all
we're going to do is lose status in the eyes of the world. What
Ford should do is cut off all the speculation and hold this very
closely. Because there are some things the CIA has to be free
to do.'

"Some of the things Ford was doing, or not doing, irritated
Nixon. He felt Ford wasn't running nearly a tight enough
ship. When General George Brown, chairman of the Joint
Chiefs, made a statement about the Jews controlling the
media, and it hit the front pages, Nixon said, 'Christ, that
really hurts. Politically. That hurts Ford. Old Brown's all
right, but goddamn, those guys have got to be held in check.
You can't have them out there making off-the-cuff remarks
like that.' "

"The first time Nixon and I talked about Watergate he said,
'I really feel compassion for John Mitchell. These poor people
who are now literally going bankrupt trying to defend themselves.' He said, 'There's no question that Watergate happened. There's no question that it shouldn't have happened.
But a lot of innocent people are being dragged into this, and a
lot of reputations are ruined.'

"It's strange, but whenever Nixon speaks of Watergate it's
always as a thing detached from him. It's never in the context
of something he was involved in. He always speaks of it as if
it were something over there—in that corner. As something
we had gone through, that the country had gone through.

"He'd say, 'God. What the country has gone through with
this Watergate business.' It's always in that vein, as if it had
nothing to do with him.

"Another thing I found surprising was that Nixon never
showed any bitterness toward some of the other Watergate
players. I went to see him one morning when the L.A. papers
were full of Martha Mitchell accusing him of every kind of
wrongdoing, and the first thing Nixon said to me about it was,
'That poor woman.' Then he shook his head and said it again.
'That poor, poor woman. She's been through so much.'

"We talked about Butterfield and John Dean, and he never
showed any feeling about them one way or the other.

"Once, though, when we were discussing Chuck Colson, he said, 'You know, Colson's a tough son of a bitch. He understood the game. There's no question about that. Now he's picking up a lot of heat for things he did or didn't do—I don't know. But Colson's a tough son of a bitch, and I feel a lot of compassion for the guy. He was a successful lawyer, and he got caught up, and God knows what the outcome will eventually be.'

"He didn't talk of Colson as a personal friend. He didn't see him as a protégé at all. But when, at one point, I made reference to Colson's miraculous conversion and said that when he'd made his million he would go back to being the tough son of a bitch that he was, Nixon just let it pass right by. He didn't pick up on it at all. He understood exactly what I was saying; he just didn't want to participate in speculation about Colson's religion.

"I was surprised again another time, when the morning papers were carrying excerpts from Woodward and Bernstein's book *The Final Days*. I expected to find him in a very, very bad mood, but he wasn't at all. And he was the one who brought it into the conversation.

"Nixon said, 'Well, I guess you've read the book that's out?'

"I said no, that I hadn't read it, but that I did know something about where they got their information. I told him that Woodward had tried to contact me, and Nixon was interested in that. He was curious about how they'd got their information, although he didn't admit what was right and what wasn't.

"I have a problem with Nixon, though. I don't feel I'm an expert on him, but then I've come to believe that *nobody* really knows Richard Nixon. The reason is that I think he does things primarily for effect, and says things for effect. That's why I was always being taken by surprise. Also, I couldn't be sure of the truth of what he was saying.

"An example of this was the part in *The Final Days* where Woodward and Bernstein describe Nixon getting down on his knees with Kissinger just before the resignation. When we were talking about the book that morning, Nixon said to me,

241

'You know, hell, Quakers don't get down on their knees and pray like Baptists. I might very well have said a silent prayer with Kissinger,' he said, 'but I certainly wasn't hanging on to Kissinger and saying "let's pray." It was nothing like what was described in that book.'

"Then Nixon said, 'And how the hell would they know? Who could tell them except me or Kissinger? *Isn't that right?*' Now you wonder. I had to wonder. Was he asking me, 'Did Kissinger tell them?' Did he want me to say it must have come from Kissinger? I didn't know. At times like that I just let a thing pass.

"I remembered what he'd said, of course, so I was surprised again when he sent me a copy of his memoirs. There in his own book he said he and Kissinger *did* get on their knees and pray. It wasn't what he'd said to me to my face, and it made me wonder.

"One of the other things he singled out was the business about his talking to pictures. He said, 'They say I was walking around the White House talking to pictures. Now how the hell could you go walking around the White House talking to pictures without the whole world knowing? With all the guards, and all the aides, and everybody following you around all the time? The whole world would have known.' On the basis of my own knowledge, I had to agree with him.

"But about the book in general, he said to me at the time, 'Hell, it doesn't bother me. I just hope it doesn't upset Mrs. Nixon. That's my concern. The bastards have got no reason to talk about her.'

"I don't think it bothers Nixon that people in general respond to him without any warmth. He's not affected by it. His one vulnerable spot is his family. You can make him damned angry by any kind of an attack on Mrs. Nixon or the girls.

"When Mrs. Nixon had that stroke, for example, he blamed it on Woodward and Bernstein's *Final Days* and some of the speculations in it about her drinking and their relationship. He talked to me about that. He said, 'I don't care what the bastards say about me. But Mrs. Nixon never did anything to anybody, and she doesn't deserve to be treated—to have speculations like that about her.'

"He's a totally different Richard Nixon when he says things like that. It's as if here's a naked Richard Nixon, telling you as a human being: I love this woman, and I may take what you do to me, but I'll kill you for whatever you do to her.

"I've never seen or heard him react that strongly about the girls, but he changes visibly, in front of your eyes, when he talks about Mrs. Nixon.

"The relationship between Nixon and Mrs. Nixon was, and is, very private. In public they've always exhibited a more professional attitude toward each other than a close personal one. But Nixon is always conscious of her. And if he feels someone is out to hurt her in any way, he becomes intensely protective.

"One of the little ways Nixon is conscious of her is that he's very careful of his language in front of Mrs. Nixon. An aide told me that one time, when Mrs. Nixon wasn't even aboard the helicopter, Nixon said 'Shit' and immediately looked around to see if she'd heard what he'd said.

"He's considerate of her preferences in other ways. There were times when he changed his mind about going to Florida and went to California instead because Mrs. Nixon preferred California. She had a close friend there, Helene Drown, who had taught school with her and who used to come and stay with her in the White House.

"Now, Helene Drown—just hearing the name drove Richard Nixon up the wall. He would just go out of his mind every time she came to visit.

"Once, Mrs. Nixon and Helene Drown had been to New York shopping and Mrs. Nixon brought her back to Camp David. They arrived at about two in the afternoon, and the President was already up there. At about four he walked over to his aide's cabin and said, 'Let's go to Washington.' They came so quickly—they got on the helicopter, left Camp David and came so quickly—that only the aide, the Secret Service agent and the doctor were with him. Everybody else was left behind.

"He literally couldn't take it; Helene Drown just drove him up the wall. Obviously she and Mrs. Nixon were very close, but just as obviously, he couldn't stand her, so he'd do anything, make any excuse, to get away. He'd do anything that was man's doings so he wouldn't have her around.''

"I don't think Nixon concerns himself with how people feel toward him. I think he's taught himself not to care, and that's what has helped him survive. Any other man probably would have taken his own life under the circumstances at the time of the resignation.''

Nixon's determination not to lay himself open to the pain of personal criticism might have hardened as a result of the way in which the Press reacted when Eisenhower was campaigning for reelection, over a secret fund Nixon was accused of having accumulated.

"The crisis of the fund,'' Nixon says in *Six Crises*, "was the hardest, the sharpest, and the briefest of my public life . . . it left a deep scar which was never to heal completely. [Pat and I] had both become perhaps too sensitive. . . .''

Nixon succeeded in growing more layers of armor coating, but the sensitivity was still there. His antagonism toward the Press was deeply rooted and virulent. No President can have a truly easy relationship with the Press for long. Even John Kennedy, who holds the record for intensity of Presidential love affairs with the Press, canceled the White House subscription to the New York *Herald Tribune*.

"Nixon not only made no attempt to woo The Goddamn-press,'' Gulley says, "but he concentrated on getting even. His feeling was: We're not going to do anything to make those bastards comfortable. We're not going to do anything to curry favor with them. Those bastards are going to have to work for everything they get. We're not giving them anything.

"Nixon had assumed he was going to get nothing from the Press, and there was nothing he could do to change that, so he concluded: We're enemies. That's Them. This is Us. And everybody in the Nixon White House knew he had no worries as far as his job was concerned if he chose to offend the Press —that went from the lowest to the highest.''

As Watergate bore down on him, Nixon became increasingly antagonistic to individual reporters.

MEMORANDUM

THE WHITE HOUSE
WASHINGTON
June 3, 1974

MEMORANDUM FOR: RONALD ZIEGLER

FROM: LTC JOHN V. BRENNAN

Last night, 2 June 1974, the President very emphatically related
to me his views regarding press pools. I am instructed to inform
you, in very forceful terms, that never, under any circumstances,
on any leg of any trip, will a representative from the following be
allowed on the press pool:

    New York Times
    Washington Post
    Time Magazine
    Newsweek
    CBS
    Richard Lerner from UPI

The President also emphatically stated that this is not appealable - do
not appeal to General Haig and do not bring the subject up to the President
as he wants to hear no more about it. This is a direct command from
the President.

The President directed that since the Office of the Military Assistant to
the President is responsible for the aircraft, he is holding us
responsible to make sure none of the above are allowed on aircraft as
part of a press pool. The President also said he wants you to continue
submitting press pools to him in advance of a trip.

Being tunnel-visioned, narrow-minded Military people, we in this
office intend to carry out fully the instructions of our Commander-in-Chief.

bcc: General Haig
        Jerry Warren

Nixon did not attempt to cultivate personal relationships. "Not only was there no personal relationship between Nixon and anybody else in the White House," Gulley says, "but professionally he stepped on a number of toes. He showed a lot of interest in economics when I saw him after he was out of office, and he always seemed to be well briefed. In part this was because he now had the time to take an interest. So many big things were going on in the foreign area while he was President that the economy seemed like a stepchild.

"Economic policy was left pretty much in the hands of the technicians. While Henry Kissinger was getting hours in the sun every day—the sun being the Oval Office—the economic guys felt they were left out in the cold simply because of Nixon's personal interests.

"The result was that the people dealing with foreign policy were impressed with Nixon's innovations and his grasp of the area, while the people on the economic side, Alan Greenspan's side, had an uphill battle with Nixon and weren't too impressed with him, because he was so tied up elsewhere. But Nixon didn't care.

"He understands where he has support in general terms, though, and what it's worth. I saw him after the third of his interviews with David Frost, and I said, 'Are you pleased with them?'

"He said, 'Yeah. The reaction, and the mail coming in has been good. I've told you before,' he said, 'there are four, four and a half million Nixon Nuts out there, that no matter what I do, it wouldn't make any difference to them. They'd still support me. Some of the mail was from them, of course. But, yes, I'm satisfied with how the interviews have gone.'

"He called those hard-core supporters 'the nutty fringe,' but he feels there are enough of them so that they can't be ignored by other Republican politicians. Nixon feels the party can't afford to alienate them.

"He would most likely deny it, but it wouldn't surprise me to see Nixon play some kind of role in the politics of the future. One thing I learned in the Johnson White House was that no matter what they say publicly or to save their own hides, what any politician admires in another is competence.

That's why I wasn't surprised that Nixon was invited back to Washington for Humphrey's funeral, or that he came.

"He and Humphrey used to talk on the telephone after Nixon left office, and certainly he and Humphrey never became enemies. If Humphrey made an attack on Nixon, it was because of political expediency, but there was mutual respect there for the other guy's ability. The fact that Carter invited Nixon to the White House dinner honoring the Chinese Vice Premier, Teng Hsiao-Ping, was another example of political antagonists recognizing each other's competence.

"That's my opinion about the situation among the politicians. But as far as the public is concerned, it's another matter, and I think Nixon has a pretty clear idea of his position there. From the minute he left office he wanted to exert some influence on the government, and he still does. It isn't because he's like an old racehorse who can't stop racing when he hears a gun go off; he believes he has an expertise, especially in foreign affairs, and he's frustrated.

"But at no point that I could see did he have any illusions about his chances of reentering public life. I was out in San Clemente the day after Goldwater had visited him in late September 1974, not long after he resigned. Goldwater, who was known to get in the bottle with the devil on occasion, had left his meeting with Nixon and gone down to the San Clemente Inn and talked to some press people in the bar.

"Apparently Goldwater told them Nixon had said he'd like to be ambassador to China; that he'd be interested in being an ambassador-at-large; that he wanted to be a voice in America's foreign policy. It hit the paper the morning I arrived, and when I walked into his office Nixon said, 'Did you see that report in the paper about Goldwater's visit yesterday?'

"I said I had, and Nixon said, 'Well, it's all a goddamn lie. I never told Goldwater a goddamn thing about wanting to be an ambassador, to China or anyplace else. Goldwater probably went down there to the San Clemente Inn, got drunk, and made those goddamn dumb statements.

" 'On the other hand,' Nixon said, 'maybe he never said a thing. Maybe The Goddamnpress printed it on their own. They might have taken whatever Goldwater *did* say out of context—that's what the bastards do constantly. They take things out of context; they print what they want to print; and you've got no recourse. Once it hits the headlines, there's no recourse.

" 'But I would never even speculate about a thing like being ambassador. Christ, I know how the American public would accept a thing like that. Not in any foreseeable future,' Nixon said, 'can I see being able to participate in any way in government. There may be a few million hard-core Nixonites out there, but there are hundreds of millions of others who are anti-Nixon. I know that.'

"Still, I knew Nixon wanted to play some kind of political role and was just waiting to be asked.

"The biggest change I saw in Richard Nixon, the thing that set him on the road to recovery, came when the Ford people asked me to find out if Nixon would be interested in giving them political advice during the campaign.

"Nixon sat in the middle of the Ford-Reagan seesaw during the Republican primaries, but all along he was aware of things he considered weaknesses in Ford. For one thing, Ford didn't appear to understand what he was dealing with in Reagan.

"One time Nixon was appalled by an off-the-cuff remark Mrs. Ford made about Mrs. Reagan, because as he said to me at the time, 'Nancy Reagan runs Ronald Reagan. She's a very strong woman, and if you make her angry, you're never going to pull this guy into camp, and Ford's really going to need Reagan after the convention. In fact, if he doesn't change his ways, he's not even going to get the nomination, Reagan's going to get it. He just cannot afford to alienate Nancy Reagan, because she's the guy's chief advisor.

" 'I'm telling you,' Nixon said, 'Nancy Reagan's a bitch, a demanding one, and he listens to her.'

"The Ford people were political amateurs; they were just thrashing around in water way too deep for them from the outset. It was obvious they were going to need help if they were going to do what should be one of the easiest things in politics—make sure the incumbent, with all his advantages, gets nominated by his own party. One thing you can say about Nixon is that he's a real political pro; he's got a better grasp of national politics than just about anybody else, and he knew all the players.

"The Ford people recognized that, and although they knew the terrible risk they were running, that the Press would find out they were holding hands with Richard Nixon, they felt they would be running a greater risk if they didn't get his help.

"So one day just before I was leaving for San Clemente in the spring of 1975, Don Rumsfeld, Ford's chief of staff, said to me, 'Would you, if the opportunity presents itself, tell the former President that we would welcome any advice that he might care to give us. Tell him it would be held in confidence, and that it would be appreciated.'

"I gave that message to Nixon, and from then on I carried back an endless stream of instructions about how they should conduct the campaign, who they should contact in which states, which states they should work on and how to go about it. It was obvious to me the Ford people lacked any real understanding of Presidential politics, because they would furiously write, they would take down verbatim, all the information I brought back from Nixon. They wrote down every word Nixon said.

"Shortly after Carter was nominated in 1976, Nixon told me which states Ford had to change over if he was going to win. He listed them. One list headed 'Carter,' the other 'Ford,' and under each he put down how every state would go unless Ford made all the right moves. This was before the Republican convention had even taken place, but in November, when the final results were in, Nixon had been right. In July he'd known to the last state which way it would go and what would happen unless Ford could pull in a few big ones like Ohio and Texas.

"Then, after the Republican convention was over and I walked in the following Monday morning, it was as if he had just been waiting for me, waiting to roll up his sleeves. The minute I walked in he said, 'O.K. Now we know who our guy is, we know who their guy is. Let's go to work.' Those were his exact words. He was excited and eager, his whole bearing was: 'O.K. We've been waiting, now we've got the meat. Let's get with it.'

"Right away we got into the point spread in the polls and how it was false. Then he had instructions for Dick Cheney, who by then was Ford's chief of staff, about what to do with this guy in this state and that guy in that state. He went into personalities, which ones had to be contacted and why. I was writing notes furiously to take back to the White House, and he was going without stopping for breath.

"At the end of that first session he said to me, 'You know, goddamn, you may be the Machiavelli of our times!' Well, and this is the honest truth, I said to myself, 'Who the hell was Machiavelli? I've heard of Machiavelli. What kind of role did this bastard play? Was he a spy? What was Machiavelli?'

"Nixon considered himself an authority on TV debates after his own experience with John Kennedy. He wrote about it in his book *Six Crises,* he's studied tapes of those debates, and he sent back pages of advice to Ford on points to remember in debating Carter. Points like what to wear, where to stand, and to be rested. How the content of the programs should be structured. What *not* to do.

"On one sheet of paper Nixon jotted down advice ranging from how Ford should react if Carter turned mean (he should be saddened, not angry) to tips such as the importance of having Ford's own TV advisor in the control truck (to prevent bias in the choice of shots to be broadcast). Nixon also reminded Ford that how he looked and conducted himself would count for more than the substance of the debates and advised him to be sure to deliver a couple of 'spontaneously' funny lines.

"Nixon kept telling them to stroke John Connally, and they didn't. They waited too long, possibly on the advice of Don Rumsfeld and others who were more worried about Connally as a possible Republican candidate in 1980 than about the 1976 election. Nixon kept saying, 'They're spending their whole time running against Reagan and Connally instead of Carter.' And, of course, in the closing days they spent all their time and money on lost causes like Pennsylvania and New York, and on a sure thing like California.

"During most of the campaign, the Ford people followed Nixon's advice, but in the last week or ten days they stopped listening to him and winged it. Just as the tide was turning toward them, they panicked. All of a sudden they thought they could carry New York, for example. Nixon had told them Carter would ride in on Moynihan's coattails; Moynihan was running for the Senate and was very popular. Nixon told them that would put New York out of reach, but they stopped listening and squandered valuable time and money there.

"In the end, when they just about had their opponent on the ropes, they knocked themselves out."

"Most of the time things were very relaxed between us, but every now and again the suspicious side of Nixon would pop out. Once, when we were deep in his giving political advice to Ford, he got very wrought up.

"We'd been talking about Kissinger. Nixon had told me that Kissinger had called him a couple of days before and said he was going to resign, that he couldn't stay in the Ford Administration. Nixon said he'd talked Kissinger into staying with Ford and said to me, 'Kissinger's absolutely essential to Ford, but he's a difficult man with a difficult ego.' Then Nixon said that about how Henry sometimes had to be kicked in the nuts, that sometimes he got to thinking *he* was President. 'However,' Nixon said, 'the need for Henry Kissinger is beyond description.'

"Then, suddenly, he became all bristling and suspicious. He turned on me, his voice hard, and said, 'I want to know exactly who you are going to talk to about this—or the game is over.'

"Mostly our visits are relaxed and easygoing. At one point, during the Ford campaign, Nixon began calling me 'the General.' And he does to this day. I just walked in one day, and he said, 'Well, General, you're back in California.' He still calls me that.

"His attitude toward me hasn't changed since I left the White House. It hasn't turned out that his only interest in me was my being at the White House. He's just as friendly and seems to be as interested as when I was there.

"My visits with Nixon are now more social visits than anything else. He talks about the book he's writing and asks about mine. I told him I would be writing about him and his Administration, and all he said was he hoped the book did well. Our conversations are loose and rambling; there are none of the ribald jokes or boyhood memories of LBJ; and they're not deeply personal. He'll occasionally talk about his daughters, but he hasn't mentioned his brothers more than five times in all the hours we've spent together.

"What he really likes is political speculation. We talk a lot about the 1980 election and the strengths and weaknesses of the various candidates. What this one needs to do to get anywhere, and why it doesn't matter what that one does because he can't get anywhere anyway.

"There's been a great change in Richard Nixon since August of 1974. He now feels that his accomplishments while he was President will be far more lasting than what drove him from office. He feels assured he has a place in history—a positive one.

"It's no longer of any consequence to him whether he's accorded the status symbols of an ex-President; for one thing, he can now afford what he wants. He doesn't care about the perks, although he's entitled to be called Mr. President, and wants to be called Mr. President. I think he feels he'll be vindicated by history. He's more or less at peace with himself."

IV

CHAPTER

Gerald Ford
and
Jimmy Carter

"SUCCESSIVE PRESIDENTS," historian Henry Steele Commager says, "have tried to wash their hands of personal responsibility for the lawlessness and corruption so pervasive in our government in the last decade or so. But whoever planned and launched the Bay of Pigs, whoever engineered the Tonkin Gulf fraud, directed the secret war in Laos . . . whoever concocted Watergate . . . for all these the ultimate responsibility lodges in the White House. It is the President who sets the moral tone. . . . It is the President therefore who must be assigned responsibility. . . .

". . . But it is insufficient, it is almost trivial, to assign full responsibility [for our current sickness] to particular Presidents. After all, it is the American people who elected them . . . our government and politics, with all their knaveries, vulgarities and dishonesties, more or less reflect American society, and even the American character . . . we are, in fact, getting the kind of government that we want. The fault, in short, is in ourselves." *

* Reprinted with permission from *The New York Review of Books*. Copyright © 1973 Nyrev, Inc.

Commager suggests that there have been significant changes in the American mind and character, a shift he attributes to a decline in individualism. "I mean," he says, "the growth of a habit of mind that responds uncritically to manipulation. . . ." He points to the militaristic moves our country has made in the name of peace: creating the world's greatest arsenal; establishing worldwide military bases; overthrowing governments—all in the name of peace. "Wonderland logic" is what Commager calls it, and he fears for the true independence of the American people when they can apparently be manipulated into accepting anything.

There is, however, another point of view about what's happened to the American electorate. It holds that rather than being manipulated, the public has become aware of its own strength and is busily unseating one President after another. When party lines are being crossed and tickets split in a way that suggests you can't count on anything; when the two Presidents with the largest election victories in American history are both driven from office, perhaps unpredictability rather than malleability has become the hallmark of the American voter.

Gerald Ford

AFTER THE EVASIVENESS and furtiveness of the previous two and a half years, the country greeted Gerald Ford with a huge collective sigh of relief. He told the people he wanted to be a Ford, not a Lincoln, and they happily settled for that. The nation took the new President to its weary heart.

The big blond midwesterner with an easy smile who had been a college football hero, had a handsome family, and lived modestly, fitted the American self-picture. His humility, candor, even his hesitancy in front of the television cameras, endeared him to the people. Gerald R. Ford, congressman from Michigan's Fifth District, who never expected it, was suddenly Vice President to the most hated President in history. Jerry Ford was in a tough spot and the public sympathized.

When he became President he was welcomed with an unparalleled outpouring of nonpartisan goodwill. The voices of Democrats and Republicans, liberals and conservatives, blended together, if not in the Hallelujah Chorus, at least in a few bars of "For He's a Jolly Good Fellow." Ford held out hope for a return to normality, to sanity in the government and the nation.

Nixon, whose judgment of men was not always sound, in one sense chose well in Ford. He had many of the right qualities for the time. That he was so patently a nice guy who had aimed for nothing higher than the post he'd reached, leader of his party in the House of Representatives, was soothing to a people who had had enough of the high-handed treatment they'd received from his ambitious and willful predecessors, Johnson and Nixon.

Ford took office pledging a time to heal, and, by and large, he lived up to that promise, although the harmony of his welcome was ruptured by his decision to "put Watergate behind us" and grant Nixon a full pardon. There were those who felt betrayed because Nixon had not been sent to trial, and others who cried that a deal had been struck: the Presidency for a Pardon. Some, like Gulley, felt that whatever Nixon had done, prison was no place for a former President; others agreed with Ford that the business of government couldn't proceed until an end was put to the Nixon question.

The merits of granting Nixon a full pardon will continue to be debated, but by the time Ford left office the country, which had been reeling when he became President, was regaining its balance. The fact that he had restored a degree of calm, however, wasn't enough to win him his own term as President. Ironically, it was some of the same qualities that made Ford such a good guy that also interfered with his ability to lead.

He was loyal to old friends, sometimes beyond the bounds of good judgment; he was tolerant of the weaknesses of others, and the Administration paid a price for it; he frequently allowed himself to be trapped by his own good nature. The same character traits that reassured the country and helped it regain emotional stability hampered him in creating a strong Presidency.

THE FORD WHITE HOUSE

The contrast with the two previous administrations, those of Nixon and Johnson, was marked. Neither of his predecessors was a "nice guy"; they were tough political animals, and their administrations reflected it. Johnson directly and Nixon through Haldeman exercised tight control over the White House, and staff members performed to their satisfaction or were dismissed.

256

When Ford took office, of course, Watergate had swept away Haldeman, Ehrlichman, Colson and most of Nixon's key aides, but a few important ones remained: Kissinger, Haig, Scowcroft and Rumsfeld—who at Ford's request returned from his post at NATO. Among those Ford brought with him were Hartmann, who had been his Vice Presidential chief of staff; Marsh, an ex-congressman from Virginia; and Buchen, a former law partner.

It was not an easy mix. The Nixon holdovers saw the Ford people as inexperienced and indecisive; the Ford staff regarded the Nixon men with uncertainty and distrust—from the start there was domestic disharmony. The disruption caused by the inevitable petty infighting and status seeking that marks every new administration was intensified and made more serious by the tensions between the Nixon and Ford groups. After Haig was replaced by Rumsfeld as chief of staff, the temperature lowered, but bitterness remained. A firm, decisive hand was needed to bring order to the White House.

"I never agreed with Lyndon Johnson's judgment of Ford, that 'he can't fart and chew gum at the same time,' but I do believe that Ford's strong feelings about his friends got in his way," Gulley says. "Hartmann was probably the biggest problem. He'd been with the President a long time and head of his staff when Ford was Vice President, so he was expecting a big job. When he didn't get one, he was frustrated, and his drinking didn't make him any easier to deal with.

"Thought was given to ways of getting him out of the White House, including appointing him Secretary of the Navy. When I was talking to Nixon about the trouble Ford was having with Hartmann and told him what was suggested, Nixon said, 'That'd be a great place for him. Why, we even had John Warner in that job. It's a job anyone can do, and he can't do any harm over there. If it'll get Hartmann out of the White House, Jerry should do it.' But he didn't; Hartmann stayed.

"In that same conversation at San Clemente, Nixon said, 'One of Jerry's biggest problems is he doesn't have the balls to take them on head to head and get rid of the people he should. He doesn't run a taut enough ship.' It was true that the White House was disorganized and drifting. Rumsfeld was a strong figure who understood Ford and brought some order into the situation, but the staff was still loose-jointed.

"Ford couldn't seem to get a firm grip on the White House, but he was a hell of a nice guy, and unlike Johnson, Nixon and Carter, he was easy to be with. It was no secret that I'm a baseball fan, and in 1976 the President asked me to join a group that was going to the All-Star Game on July 13. It was played in Philadelphia, and the Carpenters, who own the Phillies, had gone all out with a well-stocked bar in their box, so everyone was feeling very good as we climbed back on *Air Force One*.

"It was after midnight by the time we got airborne, which made it July 14, the President's birthday. The crew of *Air Force One* came up with a cake and broke out some champagne, so Ford asked the Press to join him in the staff section of the plane and help him celebrate. Joe Garagiola, the sports commentator, was one of the guests, and a Ford aide asked him to make a toast.

" 'Hell, I can't talk toasts to Presidents,' Garagiola said. Then he turned to me and said, 'Bill, you know how to say a toast; you do it.' I went completely blank with everybody quiet and looking at me, when from somewhere a toast came to me. I raised my glass to the President and said, 'Here's to honor. Get on her and stay on her.'

"Ford's eyes popped; then he broke into big guffaws while I was wondering how the hell I'd come up with something so totally inappropriate, and in front of the whole Press corps. The next morning I decided I'd made a major fool of myself, until I got an envelope with a photograph in it from Ford. He had signed it: 'To the Honor-able Bill Gulley, regards, Gerald R. Ford.' "

"To hear the stories about drinking in the White House, you could believe most of our recent Presidents have been alcoholics, which is not the case. Lyndon Johnson drank more than the next three Presidents put together, and held it better. Ford wasn't a big drinker, but he showed his liquor the minute he swallowed it.

"Coming back from his trip to Vladivostok at the end of 1974, Ford, like everyone else on board *Air Force One,* had taken precautions against the Russian winter. An hour or so after he had gone to his cabin for a nap, the pilot and copilot were totally unnerved when the door to the cockpit opened and there was the President of the United States in his undershorts. He'd been looking for the john.

"Because Ford had this embarrassing way of showing his drink, when Rumsfeld became chief of staff he decided that to protect Ford's image, liquor would not be served on *Air Force One* until the last, homeward leg of any trip. It seemed like a good idea, but nothing ever came of it.

"On the first trip Hartmann took on *Air Force One* after Rumsfeld's prohibition order came down, he asked the steward for a screwdriver as soon as he got on the plane. The steward, not knowing what to do, went to McClelland, the pilot, who called me at the White House. He said, 'Look, Bill, we can't be put in this position. We can't be expected to tell the President's senior staff they can't have a drink.'

"It was agreed there was no way the stewards could be asked to refuse to serve Hartmann or anybody else, but they were instructed to make the drinks, especially the President's drinks, as weak as they could and get away with it."

"When the President of the United States goes anywhere, it's like moving a palace. Planeloads of people and equipment precede him and go with him. The doctor, aides, communications material and personnel, Secret Service, backup aircraft, sometimes helicopters and cars. The public doesn't see it, but there's an invasion when a President arrives in a city or town. The support troops arrive as much as a week before he does, and sometimes stay two days after he leaves.

"When Ford went to Vail he used to rent what was probably the most elaborate residence there, with a heated swimming pool and all the comforts. Over Christmas of 1975 I'd rented a villa for the military that was just a little farther up the mountain and connected to Ford's by a narrow, winding road.

"We had been partying with a few of the local young ladies one evening and around midnight four of us decided to take a totally unauthorized dip in the President's pool. Among the equipment that had been flown in for Ford were guard booths, small, heated boxes for the Secret Service agents to stand in. They were worse than useless because the visibility was restricted and the agent couldn't hear anything that happened outside. As we discovered.

"The four of us went down the path, through the fence that enclosed the pool, took off our clothes and splashed around in the nice warm water for close to an hour. Which tells you something about Secret Service protection of the President, and something about the Ford White House.

"We would no more have considered sneaking into Richard Nixon's pool to go skinny-dipping than we would into Lyndon Johnson's—hell, one of Johnson's closest aides, Jim Cross, who'd been with him for over ten years, was scared to death to be sitting in his study drinking his Scotch after Johnson was *dead*."

In the Johnson White House, aides were constantly warning each other they'd be "hung" or "killed" if the President found them out; under Nixon, Haldeman was a walking threat of swift retribution. In the easygoing atmosphere generated by Ford, caution wasn't so necessary; if he liked you, you could take liberties.

"On more than one occasion," Gulley says, "Ford got boxed in by his own good nature. One of our staff, Robert Blake, who'd been Ford's military aide while he was Vice President, had brought an amateur singing group, a barbershop quartet, into the White House Staff Mess for a party the military were having. Which was fine, and we all enjoyed it. But Blake was so pleased with them he decided the President should hear this group.

"It was about nine o'clock at night, but Blake took the group up to the Oval Office, where the President was working late. Terry O'Donnell, the appointments secretary, was there and wouldn't let the little choir in, but as they were standing discussing it, the President, who was obviously tired, came out the door of his office. Blake cornered him, the quartet broke into song, and the President stood and listened—trapped because he's just a nice man."

The impact of Ford's personality on the White House affected its efficiency, which was a matter of some importance;

of greater concern was the effect it had on state business. In the wake of revelations triggered by Seymour Hersh's story in *The New York Times* exposing illegal activities by the CIA, Ford saw he would have to take some kind of action. It became clearer still when the CIA director, William Colby, briefed him on the "family jewels," documents having to do with such unsavory activities as plotting the assassination of foreign leaders.

"Ford appointed Jack Marsh to head a committee to deal with the problems in our intelligence community," Gulley says, "and one of the first things Marsh did was pick Mike Duval to be the executive director of the committee. Duval was a bright young guy, and he obviously dazzled Marsh, but the fact is that neither he nor Marsh had any background in the field. Marsh was a counselor to Ford and liaison with Congress, and Duval was on his staff, but without any expertise in the area. One of the senior National Security people told me, 'Mike Duval has just enough intelligence about the intelligence community to be dangerous.'

"This was something Nixon and I talked about in San Clemente. Nixon was concerned that Ford might overreact, particularly to the heavy criticism the intelligence community was getting about its role in the overthrow of the Allende Government in Chile. Nixon said, 'There are certain things you have to do as a world leader. You have to become involved in things you don't want to become involved in, but you do. I hope in order to keep our credibility with other governments Ford doesn't go too far in giving in to the liberals and start dismantling our intelligence community.'

"Ford took a beating on the way the investigation was handled, and on the committees that worked on it. Some of his trouble, I think, came from his feeling that if he trusted somebody and thought he made sense, he'd let him take on a job he might not be suited for.

"In March 1975, Ford sent General Frederick Weyand, the chief of staff of the Army, to Vietnam to get a firsthand account of the situation. Things were desperate there, and by the end of April it would be all over, so in all the confusion Ford wanted a direct report. While Weyand's mission was being discussed in the Oval Office, David Kennerly, Ford's pet photographer and a nice young man who came to be like a member of the family, was snapping pictures. After the meeting, Kennerly, who'd spent more than two years in Vietnam as a photographer with Time-Life, asked Ford if he could please go along with Weyand. Ford agreed.

"When Weyand and Kennerly returned, Ford was in Palm Springs on vacation, for which the President took a lot of heat since the citizens felt he shouldn't be playing golf while Vietnam went down the tubes. The general and the photographer went directly out to see him, and Weyand made his report. Then, as soon as Weyand finished, Kennerly gave *his* report, and the President, I've been reliably told, gave equal weight to the two reports in the discussions that followed.

"I don't quarrel with getting a second opinion, especially where the military is concerned. If Ford wanted a civilian assessment, then he should have sent a qualified guy, or even two or three guys. It was typical of Ford, though, to let a kid in his twenties, whose business was picture taking, share the Presidential ear on a subject as vast and terrible as the last days of Vietnam."

THE FORD CAMPAIGN

"I'd known from the time of Nixon's resignation that some kind of contact was going to have to be maintained between him and Ford. There were all the things he'd done in the foreign area, with the Chinese and the Russians; Kissinger and Scowcroft were staying on, and Nixon was their mentor; Nixon *had* to play a role in the Ford White House.

"I also knew, better than anybody, that a communications corridor would have to be established between Nixon and Ford because Nixon was a former President, and I'd seen what happened after Johnson left office. What I didn't realize was that the biggest role Nixon would play in the Ford White House and the thing that would keep them in constant contact wouldn't be foreign affairs but Presidential politics.

"From the time Rumsfeld first asked me to sound Nixon out on giving them political advice for Ford's campaign, in

March of 1975, there was an endless stream of communication going back and forth through me. The difficulty, naturally, was that it would be politically serious, if not fatal, for Ford if word of it got out. But as I've said, they needed help so badly, they ran the risk of being found out.

"The Ford campaign was basically a seat-of-the-pants operation. Campaign speeches were being written, if you can call it that, on *Air Force One* on the way to speaking engagements, by third- and fourth-level advance men. Hartmann, who was supposed to be in charge of speech writing, wasn't exercising control. They hired a so-called comedian, Don Penny, to bring some deliberate humor into the Ford campaign instead of only drawing laughs from Ford's accidental stumbles and pratfalls.

"I even got a call from a guy suggesting we pad the top of the helicopter doors so Ford wouldn't hurt himself when he hit his head, and when I pointed out what the Press would do with it, he said, 'Gee, I never thought of that.'

"When the Ford people did get an advantage, they didn't know how to use it. After Jimmy Carter's remarks criticizing Lyndon Johnson had been released by *Playboy* at the end of September, and he'd succeeded in getting Lady Bird Johnson and the girls furious with him, Dick Cheney called me.

"He said Ford was planning a campaign trip to Texas and asked me to get hold of Luci Johnson Nugent and tell her the President would like her and her husband, Pat, to be his guests at a University of Texas football game. I talked to Luci, who said she had season tickets but would be happy to give them up and sit with the President.

"It was one of those opportunities candidates dream about, and it just dropped into his hands. Carter had the Texans so mad at him that even Ford was beginning to look good—and now Lyndon Johnson's daughter was openly going to be seen with him.

"When the day came, Luci went to the University of Texas game and sat in the group around Ford—but everybody ignored her. They hardly even talked to her. Instead of having her sitting on his lap, Ford and the whole staff seemed to forget she was there.

"Nixon's campaign of 1972 was a slick, professional job,

whatever else it was, and the advice he sent back to Ford covered the whole field of campaign politics from dissecting what the polls meant to what certain Administration members shouldn't do. 'Kissinger's talking too much about black Africa,' Nixon told the Ford people. 'It's pissing off the rednecks. The Negro vote's lost; don't let it lose you white votes. The Democrats have the Negroes and the Jews, and let them have them—in fact, tie them around their necks.'

"Nixon was horrified by the amateur way the campaign was being handled. 'Jerry's running for President of the United States now,' he said, 'not just a seat in the House.' Another time, after Ford was nominated, Nixon said Ford couldn't seem to understand that the situation had changed. 'Jerry seems to have lost sight of the fact that he's running against the Democrats, not Reagan,' he said.

"Nixon was particularly concerned that Ford make use of the exposure the television debates would give him and went into detail about the big and little ways he could make them work for him.

" 'Don't worry about what you say about Nixon,' Nixon said. 'Murder me. I understand. Remember, Carter scares the hell out of me. Scare the hell out of the American people about Carter's foreign policies; bear down on it. He'll come close to making us a number two power.' Later he said, 'Hell, if Carter wins we'll never get SALT II.'

"He advised Ford to use his natural advantages. His appearance—he was big and healthy-looking—and the fact of his being Mr. Nice Guy. 'The American people wouldn't accept it if Carter went after Jerry Ford with a knife,' Nixon said. 'They'd accept it all right if it was Dick Nixon, but not Jerry Ford.' He also advised Ford to use the fact that he was the President.

" 'An international incident can be useful to Ford,' Nixon said. 'But be careful how you use it. If an international situation blows up, dramatize it. He's the President. Of course if it comes out I suggested it, they'll say, "Nixon says start a war." '

"He also suggested using John Mitchell in New Jersey and Missouri. 'He knows more about those two states than anybody around. He can be useful behind the scenes,' Nixon said, 'but it's got to be covert.' And he told the Ford people that whatever they did, they should keep Hartmann out of California. 'The Republicans in California hate him,' Nixon said."

"Nixon had been sending campaign advice since early 1975, and the Ford people were inhaling it as fast as it came in. Everybody was happy, until February 1976, just before the New Hampshire primary, when they found out Nixon was going to China. That made everybody very unhappy. Ford says he was 'astounded,' and that his aides 'couldn't believe it'; they were also in a red-eyed rage. Marsh and Hartmann said Nixon was doing it deliberately so that Ford would lose and Reagan would win New Hampshire, and the expletives were flying.

"Nixon had told Ford in January that he'd lie low the whole year so as not to stir up the pardon and remind everybody of the connection between them; then a few weeks later, on February 5, the Chinese handed Scowcroft a news release they were giving out about Nixon's trip. The Ford people were dumbfounded.

"There's never been a satisfactory explanation for why Nixon took the trip when he did. Nixon told Kissinger, for Ford's ears, that the Chinese hadn't told him until thirty-six hours before, which wasn't true, because Nixon told me about the trip when I saw him at the Annenberg estate in Palm Springs in January.

"Nixon told me then, 'Now that Ford's been to Russia and China, I can go again.' He also said, 'Jerry's got New Hampshire anyway, this won't hurt him; and it's better if I go now than closer to the election.' Which didn't explain anything, because a few weeks earlier Nixon had told me he'd thought of flying to New Hampshire to have his portrait done by Wyeth but didn't want to disturb things there for Ford since it was an important primary.

"The day of the primary, February 24, the country's newspapers were full of pictures of Nixon in Peking, and the Ford people were sure they could hear the sound of loud crowing come from the Reagan camp. But Ford won seventeen delegates to Reagan's four, so they relaxed a little, and they didn't stop welcoming, and following, Nixon's advice. But at the same time, Ford's Vice President, Nelson Rockefeller, surfaced a story that quickly did the rounds of the Washington cocktail parties.

"Rockefeller and Nixon were old antagonists since 1968 and before, and not the kind that dust each other off and walk away arm in arm after the fight's over. Rockefeller was a natural to hit back at Nixon for his timing of the China trip, and he was telling everybody that the former President had come home from Peking with a million dollars. He said the money had been laundered through the Bahamas, gone out to China and that Nixon brought it back with him. I frankly didn't know what to make of the story, and still don't; the whole China episode was so weird, anything seemed possible.

"When Nixon got back and wrote a report on his assessment of the situation in China, the Ford people came in for a round of accusations that they were maintaining secret contact with the former President. I was drawn into the controversy because both the President and Nixon wanted the report to be a confidential communication, and to be handled that way, so I flew out to California and brought it back. When the Press found out about all the special care surrounding Nixon's report, they made a big, bad mystery out of it.

"They wanted to know every move I'd made with that report—if I'd carried it or mailed it, what kind of transport I'd used, why I had been the one handling it. The transcript of the March 22, 1976, press conference dealing only with details like that runs to twenty-six pages. I wondered at the time, and still do, what would have happened if they'd ever found out I was running information back and forth between San Clemente and the White House on unmarked Jet Stars every other week."

FORD'S FAMILY

"Ford was so open and friendly, so accessible," Gulley says, "that lower-echelon staffers who would never have gone to the family quarters in Johnson's or Nixon's day, would be found sitting with Ford in his living room drinking martinis and giving him advice on how to run the government.

"One time when Rumsfeld went in to see Ford and found one of our military aides doing just that, telling the President what he should do on a foreign policy matter, Rumsfeld told us to have him transferred right away. There was a feeling among the people who cared about Ford, not only that he was being taken advantage of, but that he might be swayed by uninformed opinions.

"The situation was less serious but more extreme with Mrs. Ford. One of the first times I saw her after they moved into the White House, she came into my office arm in arm with a member of her staff who called Mrs. Ford 'Petunia.' In my opinion she was preyed upon and taken advantage of by individuals on her own staff and her husband's, ambitious people who couldn't make their mark directly on the President and tried to advance themselves through his wife.

"An aide in our office, Colonel Americus Sardo, set out to catch the First Lady's attention by telling her tales about all the plots the Nixon holdovers were hatching against her.

"He naturally offered himself as her protector, and she can't be blamed for accepting the hand of what appeared to be friendship, but it only made worse a bad situation between the old and new staffers.

"In my opinion, the brashest member of the First Lady's staff, and the most ambitious, was her press secretary, Sheila Weidenfeld. The minute she walked in the door of the White House, she seemed to view it as the place where she was going to become Somebody, started figuring the angles, and appeared determined to play on the 'A' team with the big boys, such as they were in the Ford White House. She didn't waste any time trying to work her way in.

"Seeing right away that status symbols define your position in the hierarchy, she badgered me for a chauffeur-driven limousine, a ticker-tape machine and all the same toys Ron Nessen, the President's press secretary, had. I can't judge how she handled her job, although I heard plenty of comments, but she moved right into the professional class, alongside Kissinger and Haig, in her longing for perks.

"When Weidenfeld's frontal assault on the President's staff

failed and she was brushed off, she tried to gain entry to the power structure through the Ford children, and her main target was Jack Ford. In December of 1976, Dick Keiser, one of the President's Secret Service agents, came to me and said he was concerned about a meeting Weidenfeld had set up for Jack Ford in Vail when the family would be there at Christmas.

"Weidenfeld was promoting a business deal between Jack Ford, herself and her husband, and this man who was the cause of Secret Service's concern. This person Jack Ford was supposed to meet with, Keiser told me, was considered 'highly suspect by the Secret Service, and had questionable associations.' He said a stop should be put to the meeting, and it was. Jack Ford, of course, was completely unaware of who this guy was he was supposed to meet with; all he knew was Weidenfeld had suggested it, and he'd gone along. Jack Ford, like the other children, considered her their friend.

"The waters around the Oval Office are always shark-infested, but there was something really offensive about seeing them prey on people as vulnerable as Mrs. Ford and the children, and on somebody as straight and well meaning as Gerald Ford."

"There's an incident that happened just days before Ford left office that sums up, in a particularly idiotic way, some of what was wrong with the way his Administration was run.

"On a Saturday in January 1977, Dick Cheney, who was chief of staff, called and asked me to come to his office. Jack Marsh was there, and they had a problem they wanted to discuss. Rosalynn Carter, the about-to-be First Lady, was coming to Washington to interview people for her staff on Monday and was arriving the next evening, Sunday, expecting to stay at Blair House overnight. The problem was that Phil Buchen, Ford's legal advisor, had been given permission to have a party at Blair House Sunday night.

"Scowcroft had joined us, and when Marsh and Cheney outlined the situation, he immediately said, 'Where's the problem? Tell Buchen he'll have his party somewhere else.' Instead of saying O.K., picking up the phone and calling

Buchen, they said, 'Oh, no. We can't do that. Buchen would go right to the President, and you know how the President feels about Phil. He'd get all upset.'

"I couldn't believe what I was hearing, but it got even more unbelievable. Jack Marsh actually suggested they bring Mrs. Carter in through the back door of Blair House and up the rear stairs. Scowcroft was speechless, and although I found a few words to say about hustling the future First Lady through the back door, they wouldn't budge. They were determined Phil Buchen would have his party at Blair House—which he had no right to use in the first place.

"The end of the story was that I suggested calling Mrs. Carter and telling her I had a plane that would be near Plains early Monday morning and could pick her up, saving her spending a night away from home, at Blair House. Cheney and Marsh clutched at the idea. I set it up with Mrs. Carter, and, since, of course, I didn't have a plane in Georgia, I sent one down to get her first thing Monday morning. The entire exercise cost the American taxpayer about $3,000.

"Shortly before Ford left office, Nixon sent a message to him through me. It was a handwritten letter in which he quoted a verse he said he'd run across while doing research for his book. The theme is that what appears to be an end is really a new beginning and that although one fight may be lost there will be another equally worthwhile."

"The other Presidents I saw tried to be two people; they schemed to show the electorate somebody they thought it wanted to see and cover up the rest. Except for a few tries to polish him up and make him look 'Presidential,' Ford was just himself, and he was tossed into a no-win situation. The citizens demanded a good, open man who wouldn't mislead them; but to control the politicians, he needed to be a tough, hardball player. Gerald Ford didn't have the son-of-a-bitch factor."

Jimmy Carter

ONE OF THE VERY THINGS that made Ford desirable to the American electorate, his easygoing good nature, ultimately hampered his effectiveness and helped defeat him in his bid for his own term as President. In the same way, one of the qualities that most attracted the public to Jimmy Carter—that he was an outsider without ties to Washington and all that conveyed—has contributed heavily to *his* difficulty in becoming an effective leader.

In discussing the Presidency, Wilfred Binkley wrote, "Curiously enough, it is when the electorate is most thoroughly aroused that it usually elects a symbol rather than a candidate distinguished by demonstrated competence for the Presidency." He was talking about the postwar elections of General Grant over Governor Horatio Seymour in 1868, and General Eisenhower over Governor Adlai Stevenson in 1952, but the point is valid when applied to the post-Watergate period. Carter's experience was considered virtually irrelevant; what mattered was that he was An Honest Man. Even when a majority of Americans later criticized him harshly for incompetence, that same majority reaffirmed its view of him as essentially sincere.

Men and women who have had the opportunity to talk to Carter alone or in small groups have come away impressed with his intelligence and desire to help the country solve its problems. At the same time, they have left discussions with him disturbed and concerned about whether he would be able to develop strong positions and then hold to them.

Through it all, however, Carter the man has been viewed, by and large, as honest and without duplicity.

Gulley's view of Carter is considerably harsher and is based on his experiences during the first ten months of the Carter Administration. "After eleven years at the White House," Gulley says, "my rose-colored glasses were long gone; in fact they broke right after I got to the LBJ White House. It's just not possible to spend any length of time close to the Presidency and have any illusions left, so I wasn't expecting a saint when Carter was elected, even if he had won on a preacher's platform of 'Trust Me.'

"The first time I went down to Plains to brief him on the military support available to the President, on December 10, before Carter took office, I was aware, of course, that he hadn't had any experience in Washington. Hell, it was one of the things that got him elected. So I was surprised at the way he got right into specifics in areas in which he couldn't, and didn't, have any knowledge.

"Carter met me at the door of his house, and I was struck by his size; I was as surprised by how small he was as I had been at how big Johnson was. We went into the study, and I hauled out copies of the briefing papers I'd sent ahead and the talking papers I'd brought with me, and we got right into details.

"Carter immediately started punctuating one item after another by saying, 'I want that cut 70 percent,' and 'That will be reduced by 30 percent,' and so on right down the list. I was really taken aback, because here he was in Plains, Georgia; he hadn't set a foot inside the White House, didn't have the first idea of what it takes to run the Presidency; yet he was telling me by what specific percentage each thing was to be cut. We weren't talking in generalities or symbols; we were talking numbers.

"When we got to Camp David, for example, he said, 'Camp David costs too much money. I want it closed.' When I asked him if he knew what all was at Camp David, he said, 'Yes.

271

Cabins.' I asked him if he was aware of the other facilities that were there, and he said, 'I don't know anything about it. I don't even know anyone who's been there.' I explained about the bomb shelter, and the emergency communications center, and it was all news to him. But without knowing anything about it, he'd been ready to order it closed. It's especially ironic in view of what Camp David has come to be for Jimmy Carter, but it was the same with everything. He had the answers before he'd added up the numbers.

"I thought Carter would have done better to wait a while, take the time to learn, ask a few questions, before getting specific and making decisions that could be critical. It wasn't too encouraging a start.

"Carter hadn't sold himself to the country as being an authority on government, so it was disturbing to have him making wild-sounding statements about cuts and reductions, but it wasn't the same kind of surprise as discovering he wasn't some of the things he *had* sold himself as being.

"Carter's first trip overseas as President was in May 1977, for a European economic summit meeting in London. Our ambassador to England hadn't arrived in London yet; so the President decided to stay at Winfield House, the official ambassador's residence.

"The people on the embassy staff had taken the Carter publicity seriously, and there wasn't a drop of liquor in the house when the President arrived. That created quite a stir in the Carter entourage because by the time they got to Winfield House and reported this discovery to the President, it was about eleven-thirty at night and everything was shut, including the pubs, because of British licensing laws. But Carter, it turned out, wanted a drink, so the naval aide had to go scurrying out into the London night, back to *Air Force One*, to find the new President a bottle of booze.

"I'm not suggesting there's anything wrong with Carter or with anybody else wanting a drink. But it seems to me the guy got himself boxed in by representing himself as holier-than-just-about-everybody during the campaign.

"That's why it comes as such a shock when he says things like he can 'whip Teddy Kennedy's ass,' or gives an interview to *Playboy* and talks about a guy who 'screws a whole bunch of women,' or wants a drink enough to send an aide out at midnight to find one. It casts a shadow of doubt on the man and makes you wonder what else isn't what it seems to be.''

"After my first trip to Plains to see Carter, it was agreed I would go back and talk to brother Billy about plans for putting a support compound for the President on his land. We had to install a helicopter landing pad; trailers for the doctor, the military aides and other personnel; communications facilities; and a lot of other things. So I went back to Georgia in January.

"After Billy and I had talked for a while he suddenly said, 'Look. We may as well go and see Rosalynn. She's the one who makes all the decisions anyway, so we might as well talk to her now. Whatever she says will go.' It was a memorable drive if only because of the smell. A bottle of whiskey had spilled all over the front of the car, and his dog had crapped all over the back.

"When we saw Rosalynn Carter, she wasn't so much concerned with what went onto Billy's land as she was that nobody do any damage to theirs. We went back and forth on it for a good while until Billy broke in and said, 'I tell you how we can settle the whole goddamn thing. Keep the bastard in Washington and we won't have to worry about any of it.'

"You could say, all in all, the Carters took some getting used to.

"Carter's White House took some getting used to, too. The formality level that was observed on *Air Force One* would rise and fall with the different administrations, largely owing to the personality of the chief of staff. It was highest with Nixon and most comfortable under Ford when Dick Cheney was in charge of the President's staff, because he's a relaxed kind of a guy who's easy to be with.

"The level reached rock bottom on that first trip we made out of the country with Carter. On a flight from London to Geneva the Georgians—Jody Powell and Hamilton Jordan and the others—were having such a fine old time that before long they started throwing fruit at each other and rolling beer cans down the aisles of *Air Force One*.

"Rowdiness on the part of the top Carter staff people is

neither here nor there, but when they didn't know what they were doing on substantive matters, then it got serious. Jack Brooks of the House Government Operations Committee dogged my days in the White House; he was like a terrier snapping at my heels to get information about military expenditures, and we finally reached a standoff. He'd badger me for information about Nixon and Ford, and I'd tell him if I had to go and testify I'd have to bring up what had been done with military assets in LBJ's time, too. 'And that,' I'd tell him, 'will make Lady Bird Johnson very unhappy.'

"Jack Brooks is a Democrat from Texas, and one thing he didn't want was an unhappy Mrs. Johnson, so he'd say, 'Goddamn it, Bill. I get so frustrated with you. I didn't ask you about Johnson, I don't want to hear about Johnson, don't tell me about Johnson.' But he knew I would if he made me go to the Hill and testify.

"We went on like that for years, Brooks asking, me not telling, until Carter came in. Then Brooks got his second wind. Being nobody's fool, I'm sure he saw that with this new, green administration, he'd finally have a chance at prying some information out of the White House.

"He sent word to Hugh Carter, Jr., Jimmy Carter's cousin, who was in charge of administration for the White House, that he'd like to have him come up to the Hill and meet with him and some of the committee staff. He also invited me.

"Now, Brooks was a Democrat in a Democratic Congress with a Democratic administration, and he wasn't looking for scandals from the Carter White House. The idea was that Gulley was going to tell them Nixon was a crook, and Ford abused assets right and left, and then Hugh Carter, Jr., and Gulley were both going to say that the new Democratic President, Jimmy Carter, wasn't going to do any of that stuff.

"What they also wanted, most of all, was access to information about what was going on inside the White House; it's what every agency, department and committee in Washington wants.

"It became clear the minute we sat down that this Carter kid didn't understand what was going on. He kept saying, 'Don't you worry. We're going to tell you everything. We've

274

got nothing to hide. Bill Gulley and I are going to tell you everything you want to know.' Then he said, 'I want you to know that Jimmy is very conscious of expenditures. Have you gentlemen ever heard of zero-based budgeting?'

"Most of these guys were from Texas, and they were slickers, every one of them. They'd been on the Hill a long time, and they were all looking at each other. Who IS this guy? What is he doing giving us all this zero-budgeting bullshit? I was kicking Hugh, Jr., in the leg, and he'd stop and look at me, then go right on.

"Before we finally got out of there, Brooks had a commitment from Hugh Carter, Jr., that we would turn over details of the military assets Carter used, particularly the aircraft, and specifically including the passenger manifests. In the car going back to the White House I explained a few facts of life to Hugh, Jr. I told him, 'Don't you see? They don't give a shit about expenses in this administration. It's all political. They want to know who the President is seeing, what he's doing; they want a foot in the door.'

"Within hours of my getting back to the office a letter came from Brooks confirming that it had been agreed we would have copies of the passenger manifests of every trip the President took sent over to his committee monthly. What my successor has done about it I don't know; during my remaining months at the White House, Brooks never got what he wanted."

"Carter was personally concerned with appearances, how his Administration was going to *look*, and when Jerry Rafshoon, his full-time image-maker, moved into the White House, it turned into an official concern. But Carter worried about it from the outset.

"A week after the inauguration I met with him in his inner office, and he had classical music playing. The music was loud, and his voice was soft, which created a problem for me, but we managed to communicate. We were discussing how White House ceremonies were to be conducted, and he had some definite ideas.

"There was to be no dancing, the herald trumpets were to

275

go, and he said, 'I think one reason the American people elected me is because they see me as a man who doesn't like to high-side things.' It was an expression I didn't understand, but I later found out it meant he believed the public liked him because they thought he wasn't a show-off, and he wanted the people to go on seeing him that way. That's what led to the short-lived cardigan sweaters and carrying his own bag.

"Carter wasn't going to have his staff 'high-siding things' either. They were told, along with NBC, CBS, AP and anybody else who would listen, that there would be no chauffeured cars or other special privileges for those in the White House. But Carter's people were no different from any other people; they knew a status symbol when they saw one. The leader of the pack that was on the hunt for them was Zbigniew Brzezinski, the Georgians' answer to Henry Kissinger. Before long, and quietly, he and then others began to taste the good life.

"It seemed to me Carter had a double standard about who was allowed the perks of being near the President. Family, or those close to it, were allowed advantages others weren't. During the transition, before Carter was even inaugurated, his son Chip and wife Caron, and their dog, lived in a government-owned house in Lafayette Square, across from the White House.

"The house had been renovated for use as a former President's residence, and with Ford's approval, Chip lived there and was working at the Democratic National Committee. The American taxpayer not only paid his rent; he even paid a ticket Chip Carter got and handed over to Jack Marsh to take care of when Chip's car was towed away.

"Carter's Secretary of State, Cyrus Vance, didn't do so well. When he was abroad working on the peace negotiations between Israel and Egypt, he wanted to fly back to the United States for his son's graduation from college. When inquiries were made about bringing him back from London on a military aircraft, Carter said no and made him fly back commercial."

A thread that runs through Gulley's account of the administrations he served is the abuse of military assets in general, and the Military Office Secret Fund in particular. Gross abuses occurred under Johnson and Nixon; in Ford's Administration some improper use was made of these things but on an infinitely smaller scale.

The question of what use Carter has made of military assets, including the Secret Fund, since Gulley left the White House is one probably only Carter can answer. "All I know," Gulley says, "is what was said between us before I left the White House.

"Among the briefing papers I sent the President-elect during the transition I did not include any information on the Secret Fund. It was highly classified material, and I wasn't sure who had clearance and who didn't. Jody Powell, for example, had been dismissed from the Air Force Academy, and I didn't know how that would affect his position when it came to getting cleared. And Amy's nanny had been convicted of murder, so I didn't know what that would do to *her* clearance.

"When I saw Carter in Plains, though, I told him about the fund. I described what it was designed for, that it was secret, and alluded to the fact that in previous administrations it had been used for things other than what it was meant for. The first question he asked me was who controlled the fund, and when I told him he and I did, he said, 'In other words, you on your own, or you with my approval, can use this fund for just about anything?' and I told him that was true.

"He asked me for some specifics about how the fund had been spent in other administrations. I told him about expenditures at the LBJ Ranch, rebuilding and redecorating Camp David in Nixon's time, renting houses for the staff at Vail during Ford's day, and so on. When I finished he asked me who audited the fund, and when I told him there was no audit and never had been, he asked me, 'Could you withstand an audit?'

"I said, 'No, I couldn't. For one thing, there were no records kept of a lot of what was spent.'

"Then Carter said, 'That could be an advantage, couldn't it?' I answered, 'It could be an advantage to you, yes.'

"I know what I meant in that exchange. I meant that the fund, the secrecy of it, could be an advantage to him because

277

he could spend it any way he wanted and no one would know. What Carter meant when he said, 'That could be an advantage, couldn't it?,' I don't know. All I know is what he said; only he knows what he meant.

"The only other time the fund was mentioned, except for when I told the President I was paying for the Plains compound plans out of it, was when Hugh Carter, Jr., asked me about it. In February 1977 he talked to me about the fund and suggested that he and I be coresponsible for it in the future. I told him that was out of the question on two grounds: one, it was a military fund, established to be handled through the Military Office, and, two, I wasn't going to be coresponsible for that stick of dynamite with anybody but the President.

"That was the last I heard of it, and for the remainder of my time at the White House, I administered the fund and made expenditures from it. How it's being handled now, I just don't know."

Gulley has no soft parting thoughts about Carter, and no feeling that he was hasty in his judgment of the man, the men around him or his Administration. "Looking at the way he's handling the Presidency," Gulley says, "I feel my early impression of Carter as a feather merchant and my decision to leave his White House were correct. His lack of commitment to any course of action, and his evasiveness, soon showed through, and his country-slick religious approach has worn thin under the pressure to produce.

"I remember the first television debate he had with Ford during the campaign of 1976. The subject was domestic affairs —the economy, inflation, unemployment—and suddenly Carter turned to Ford and said, in words very close to these: 'Mr. President, you should be ashamed of the way you have handled your responsibilities to the people of your country.'

"Gerald Ford had been in office two years at the time. It seems to me that any Presidential challenger, or any citizen looking over his longer time in office, has the right to say the same thing to Jimmy Carter.

"Of the incidents I was involved in that had to do with the

278

Carter Presidency, one that occurred during that first visit to see Billy in Plains stands out.

"I met him at the peanut warehouse in the middle of the town, and since his office wasn't big enough for us to spread out the blueprints and plans I had, we went next door into a sort of lounge area. It had a broken-down sofa and a couple of overstuffed chairs, but there was a good bit of floor space.

"Billy and I got down on the floor with our diagrams, and as we were looking at them the citizens of Plains began drifting in so that before long we'd assembled a pretty good crowd. I thought it was strange, but, what the hell, if it didn't bother Billy, why should it bother me?

"Suddenly Billy stood up and said, 'Momma, this is Mr. Gulley from the White House. He's here to talk about the military putting a compound on my place.' He was talking to Miss Lillian Carter, of course, and as I got to my feet she said to Billy, and these are her exact words: 'Get all you can, honey. If they'll give you a hundred thousand, take a hundred thousand. Get all you can, because you'll never get another chance like this.'

"I knew right then that at the White House it was going to be business as usual."

INDEX